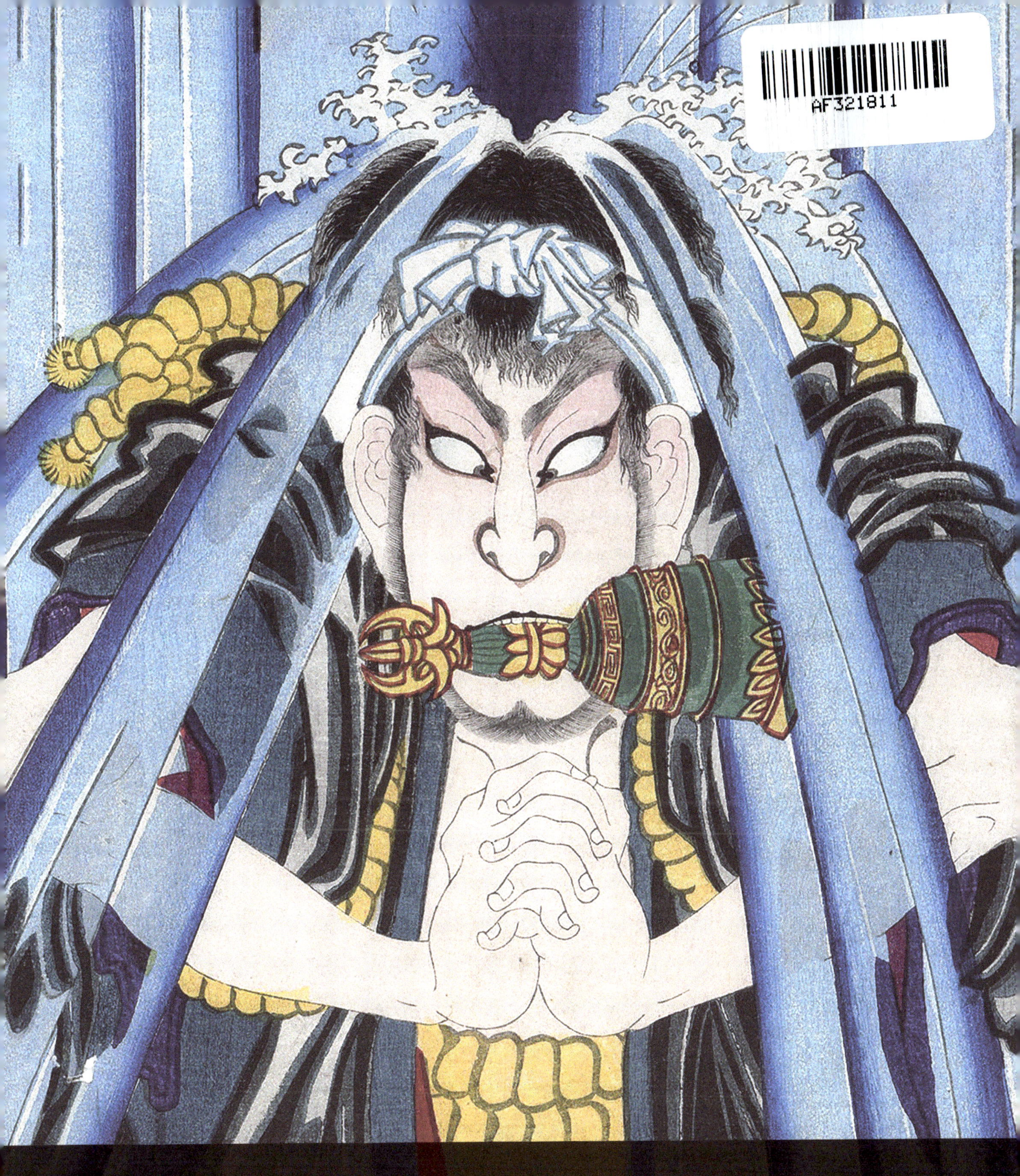

DOYENS OF DELIRIUM

100 ACTOR PORTRAITS BY KUNICHIKA

DOYENS OF DELIRIUM
100 Actor Portraits By Kunichika
Series: Floating Worlds
Publishing: Bonefyre Books
Date: 2024
Place: Gardena, CA
ISBN 978-1-917285-29-2
Editing: Ringo Yoshida
Editorial assistance: Kanako Wakamatsu @ Kobayashi Foundation
Japanese-English translation: Outer Rim Sensation, Osaka
Concept: Fabbrica Sodoma
Design: Fever Claw

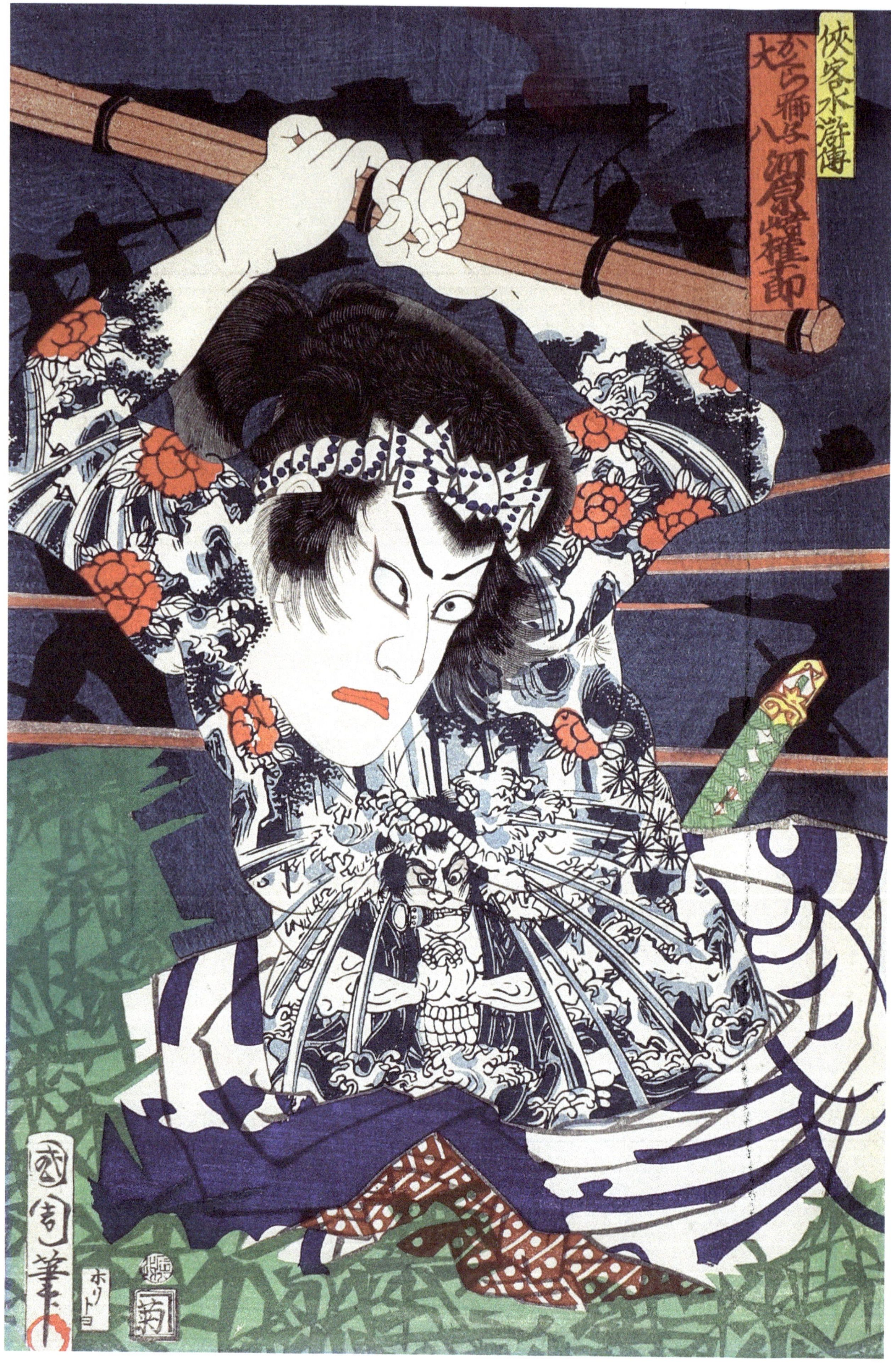

俠客水滸傳
むら雷八　河原崎權十郎

FOREWORD

Ukiyo-e

"Pictures of the floating world." The floating world – a transient realm of pleasures, horrors, and dreams. *Ukiyo-e*, depictions of this shadowy projection of the human mind, formed the mainstay of Japanese paintings and woodblock prints produced between the 17th and 20th centuries.

Yakasha-e

"Pictures of actors". This sub-division of *ukiyo-e* was dedicated to illustrating famous scenes and players from the *kabuki* theatre, the decadent epicentre of Edo's floating world.

Toyohara Kunichika

Born Oshima Yasohachi in 1835, in the Kyobashi area of Edo, and also known as Arawaka Yasohachi, Toyohara Kunichika derived his artist name from the two teachers who schooled him from the age of eleven onwards – Toyohara Chikanobu and Utagawa Kunisada, the latter a recognised *ukiyo-e* master. Kunichika's first published prints appeared in the early 1850s, and he first came to public attention in the early 1860s when his output consisted largely of *musha-e* ("warrior pictures") derived from designs by Kuniyoshi and Yoshitoshi. Around 1863 Kunichika clearly experienced an artistic ephiphany, the realization that his talents were better served in producing *yakasha-e*. Although, like other *ukiyo-e* artists, Kunichika ventured into several genres, including *shunga* (erotic prints), book illustration, and also *shinbun nishiki-e* (news-sheets), producing several works for the *Tokyo kakushu shinbun* around 1876, his first love remained the *kabuki* theatre and its swaggering, often omnisexual stars.

Tattoo designs in *ukiyo-e* were popular ever since Kuniyoshi's innovative 1827 series of 108 **Suikoden** subjects; tattooing had a forbidden glamour associated with those on society's fringes: samurai, outlaws, prostitutes, gamblers. Some of Kunichika's most intense and intricate designs were portraits of actors as characters whose skins were daubed with tattoos of demons, dragons, snakes, beasts and similar creatures in all manner of diverse configurations. These intimations of violence flower in Kunichika's 1868 portrait series **Zan-aku kijin kagami** ("Demonic Mirror Of Good And Evil") which often rivals Yoshitoshi's innovative **Kaidai hyaku senso** ("100 Faces Of War"),[1] from the same year, in its confrontational power.[2] The fundamental difference between these two series, however, is that whereas Yoshitoshi was drawing inspiration from real life (having witnessed first-hand the bloody Battle of Ueno), Kunichika's figures were derived solely from the *kabuki* stage.

In 1869, Kunichika intensified his production of *yakusha-e* with an iconographic 22-part series showing *kabuki* actors' faces in extreme close-up, and set against richly coloured backgrounds created with imported chemical dyes. From that point onward Kunichika became the foremost chronicler of *kabuki* theatre, developing a comprehensive knowledge of plays, players, and performances. In particular, he would document the many roles essayed by the leading actors of his

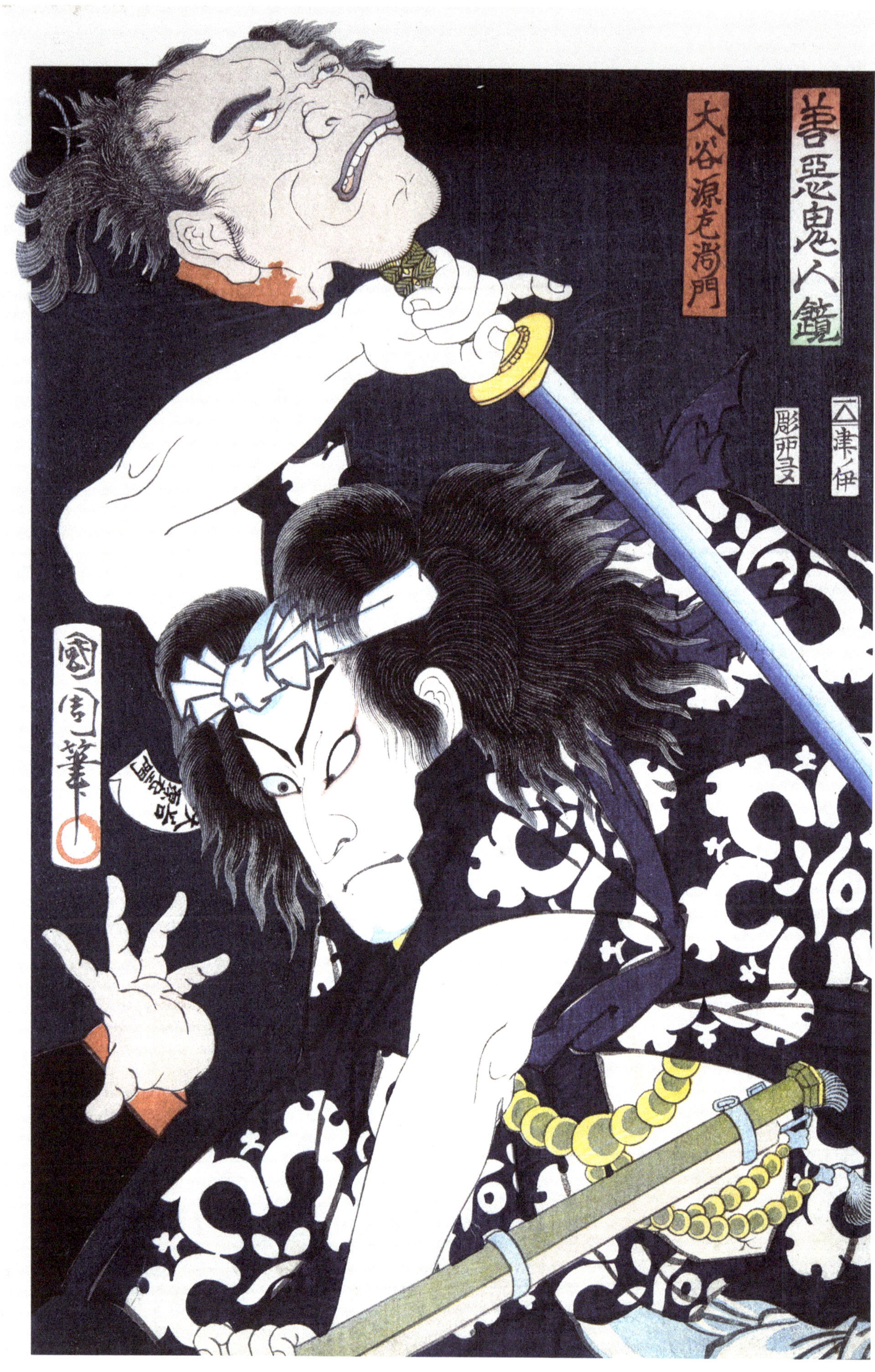

善惡鬼人鑑
大谷源左衛門
一勇斎
彫卯ニ
國周筆

time, especially Ichikawa Danjuro IX (1839-1903), Onoe Kikugoro V (also known as Baiko, 1844-1903), Bando Hikasaburo V (1832-1877), Nakamura Shikan IV (1830-1899), and Ichikawa Sadanji I (1842-1904). For Kunichika, these *kabuki* stars were the "flowers" of newly-named Tokyo, a delinquent aristocracy who ruled the night as lords of illusion, doyens of a delirious stagecraft emanating from the heart of the floating world. By 1874, Kunichika was being acclaimed as one of the leading "experts" in the art of *ukiyo-e*, and fulfilled this role over the next two decades with numerous series that culminated with extensive tribute sets dedicated to two of his *kabuki* heroes – **Baiko Hyakuju no uchi** ("100 Roles Of Baiko", 1893) and **Ichikawa Danjuro engei hyakuban** ("100 Roles Of Ichikawa Danjuro", 1893).

DOYENS OF DELIRIUM collects 100 of Kunichika's most striking and vivid *yakusha-e* portrait designs, in a testament to the enduring innovation and power of his prolific output. The selection presented here draws from two decades of the artist's work, and features a wide range of seminal *kabuki* subjects produced between 1864 and 1883 (after which his artistic focus turned more to the triptych format). Prints from the following series are included: **Haiyu shiranami atari goketsu** ("Actors As Outlaws In Popular Plays", 1864, eight prints); **Satomi hakkenshi no uchi** ("Eight Dog Heroes Of Satomi", 1865-66, eight prints); **Chochidori juban-kiri** ("Ten Deadly Camellias", 1868, fifteen prints); **Tokyo hana Kunichika manga** ("Flowers Of Tokyo: Kunichika Sketches", 1872, eight prints); **Tokyo ichini date kurabe** ("Comparing A Few Of Tokyo's Most Dashing", 1874, ten prints); **Kijutsu junishi no uchi** ("Magic For The Twelve Zodiac Signs", 1877, twelve prints); **Chimei junikagetsu no uchi** ("Places For The Twelve Months", in collaboration with Kawanabe Kyosai, 1882, twelve prints); **Mitate hakkenden no uchi** ("Imagining Eight Dog Heroes", 1883, eight prints); and **Gishi meimei-den** ("Legend Of The 47 Ronin", 1883, sixteen prints).

Like his friend and sometime collaborator Kyosai, Kunichika apparently cultivated a flamboyant, alcohol-fuelled lifestyle to match his garish and audacious prints; he reputedly had over forty serial mistresses, moved house over one hundred times, and was unable to keep money in his pocket for more than a day. He became renowned as a dissolute, to be found politely drunk either in brothels or backstage at the theatre, and declared in his self-penned epitaph: "Since I am tired of painting portraits of people of this world, I will paint portraits of the King of Hell and all his devils". This self-ordained trip to the underworld finally occurred on July 1, 1900, after a particularly heavy bout of drinking inspired by the premature death of his daughter.

NOTES

1. Kunichika and Yoshitoshi actually collaborated on a slightly more sedate series, **Shinzo gekijo iroha awase** ("Pairs For The Iroha Alphabet"), juxtaposing warrior and actor profiles, the following year. Kunichika, Yoshitoshi, and Kyosai – and perhaps Kiyotaka Kobayashi, with his detonative scenes depicting the Sino-Japanese war of 1894/5 – were the last greats of *ukiyo-e* in the Meiji era, before the art form began to die out with the advent of Western influence and new imaging technologies.

2. Scenes of bloody combat also feature in **Chochidori juban-kiri** and **Shi-kyaku Suikoden** ("Outlaw Agents", also 1868). Blood-letting in Kunichika's later prints is mostly confined to scenes of onstage *seppuku* (ritual suicide).

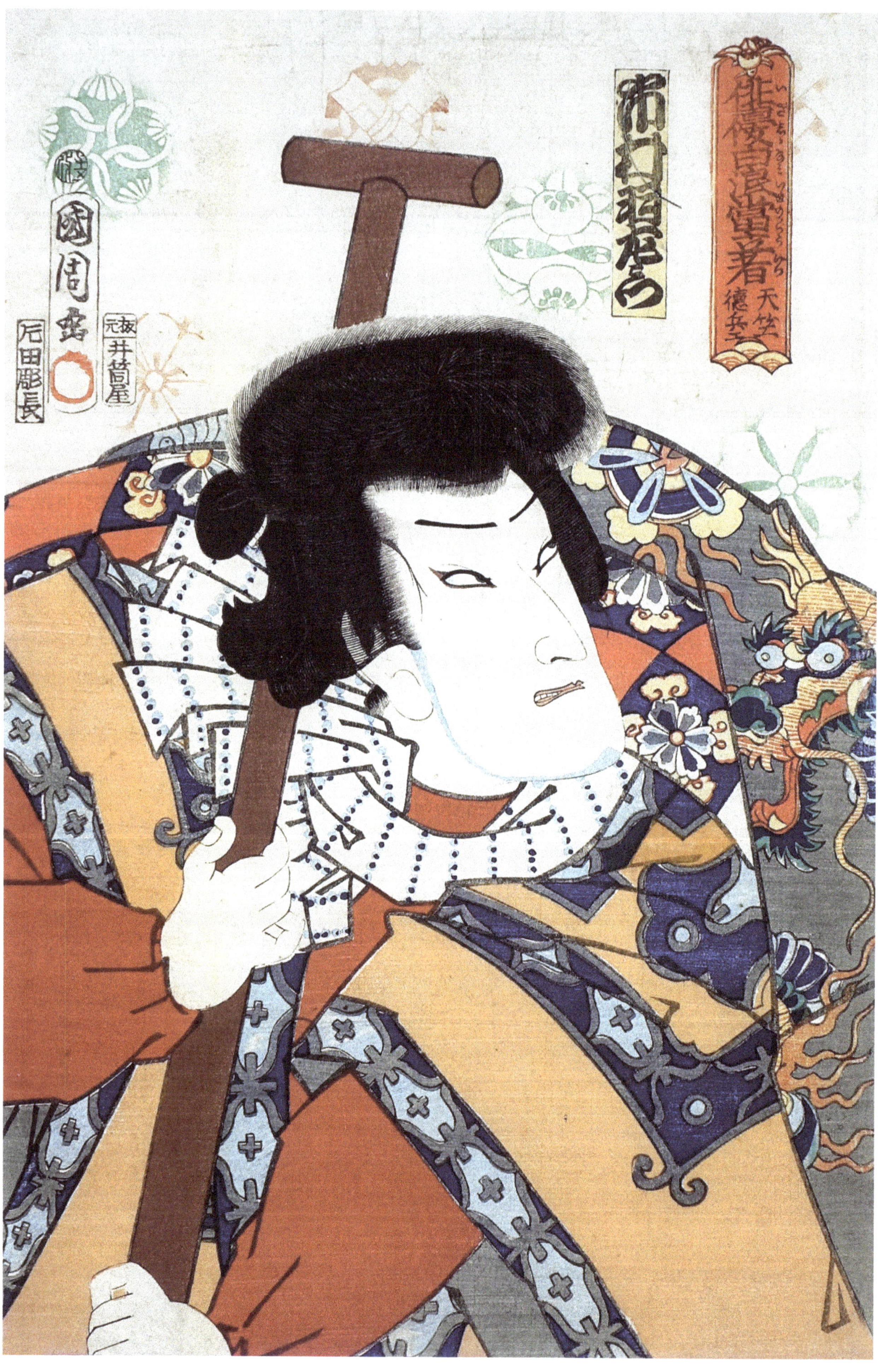

俳優自浪當者　天竺徳兵衛
應需　國周画
石田彫長
板元　井筒屋

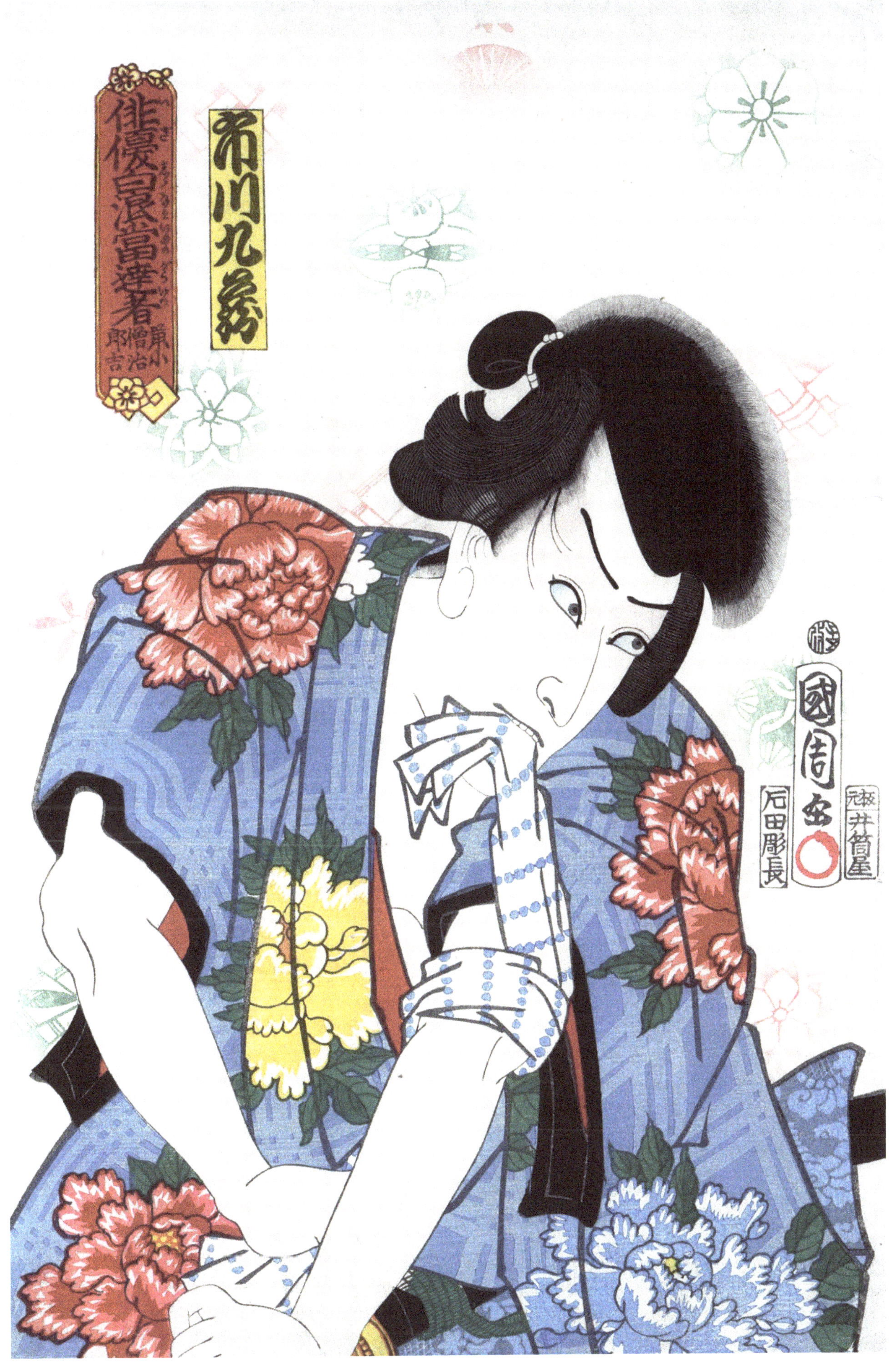
市川九蔵
俳優白浪當邊者
小猿
僧治
郎吉
國周画
石田彫長
板元井筒屋

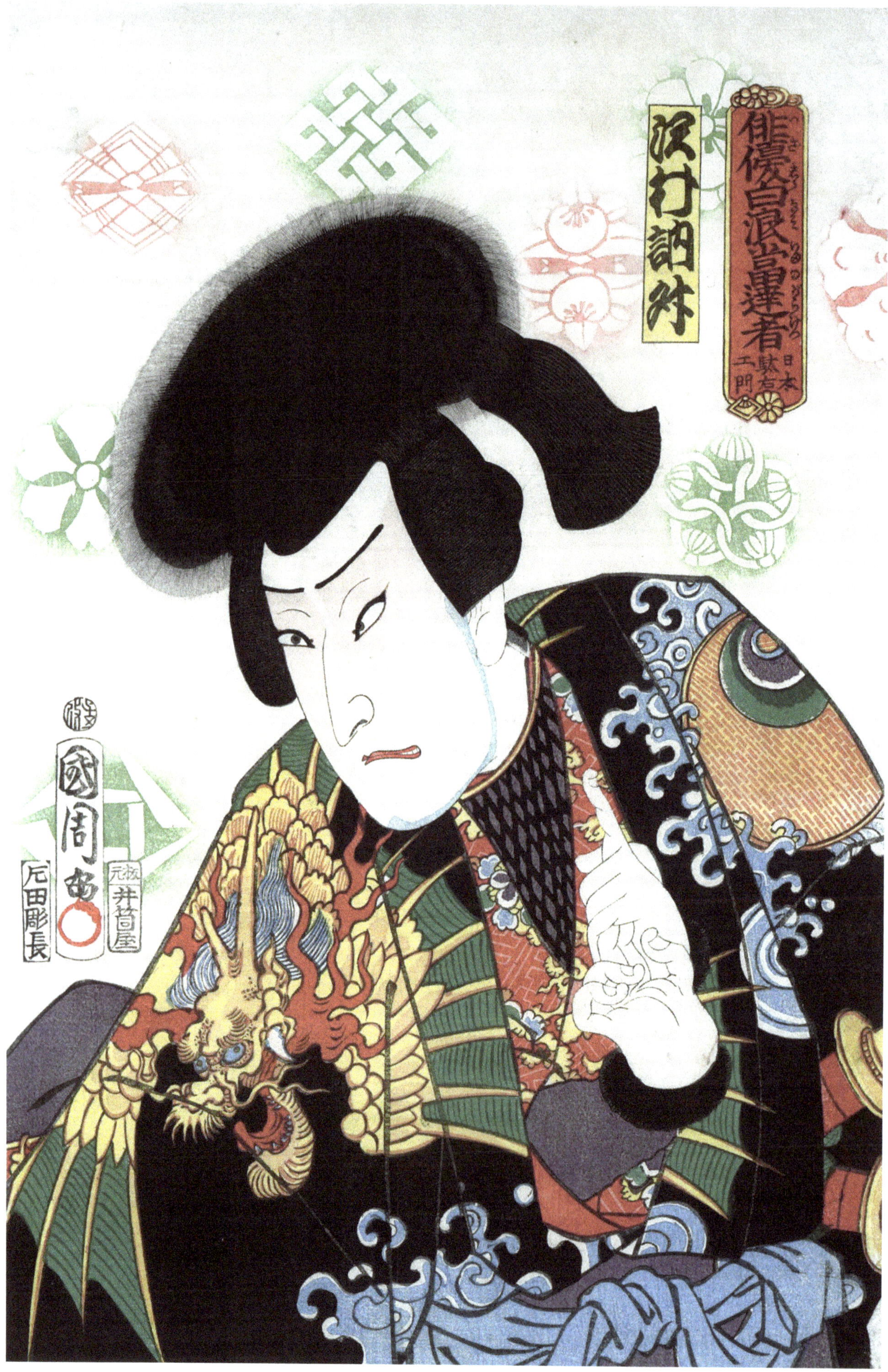
俳優當浪當運者
沢村訥升
國周筆
井筒屋
大田彫長

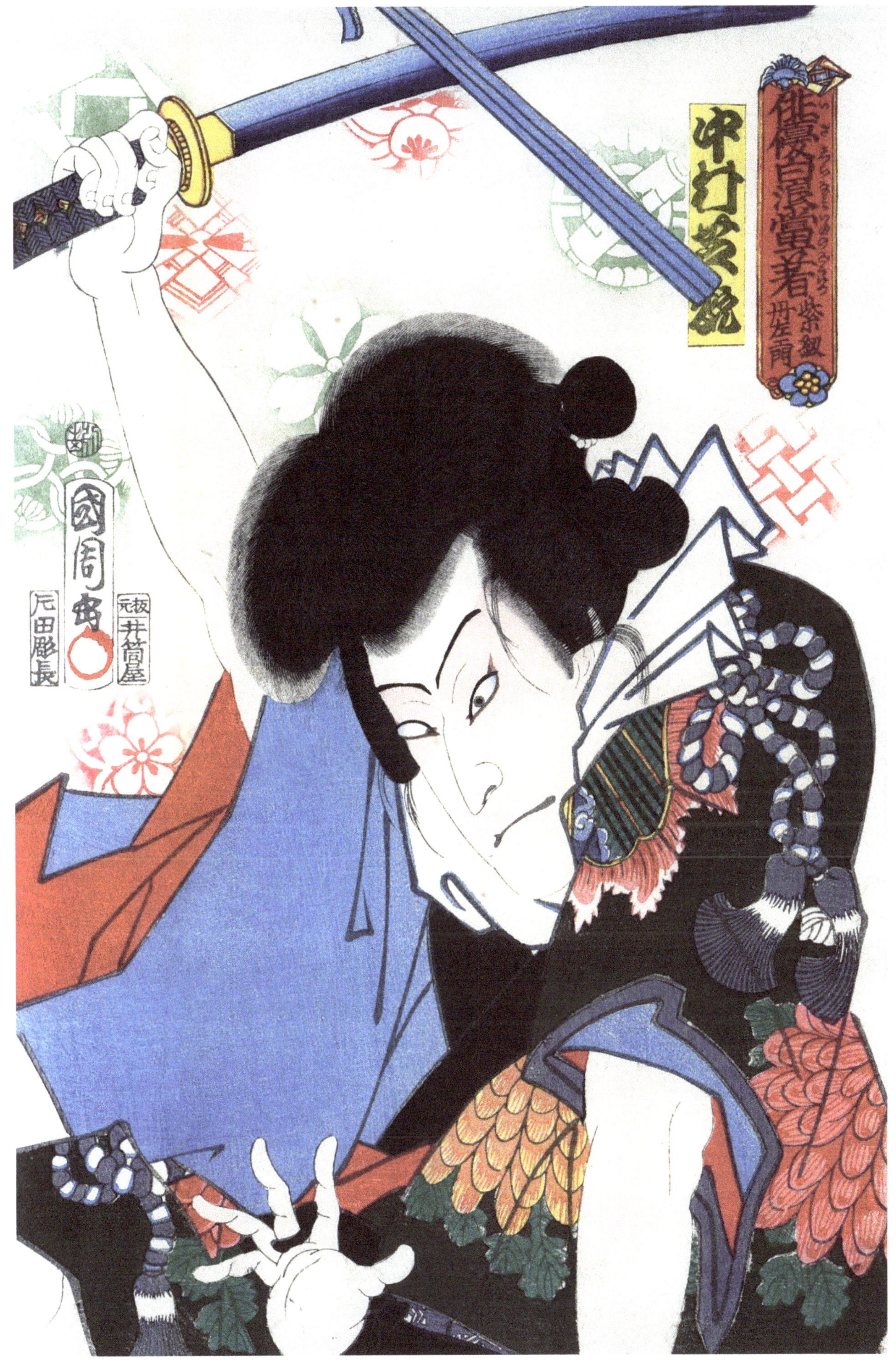
俳優自漫當者
中村芝翫
國周画
板元井筒屋
彫長

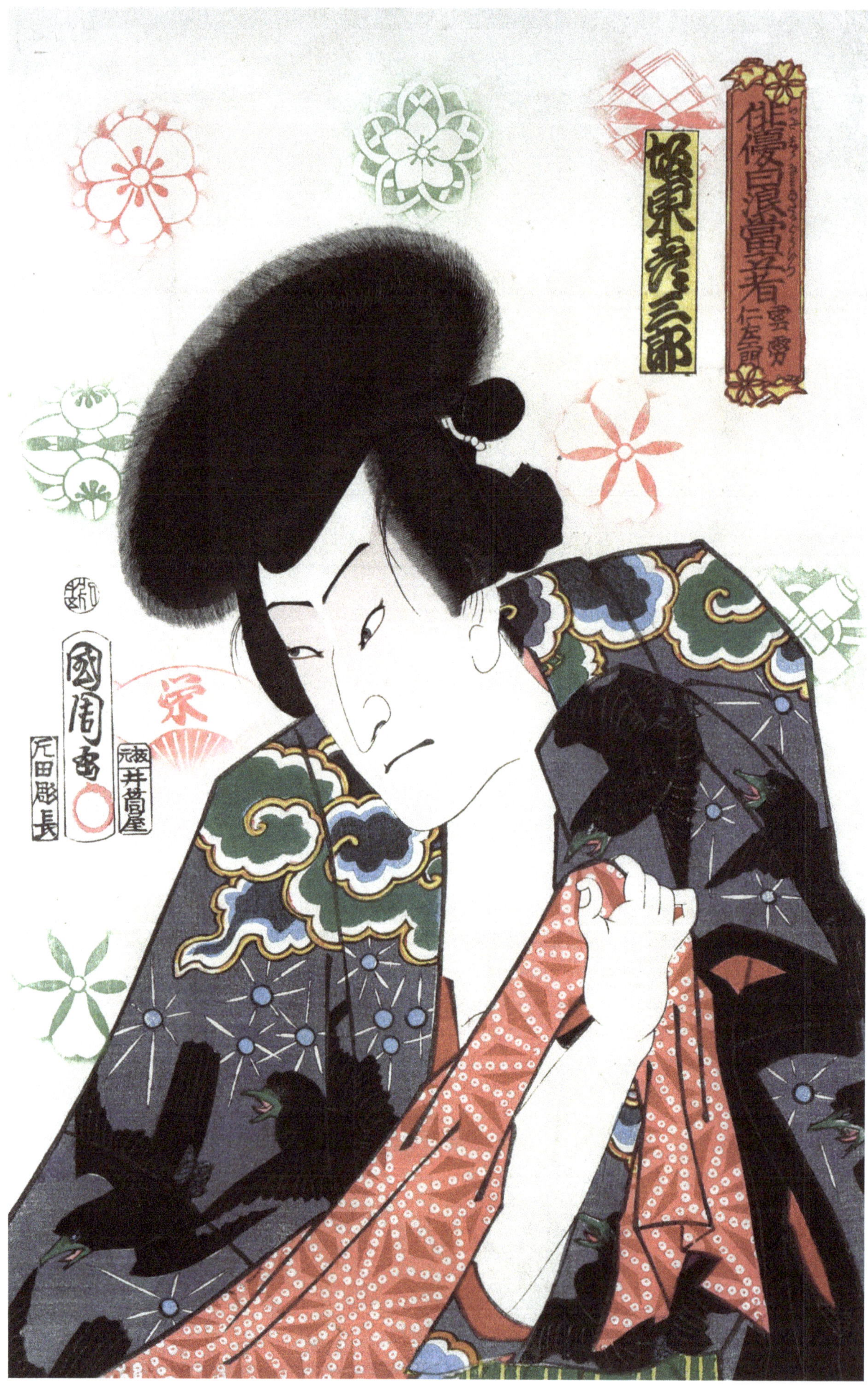
俳優白浪賣者
坂東秀三郎
國周画
元田彫長
板井筒屋

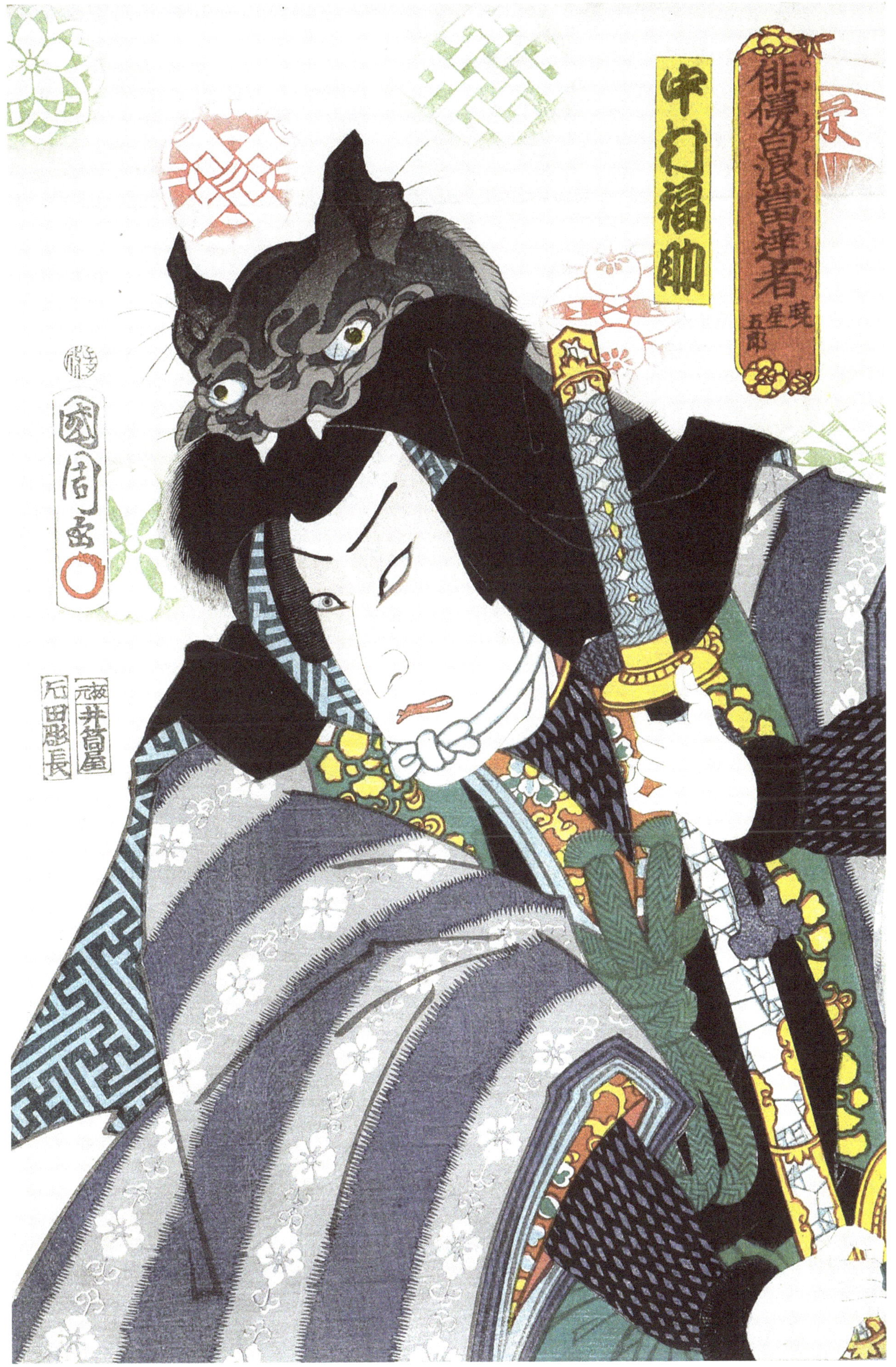
俳優當世連者
中村福助
國周画
元井筒屋
石田彫長

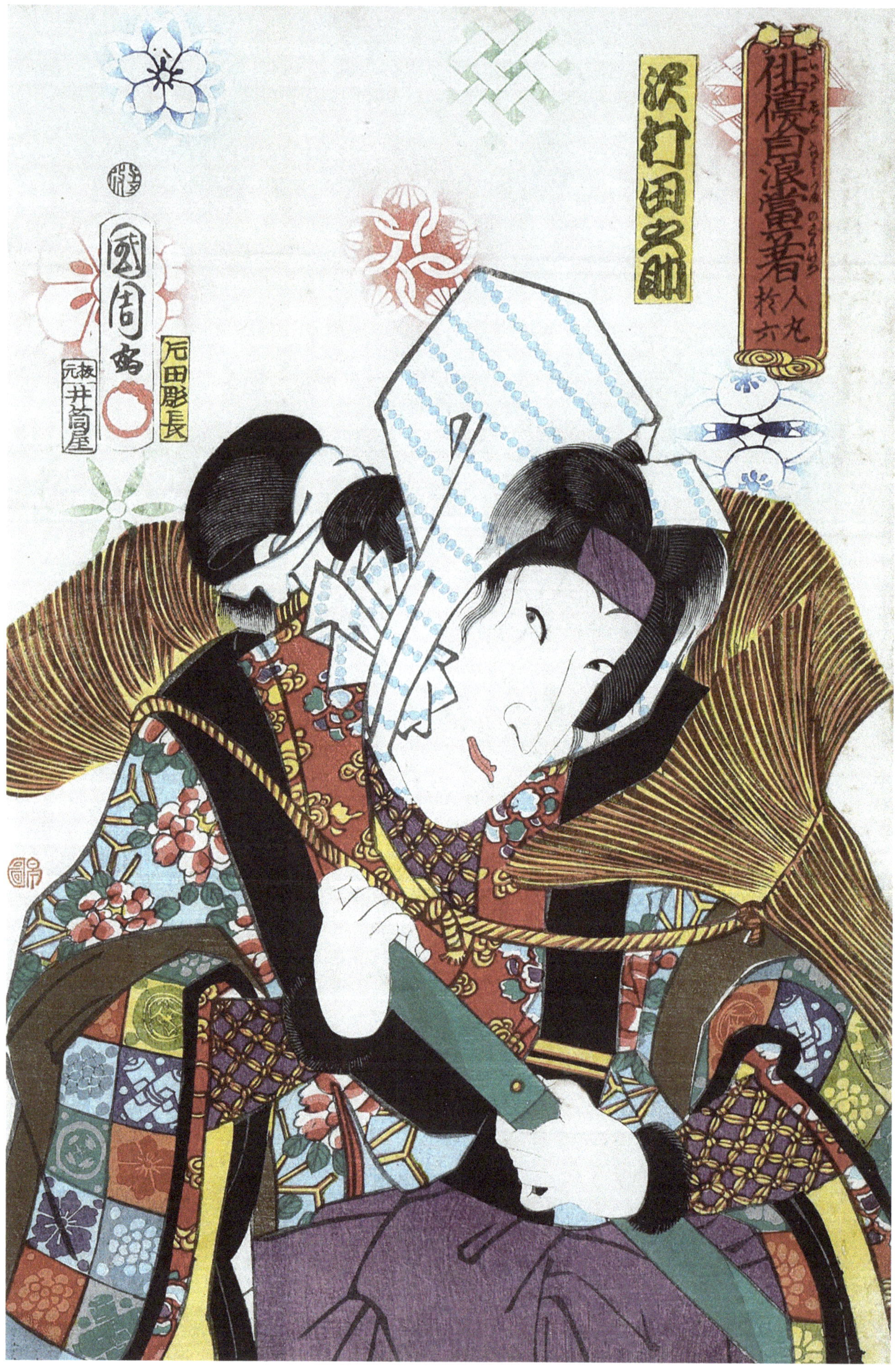
俳優百浪當著　入丸　於六
沢村田之助
國周筆
石田彫長
板元　井筒屋
16

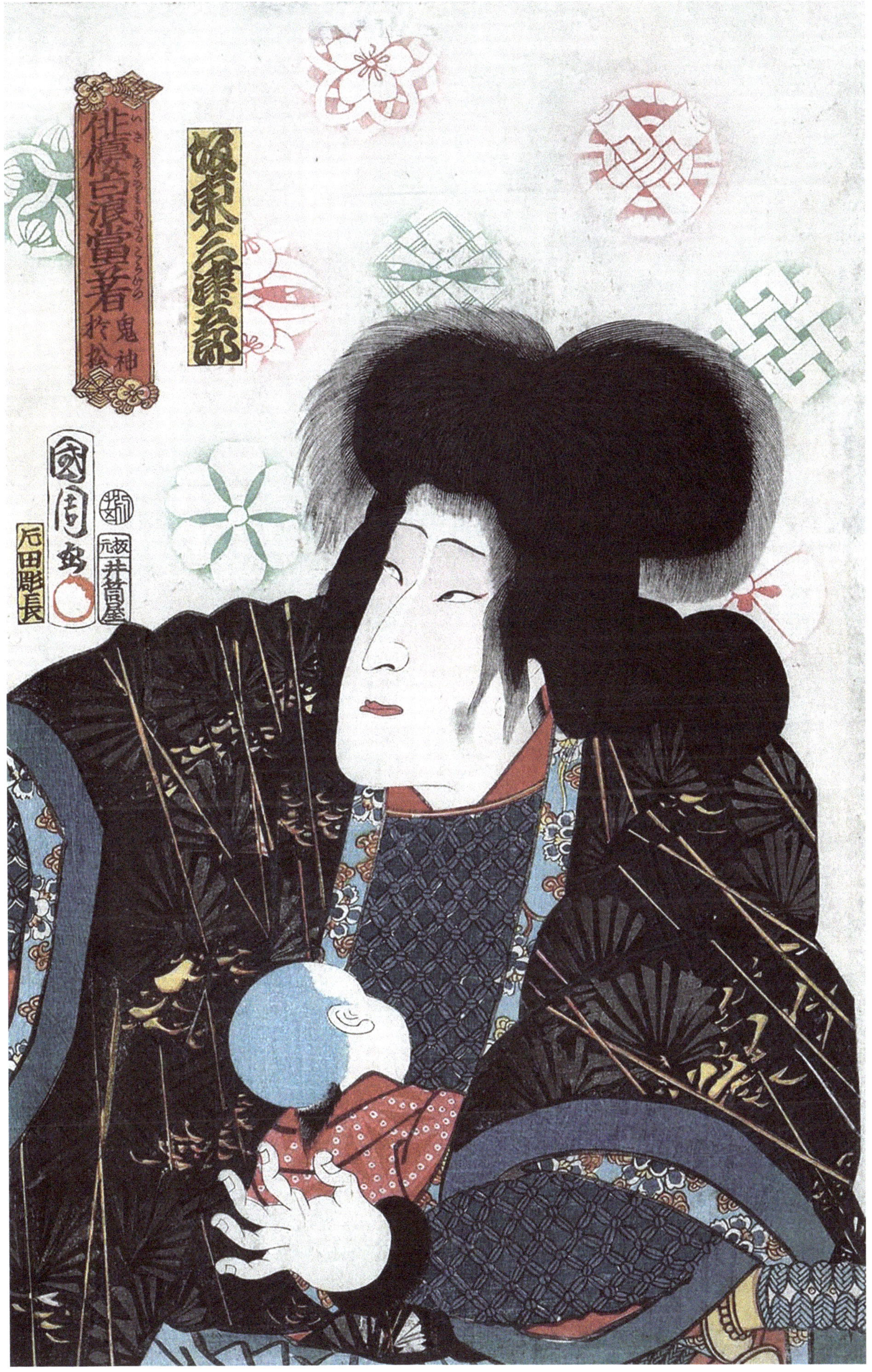
坂東三津五郎
俳優白浪當者 鬼神 於松
國周画
板井筒屋
石田彫長

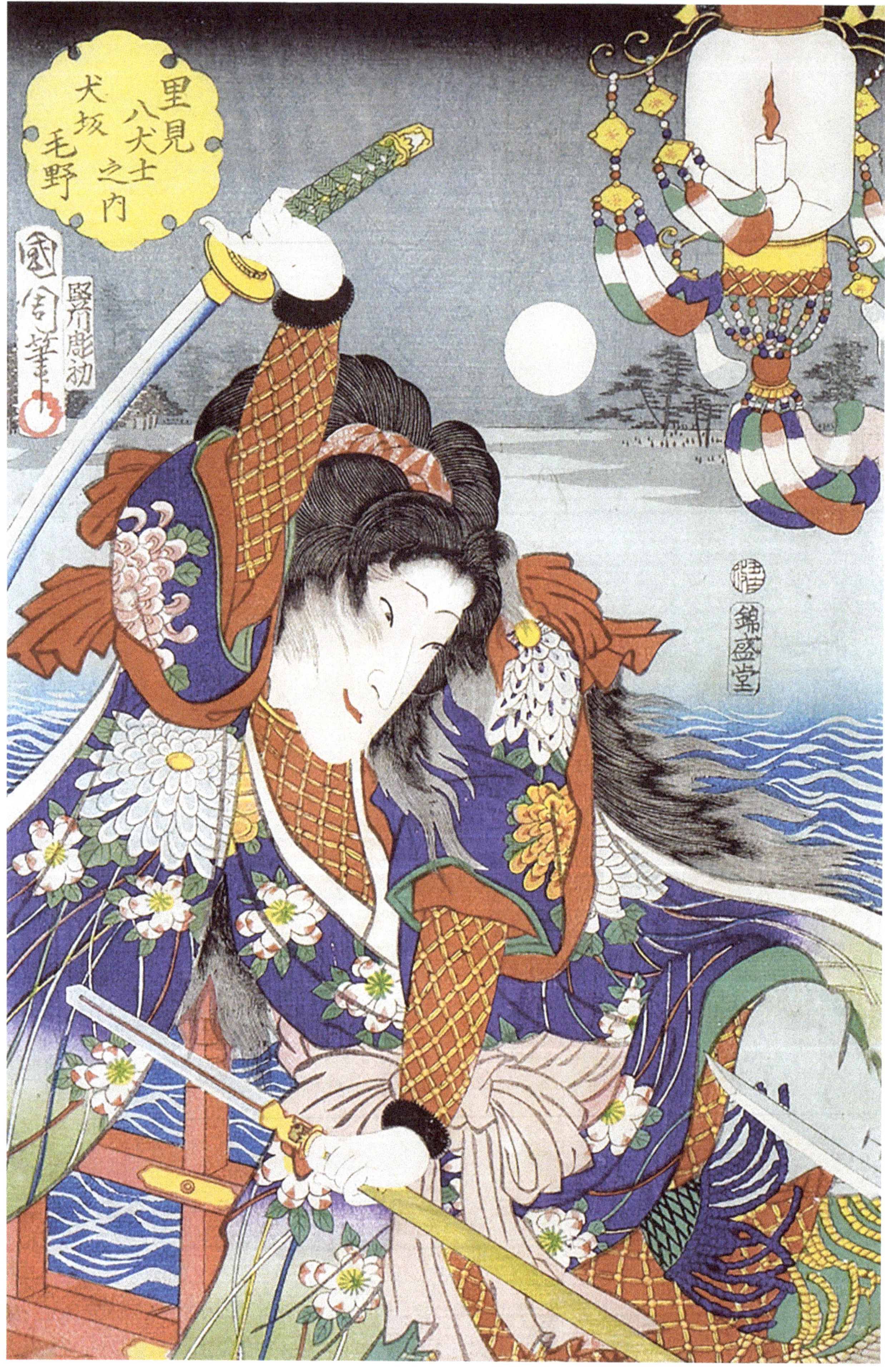

里見八犬士之内
犬坂毛野
國周筆
堅川彫初
錦盛堂

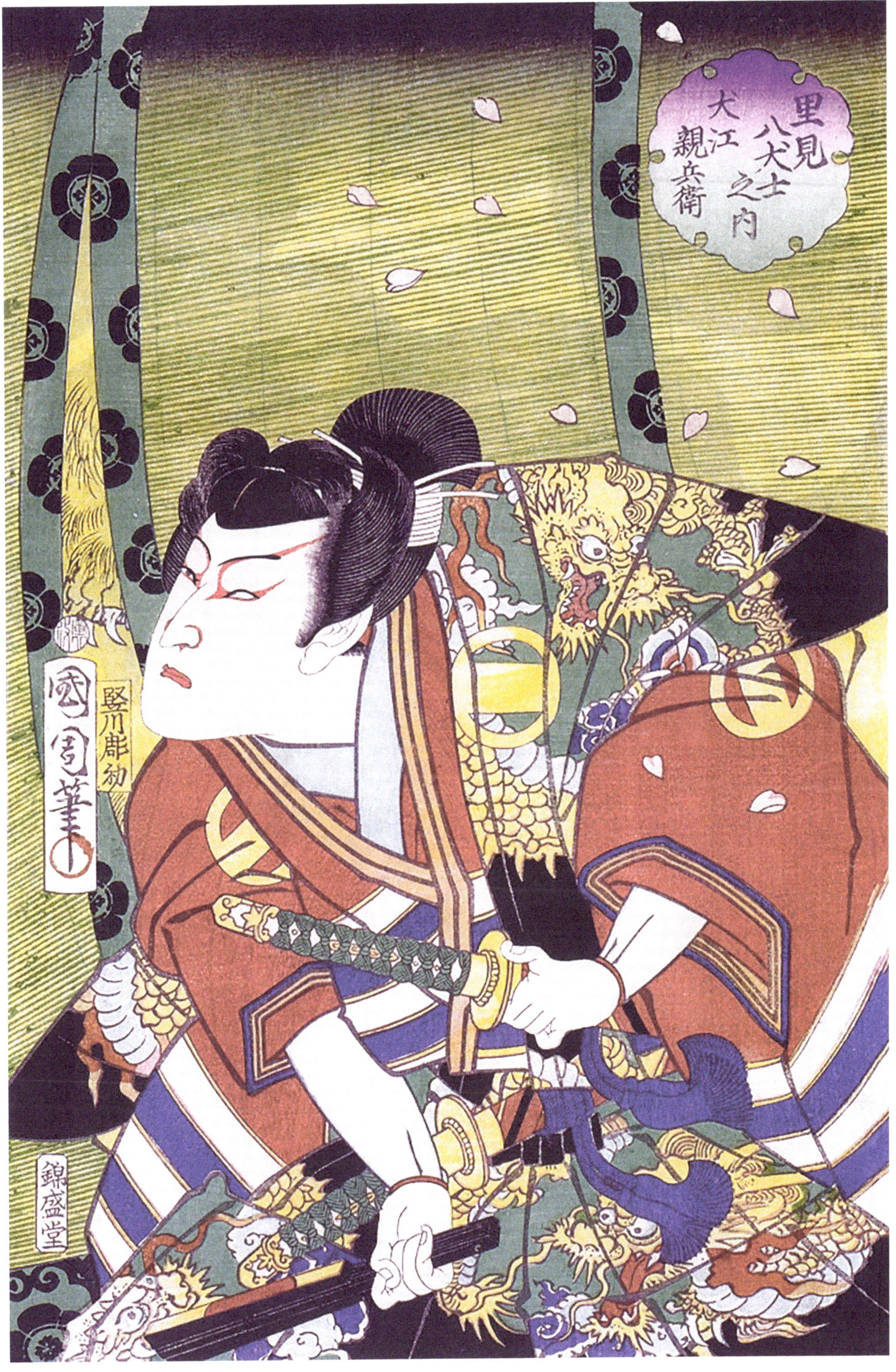
里見
八犬士
之内
大江
親兵衛
堅川彫初
國周筆
錦盛堂

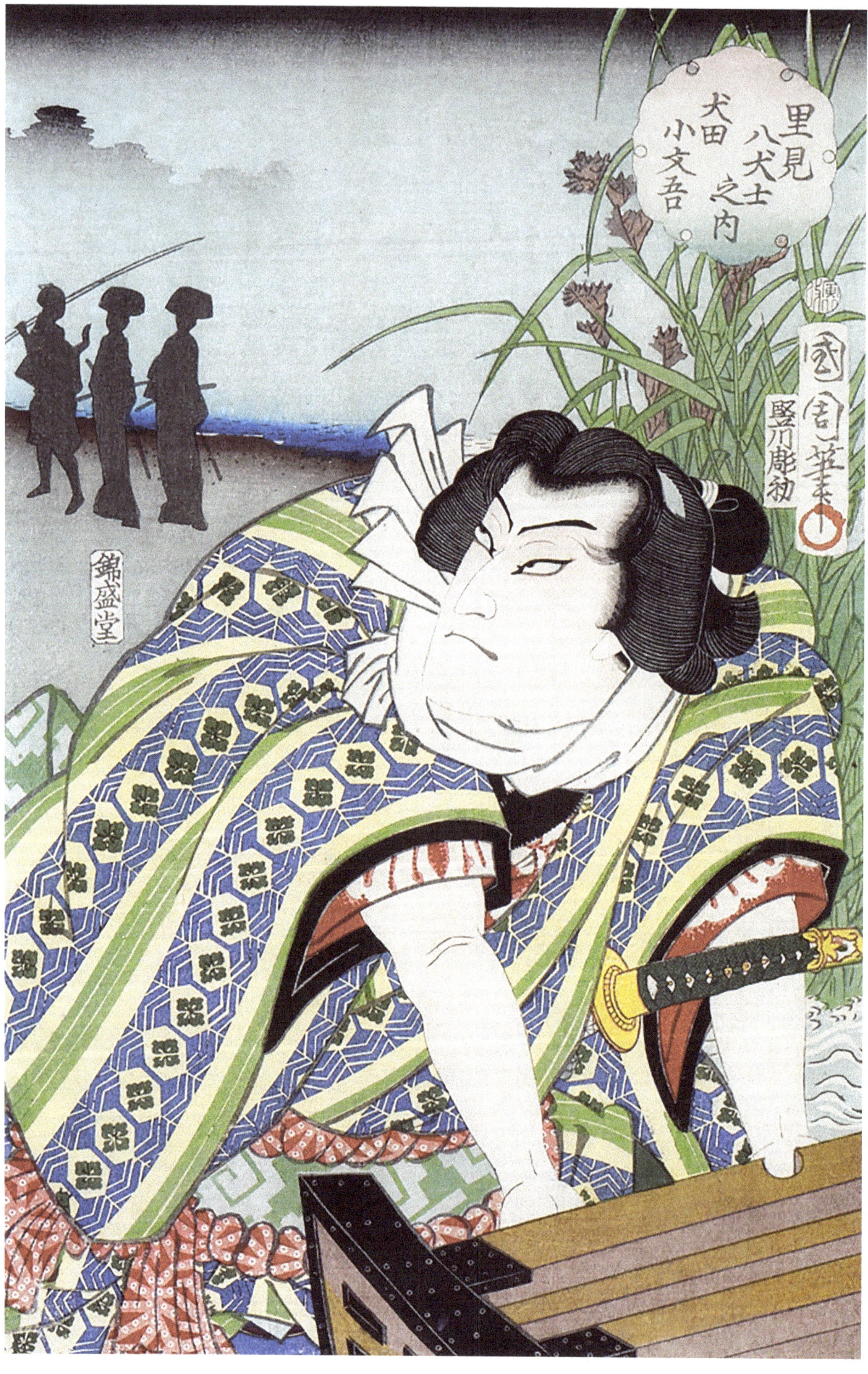

里見八犬士之内
犬田小文吾
國周筆
堅川鹿初
錦盛堂

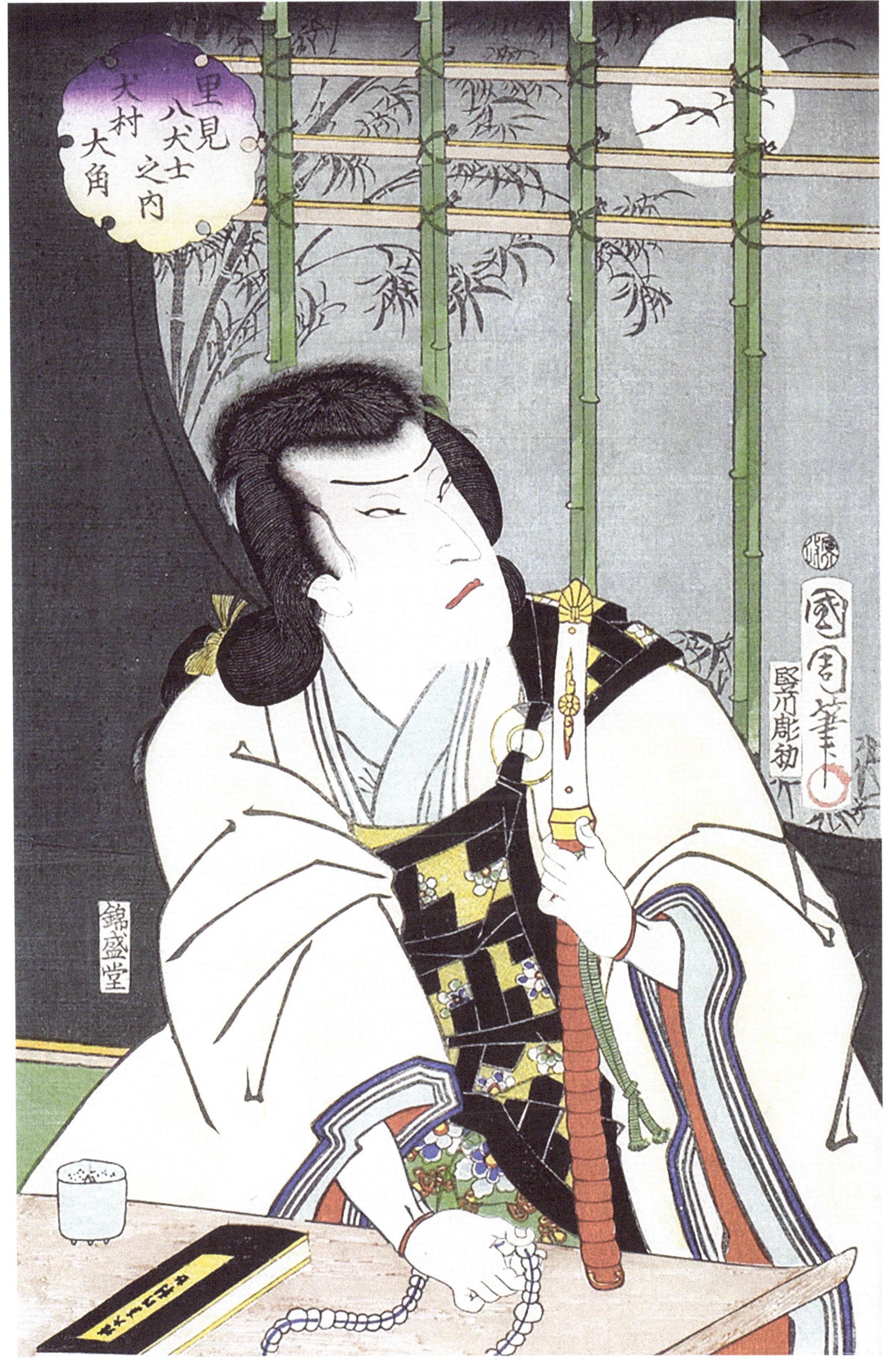

里見八犬士之内
犬村大角
國周筆
竪川彫初
錦盛堂

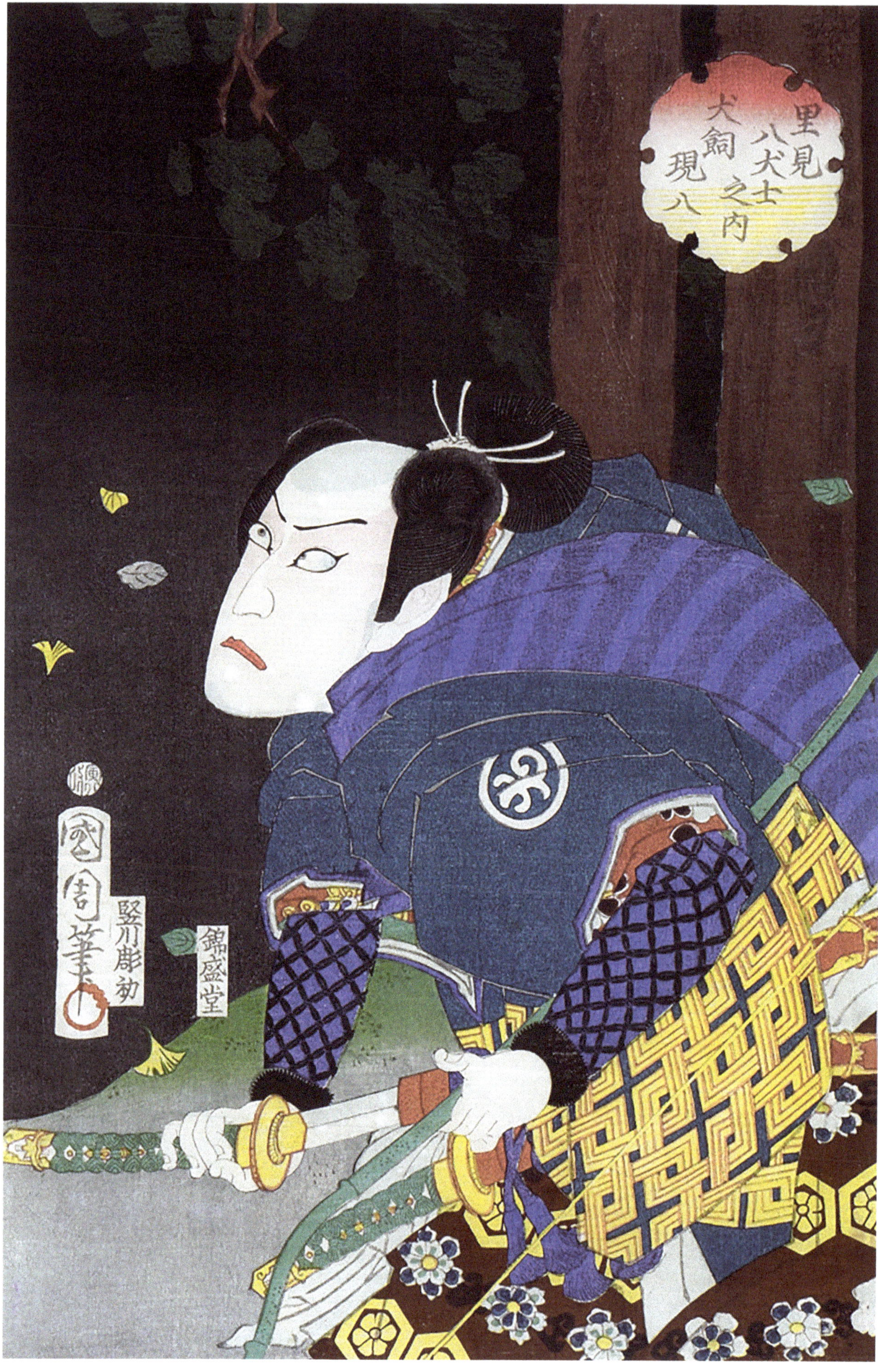

24

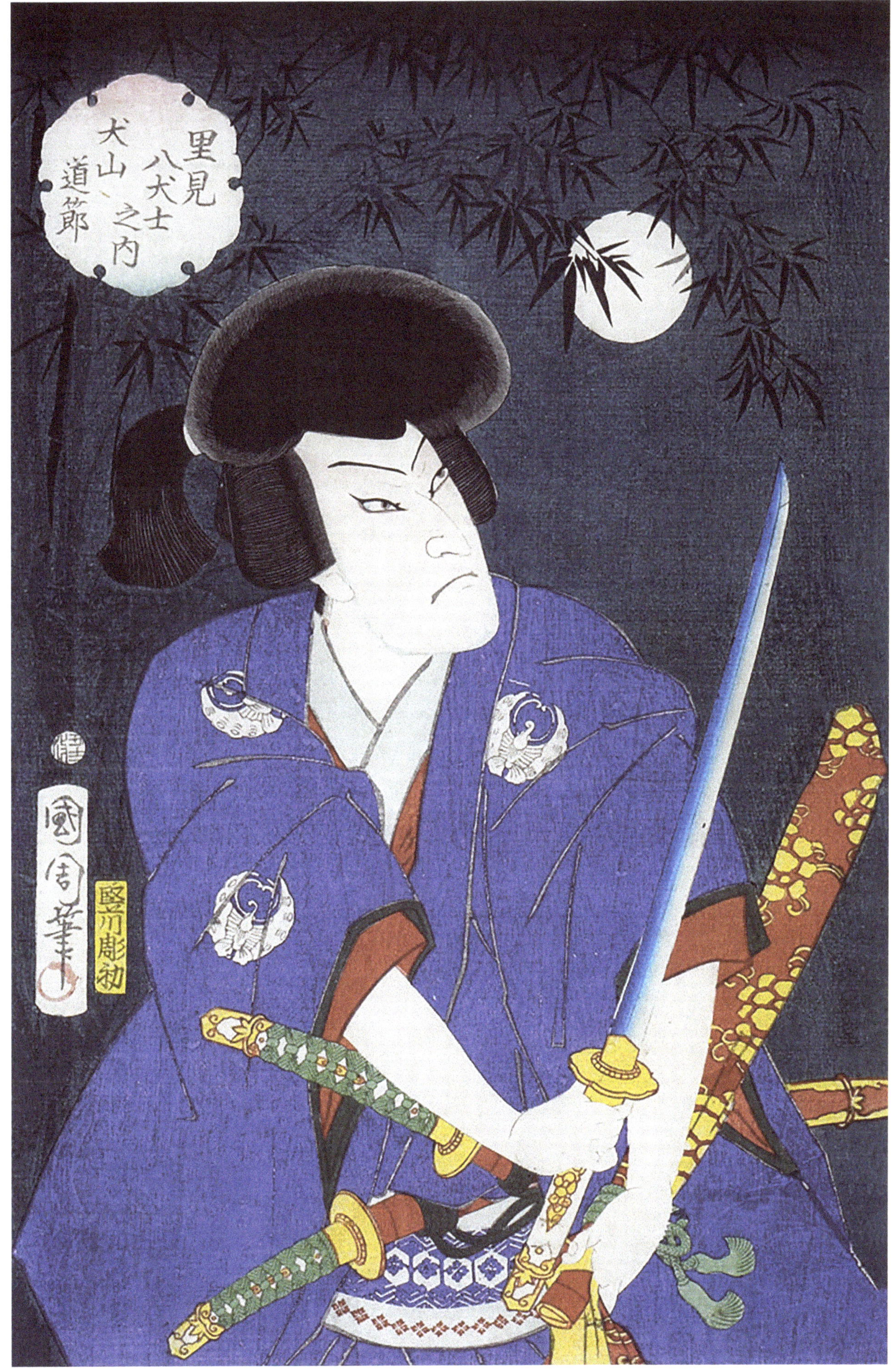

里見八犬士之内
犬山道節

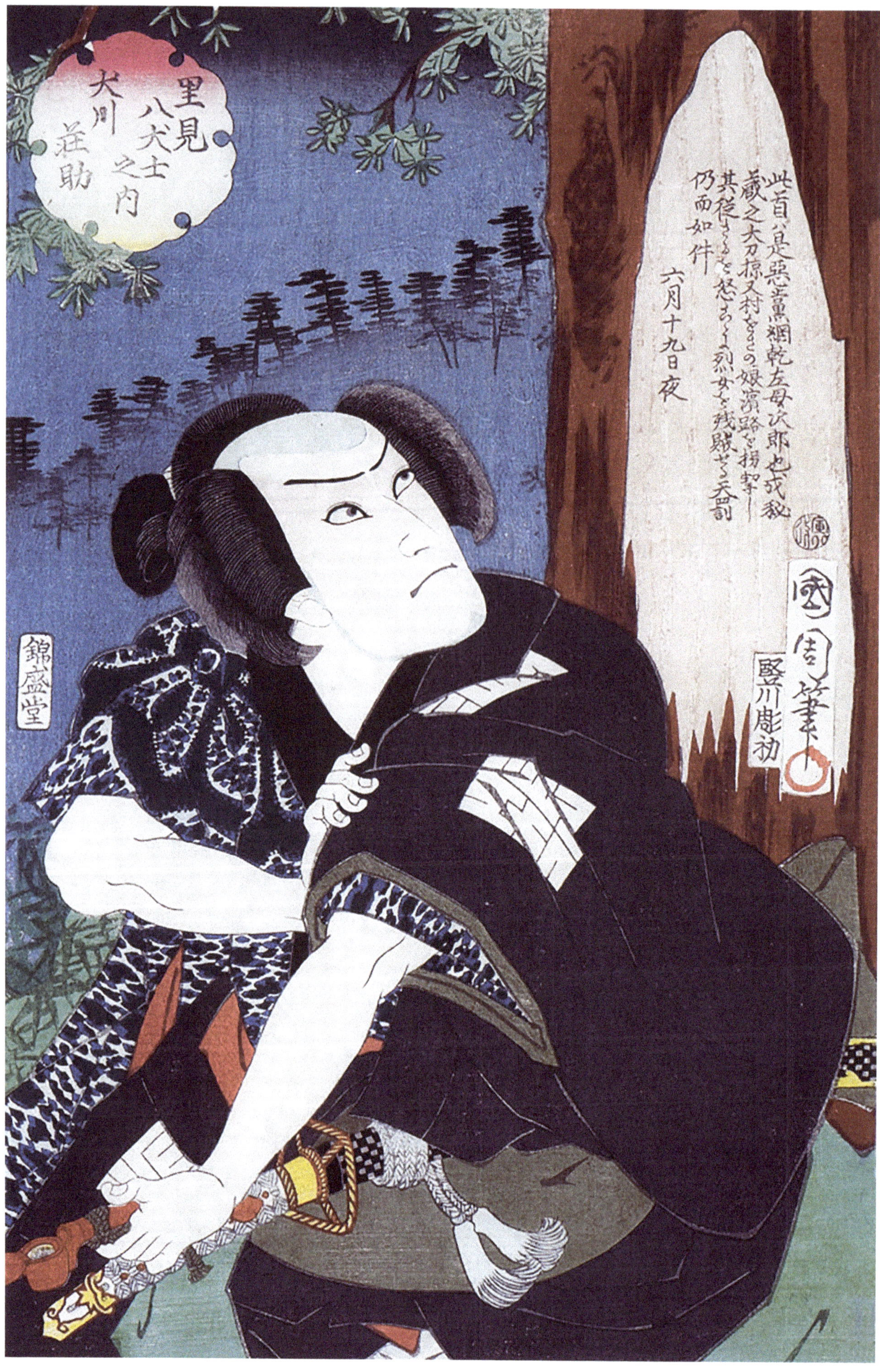
里見
八犬士
之内
犬川
荘助

此首ハ是悪童黒網乾左母次郎也戌秘
蔵之大刀捄又村をその娘濱路を掲挙
其従さるを怒るゝ烈女を残賊せる天罰
仍而如件

六月十九日夜

國周筆

堅川彫初

錦盛堂

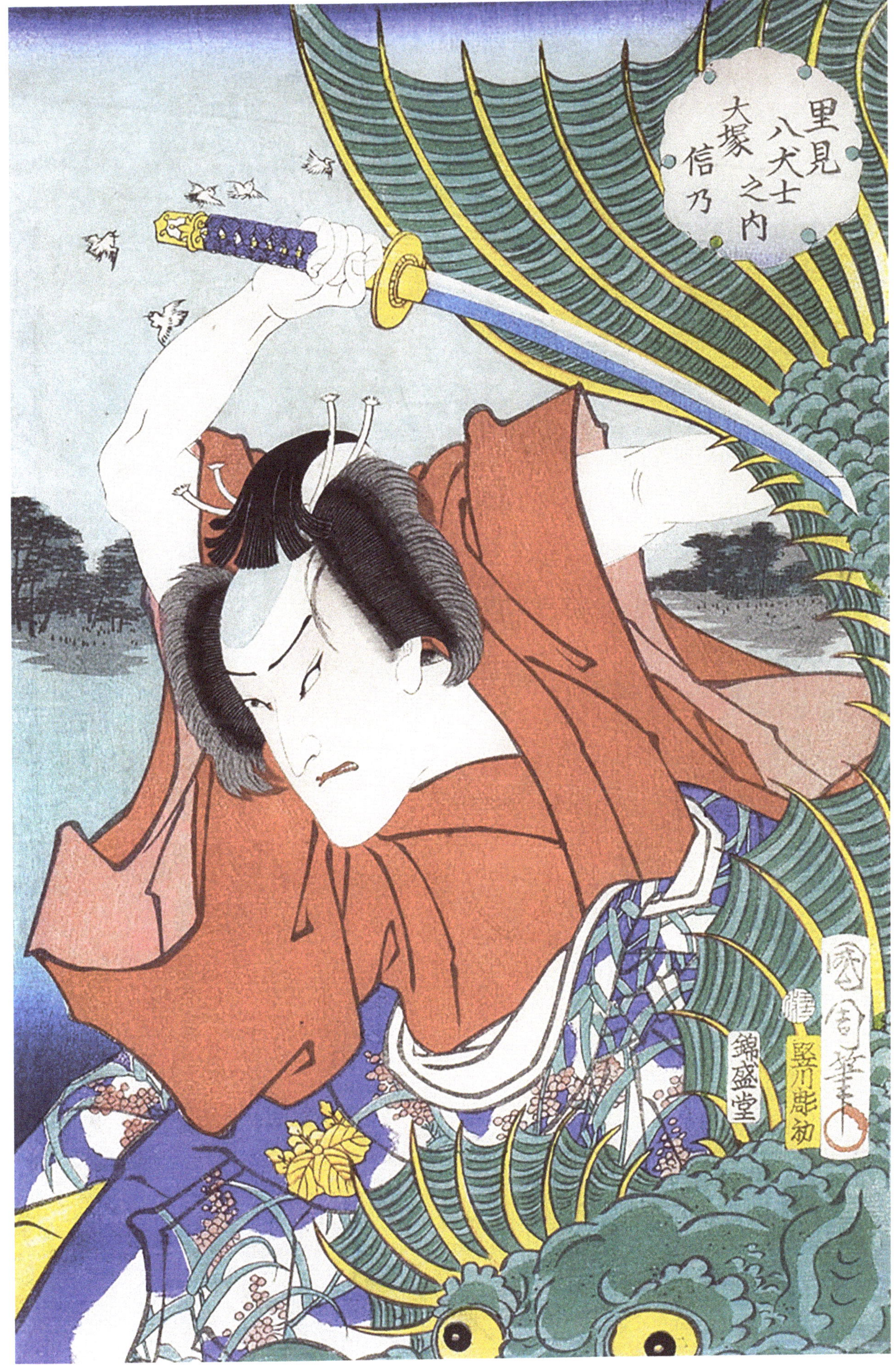
里見八犬士之内
大塚
信乃
國周筆
堅川彫初
錦盛堂

CHOCHIDORI JUBAN KIRI

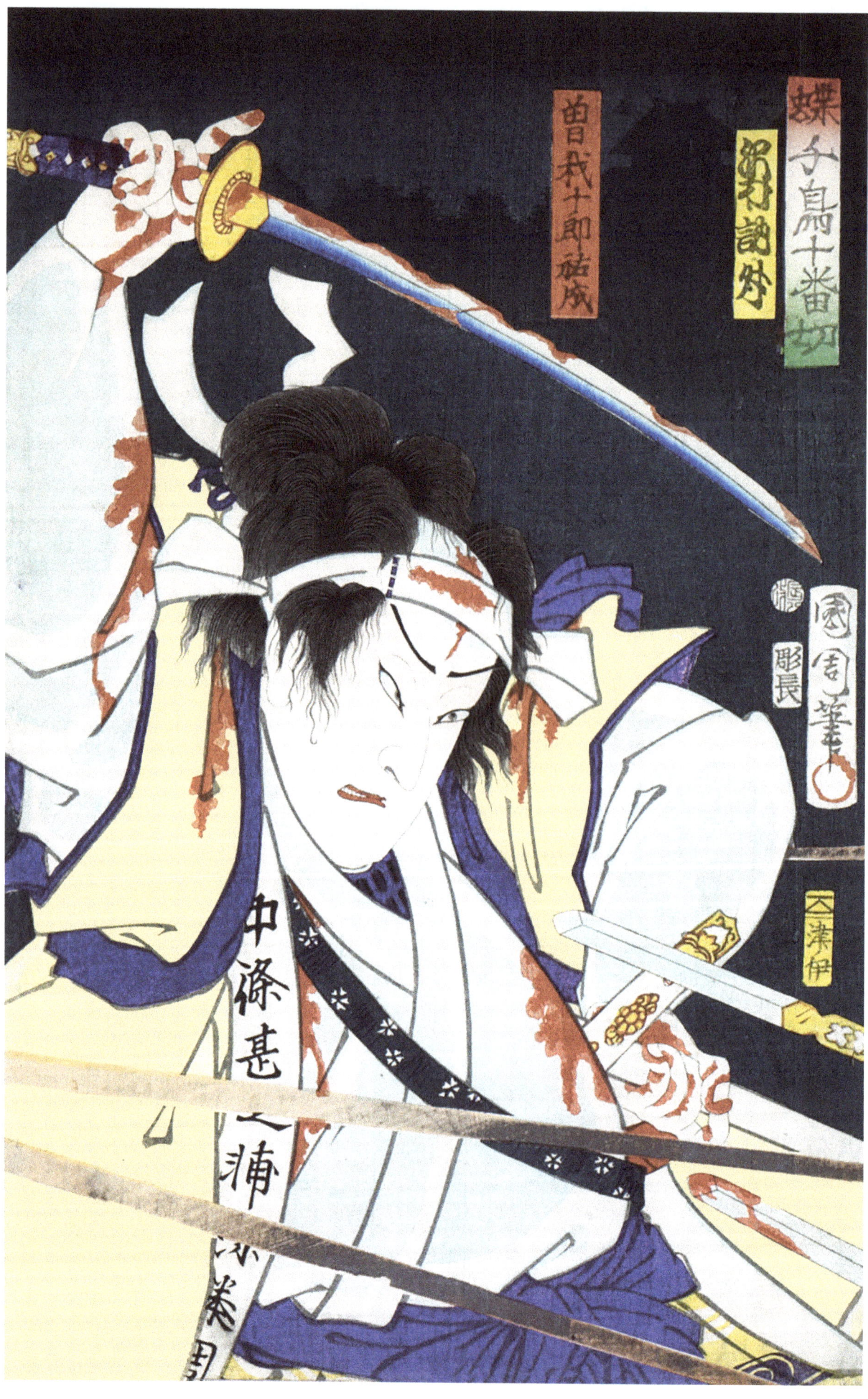

蝶千鳥十番切
梨諛分
曽我十郎祐成
國周筆
彫長
中條甚之輔

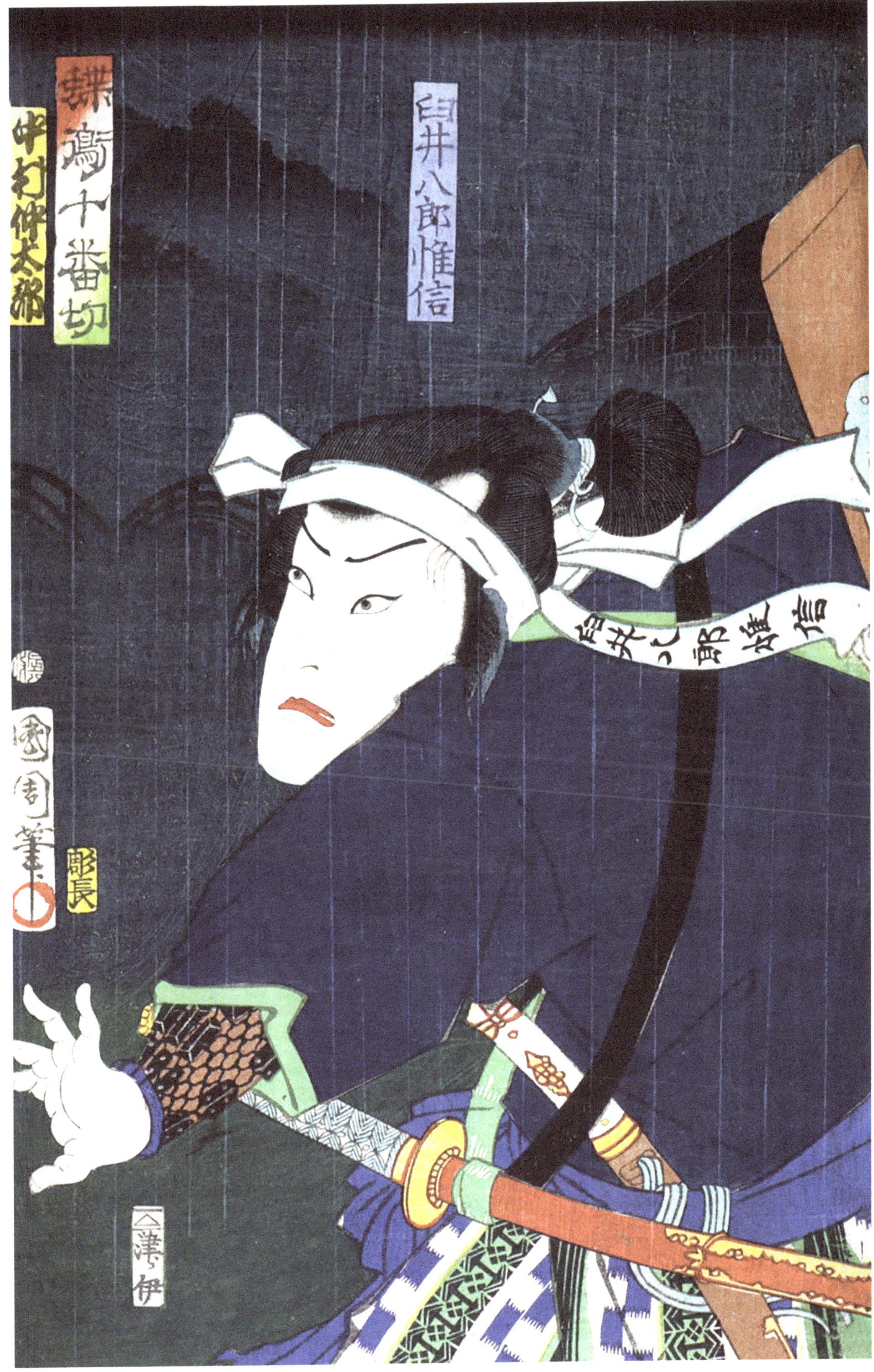

蝶鵆十番切
中村仲太郎
臼井八郎惟信

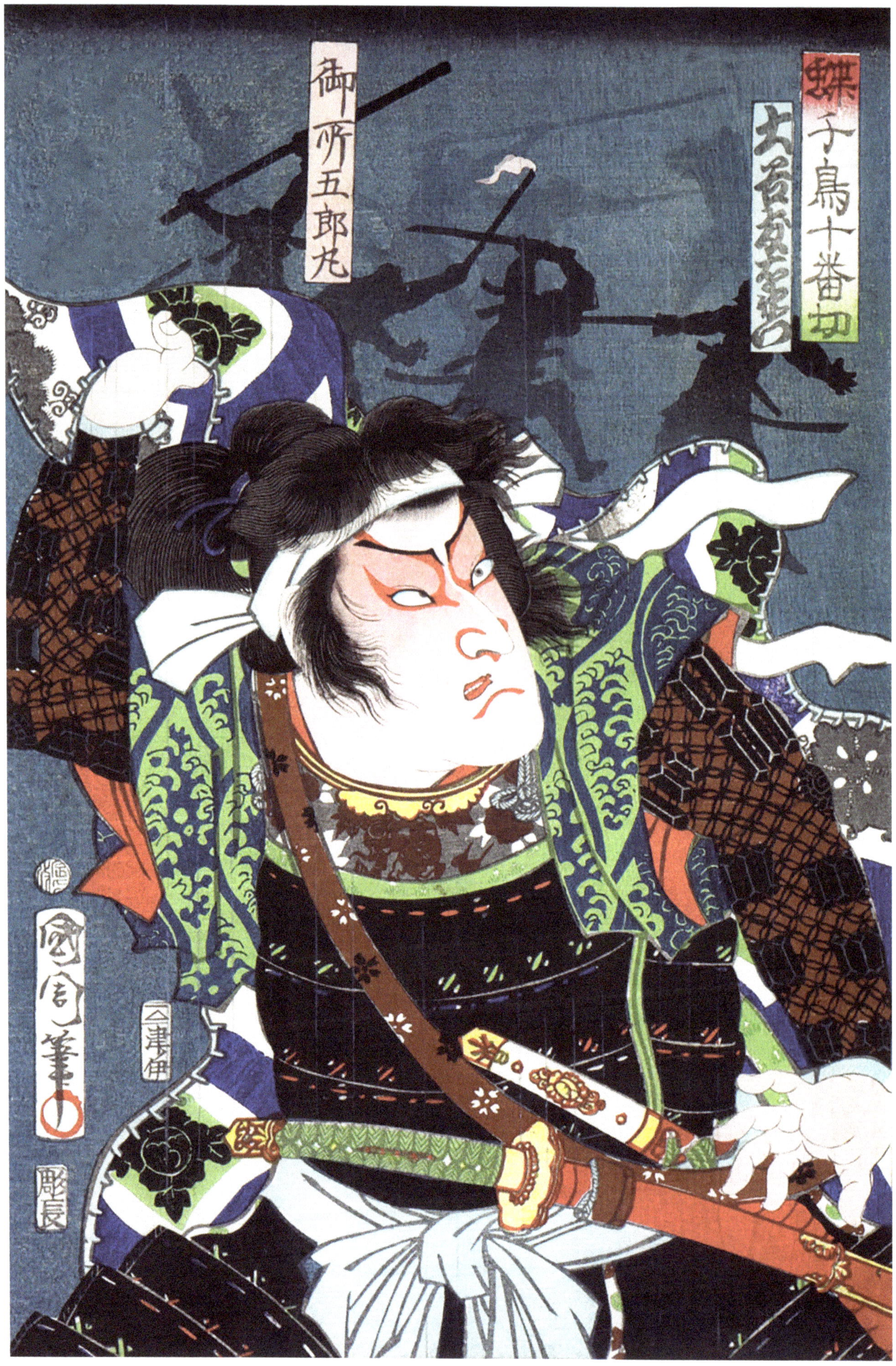
御所五郎丸
蝶々鳥十番切
六名儀左術の
国周筆
会津伊
彫長

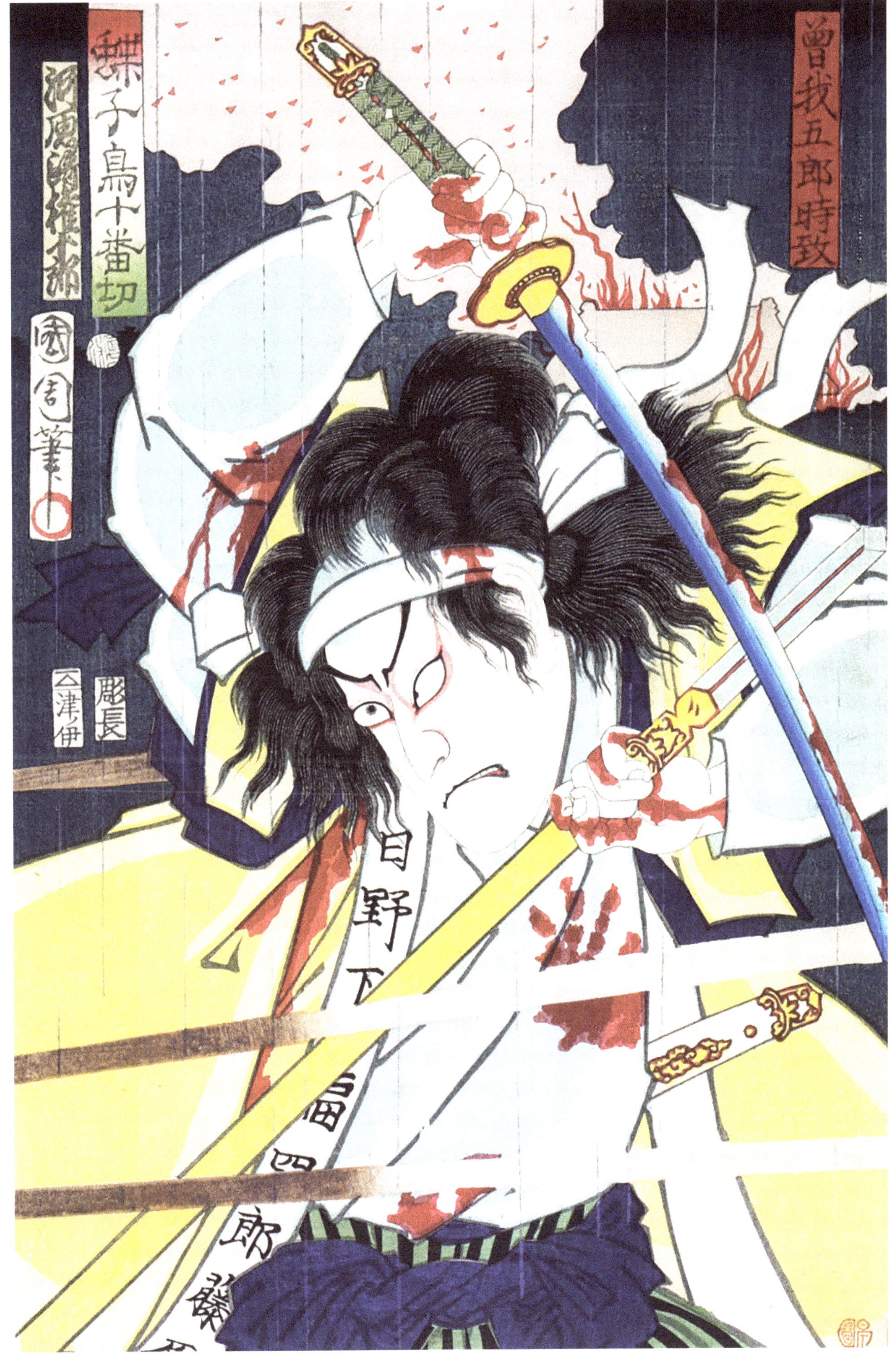
曽我五郎時致
蝶子鳥十番切
河原崎権十郎
國周筆
彫長
二津伊
日野下
四郎藤

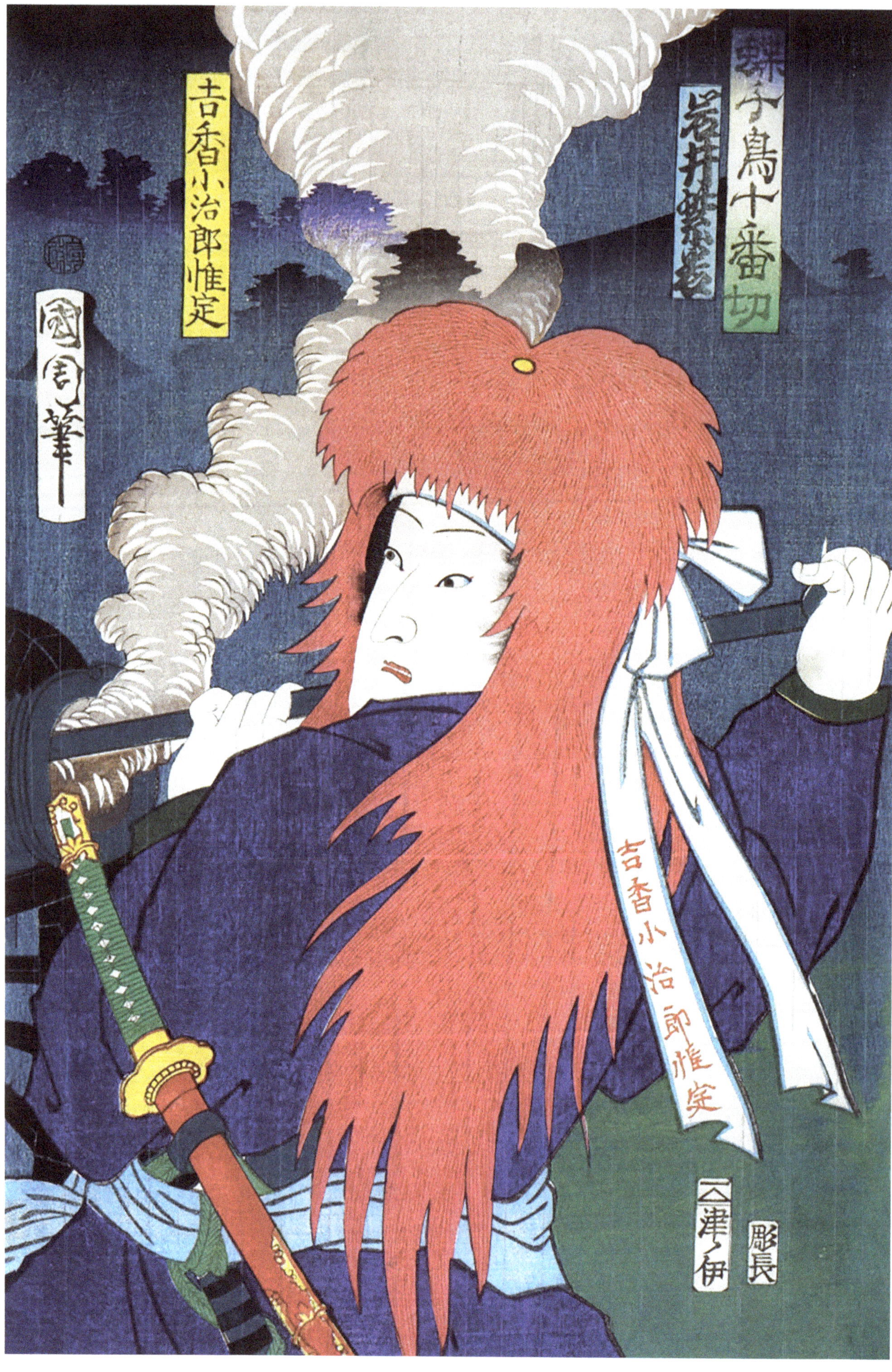

蝶千鳥十番切
岩井紫若
吉香小治郎惟定
國周筆
吉香小治郎惟定
彫長
三津ノ伊

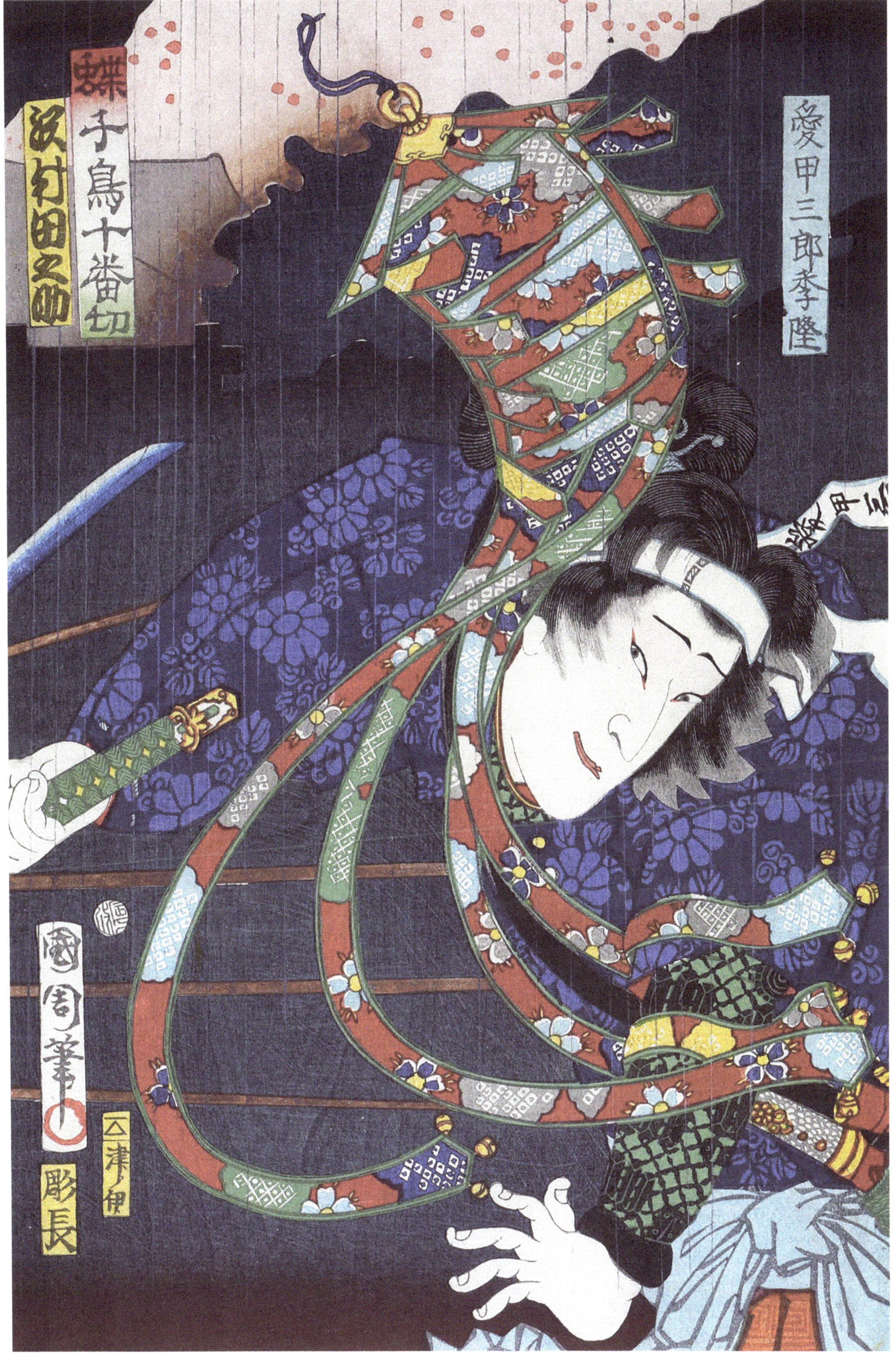
蝶千鳥十番切
沢村田之助
愛甲三郎季隆
國周筆
彫長

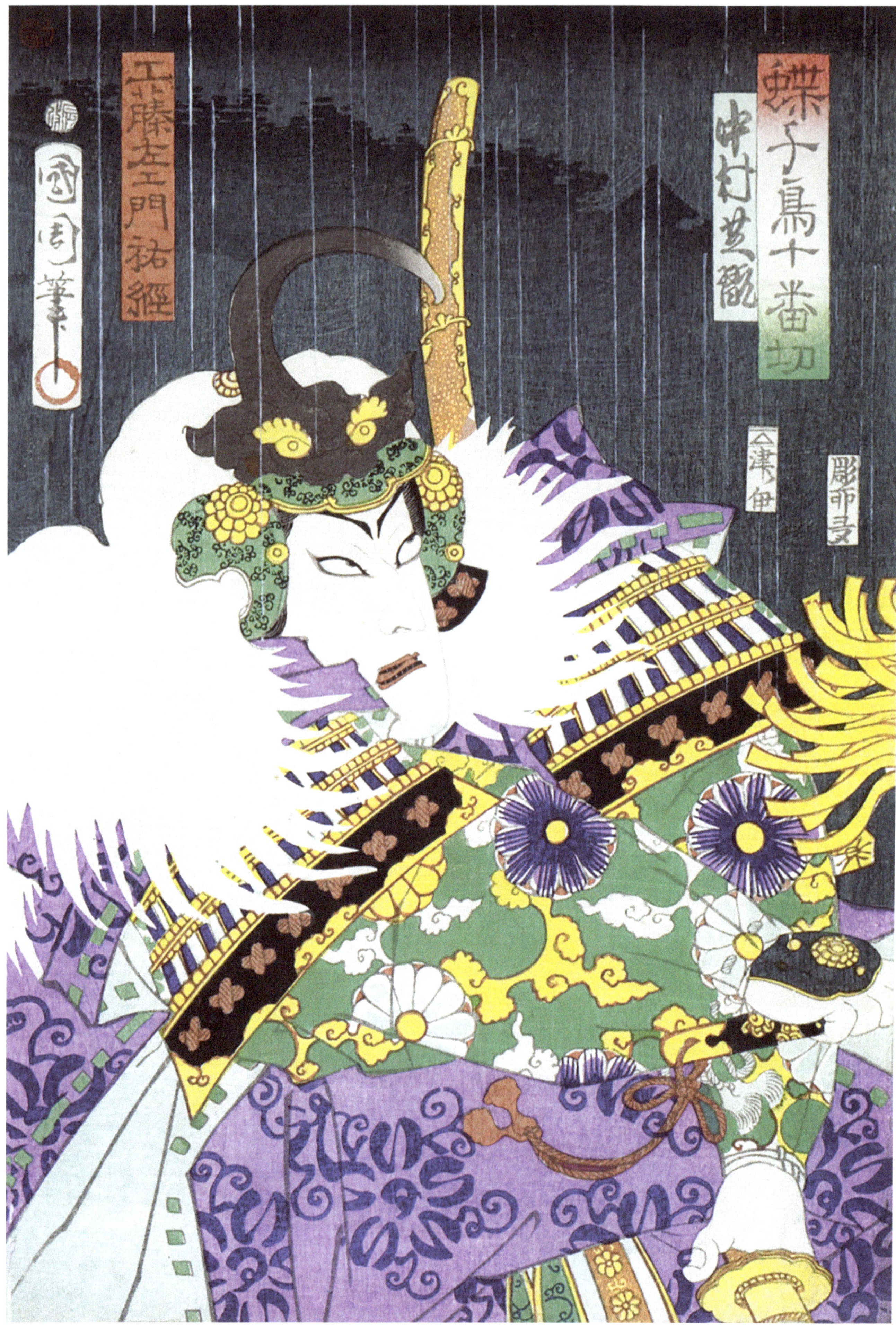
工藤左エ門祐經
國周筆

蝶千鳥十番切
中村其歡

會津ノ伸

彫市号

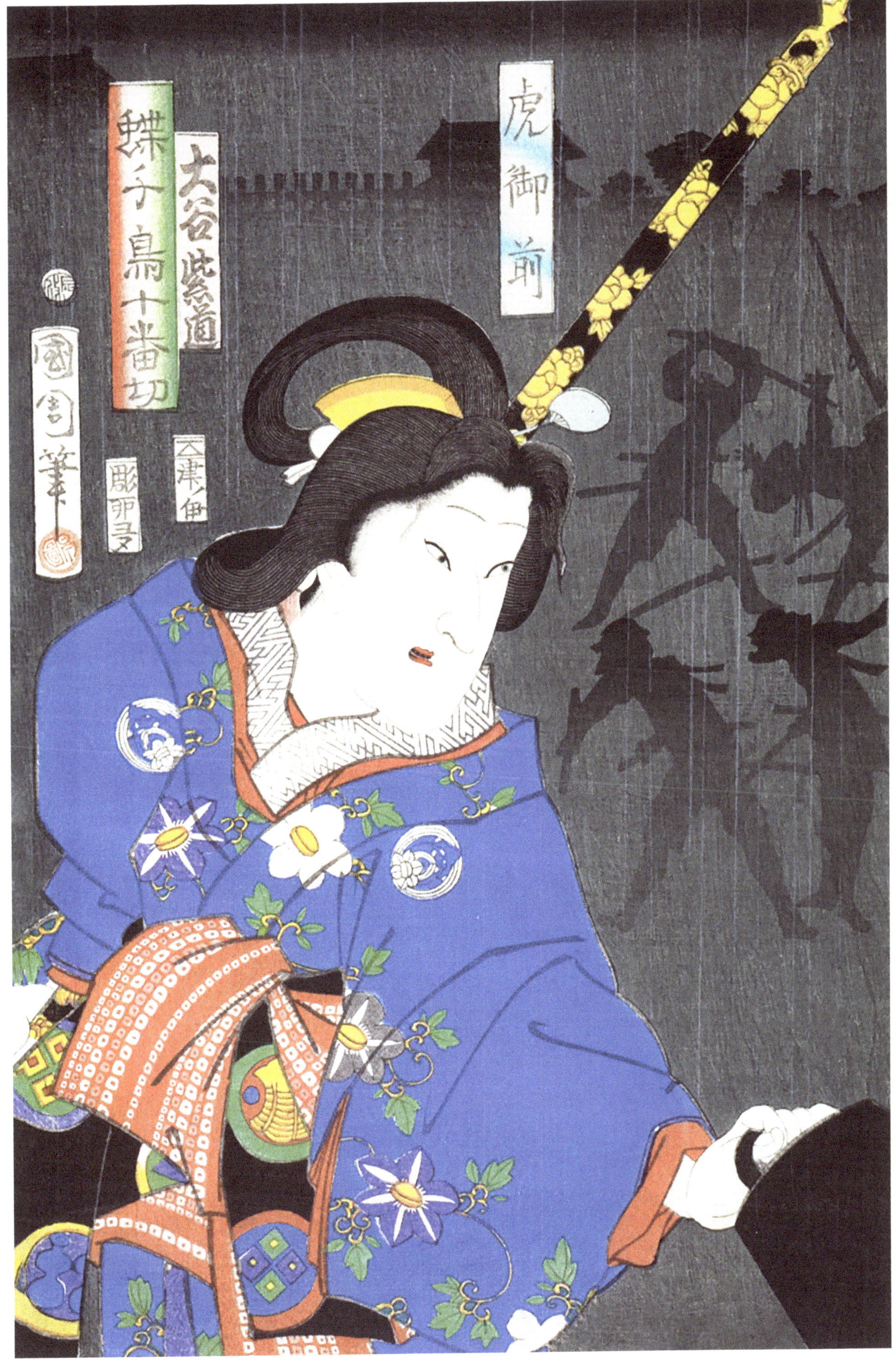

虎御前
大谷紫道
蝶千鳥十番切
國昌筆
彫卯号
六津伸

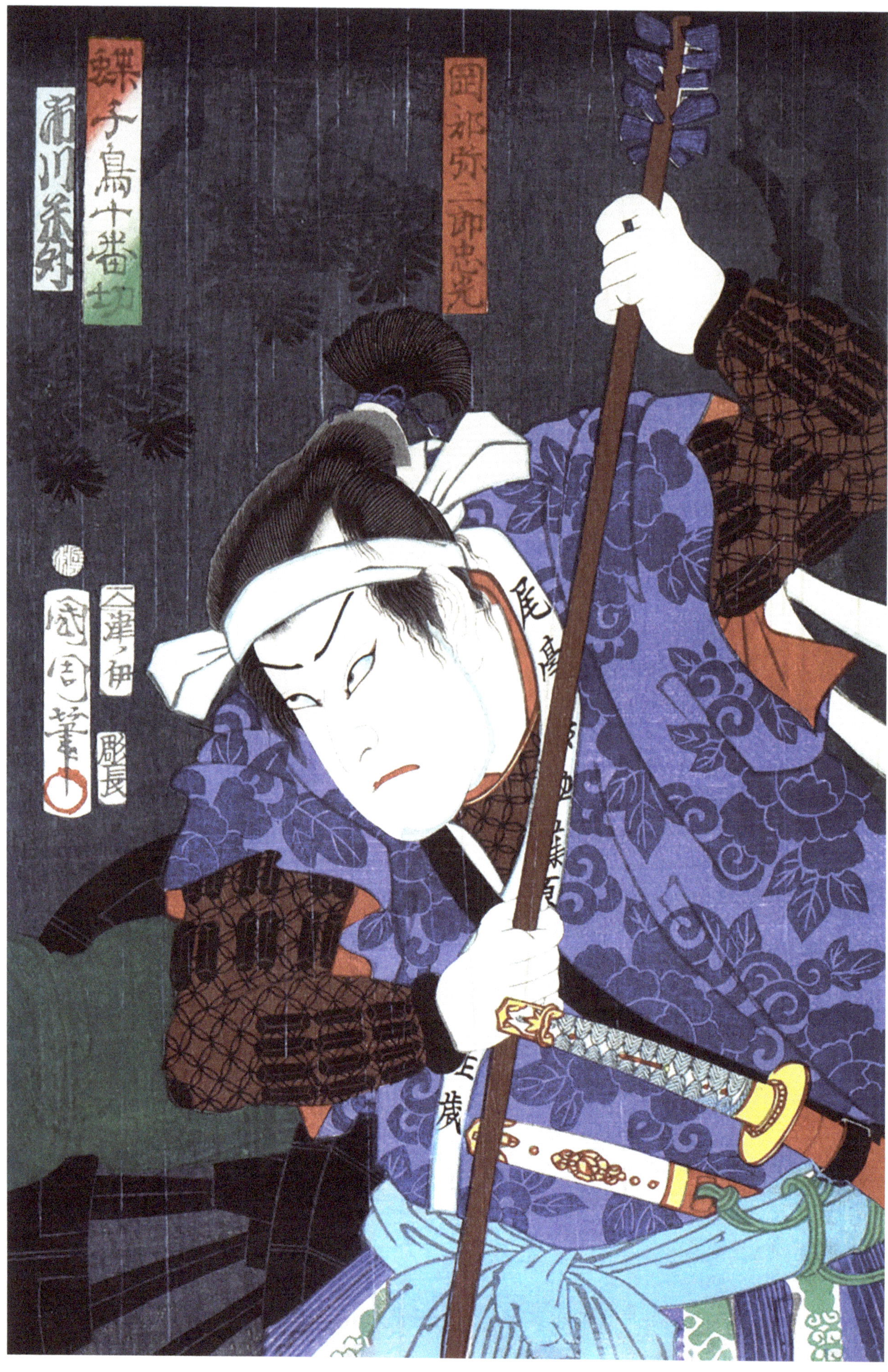
蝶子鳥十番切
市川糸升
囲祁弥三郎忠光
〈津ノ伊 彫長
国周筆

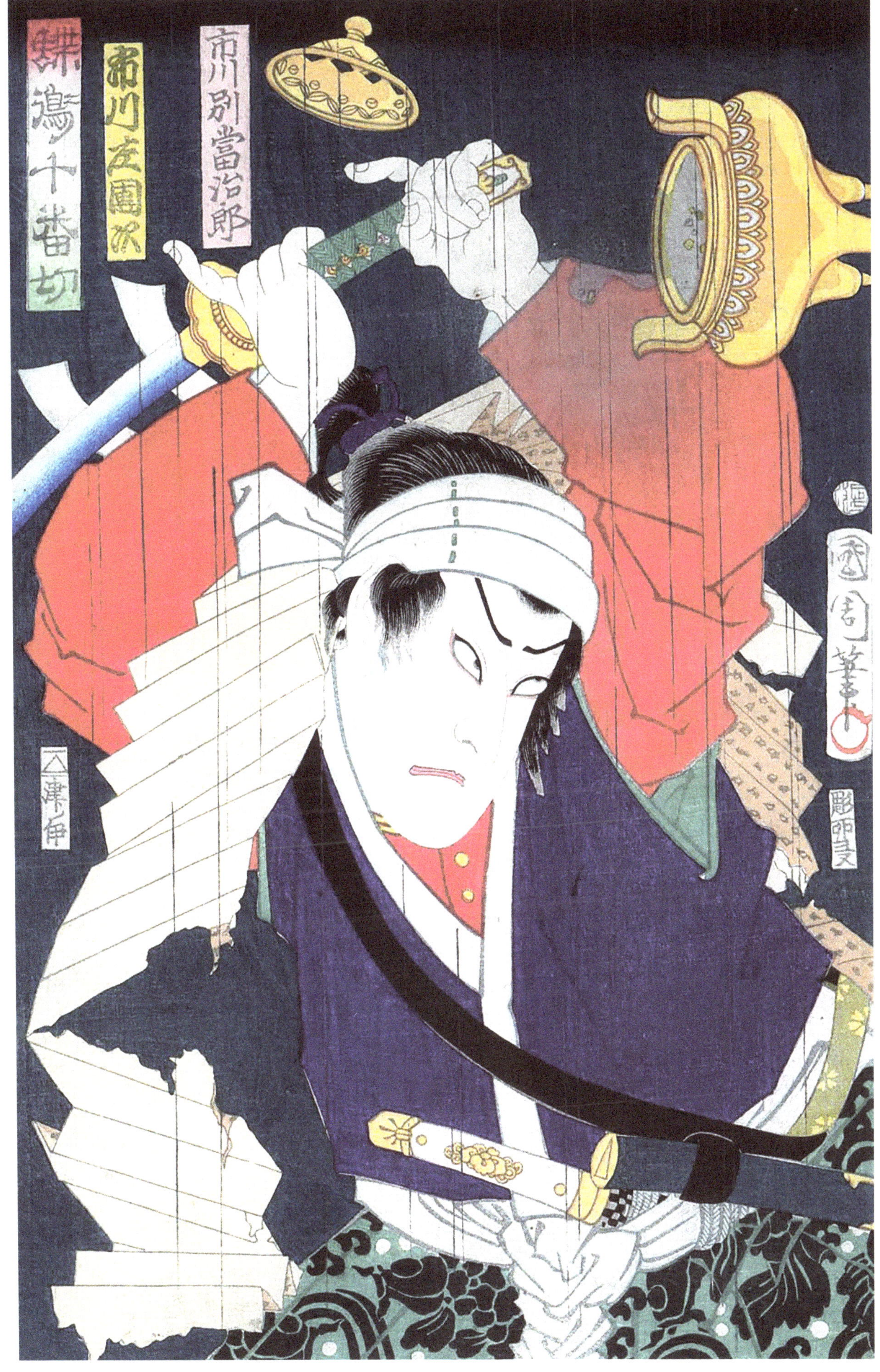
市川別當治郎
市川左團次
緋鴈十番切

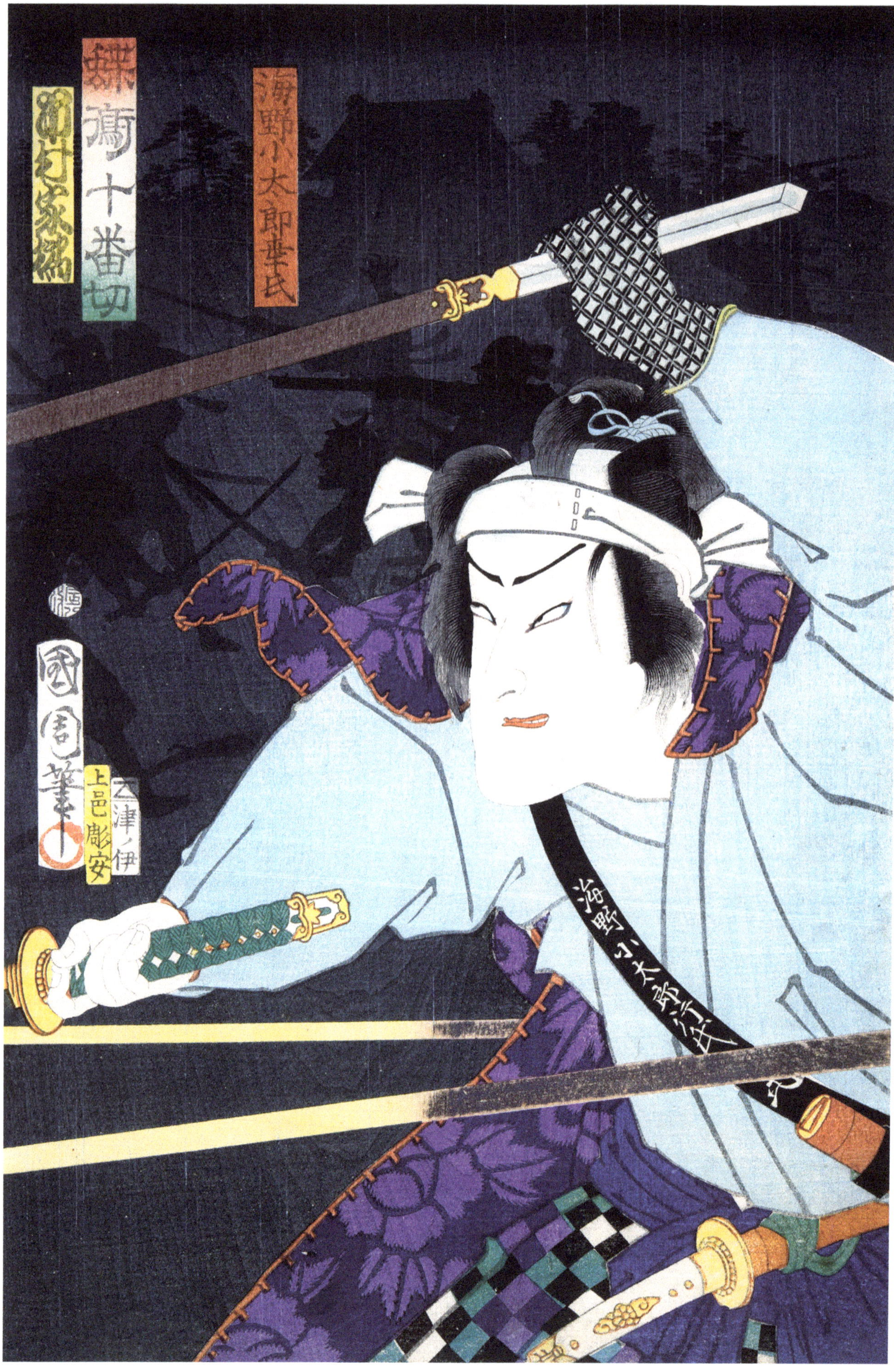
蝶鶺十番切
御江家綱

海野小太郎平氏

國周筆

二津ノ伊
上邑彫安

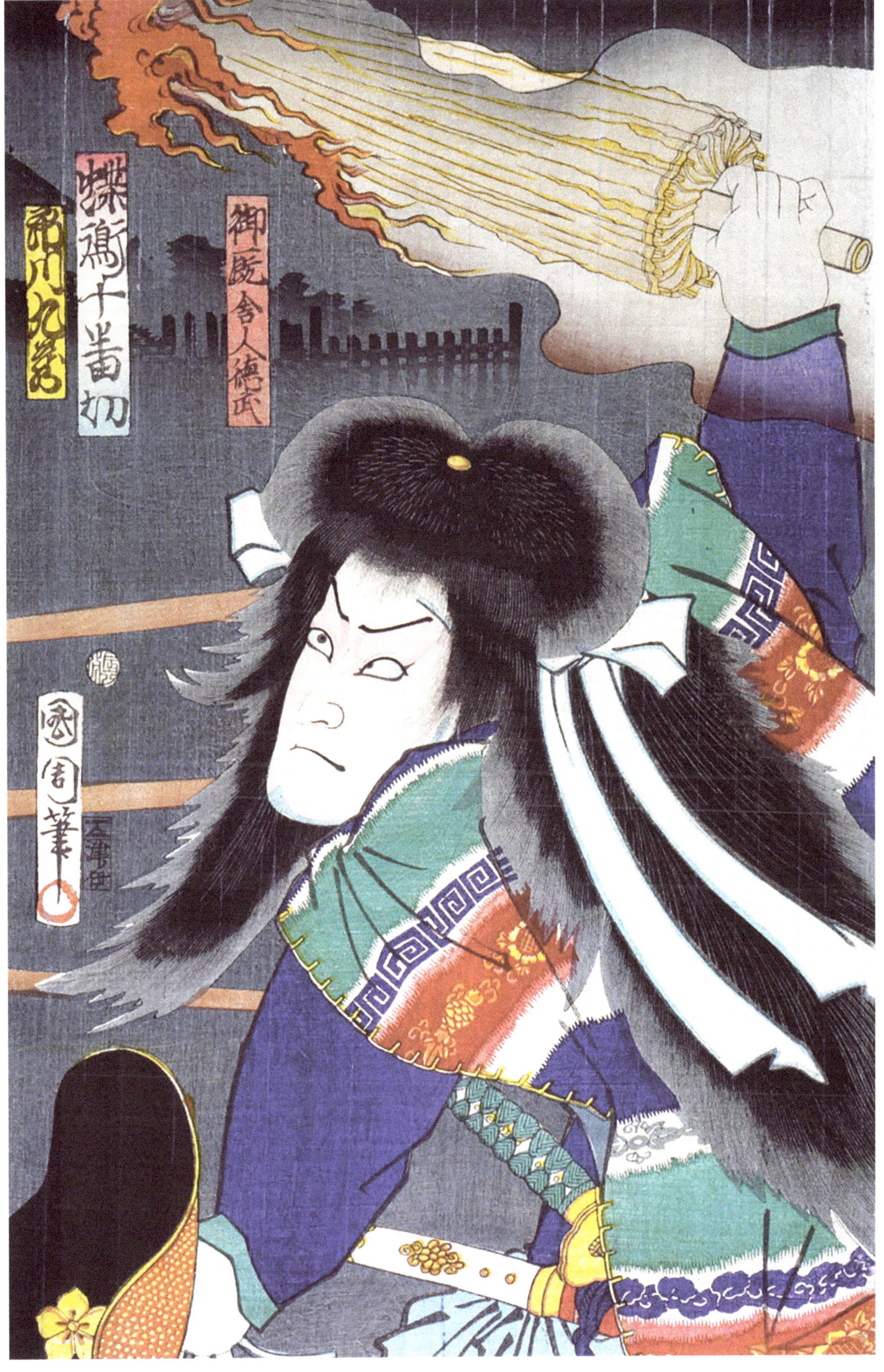
御廐舎人徳武
蝶鵆千両切
市川九蔵
国周筆

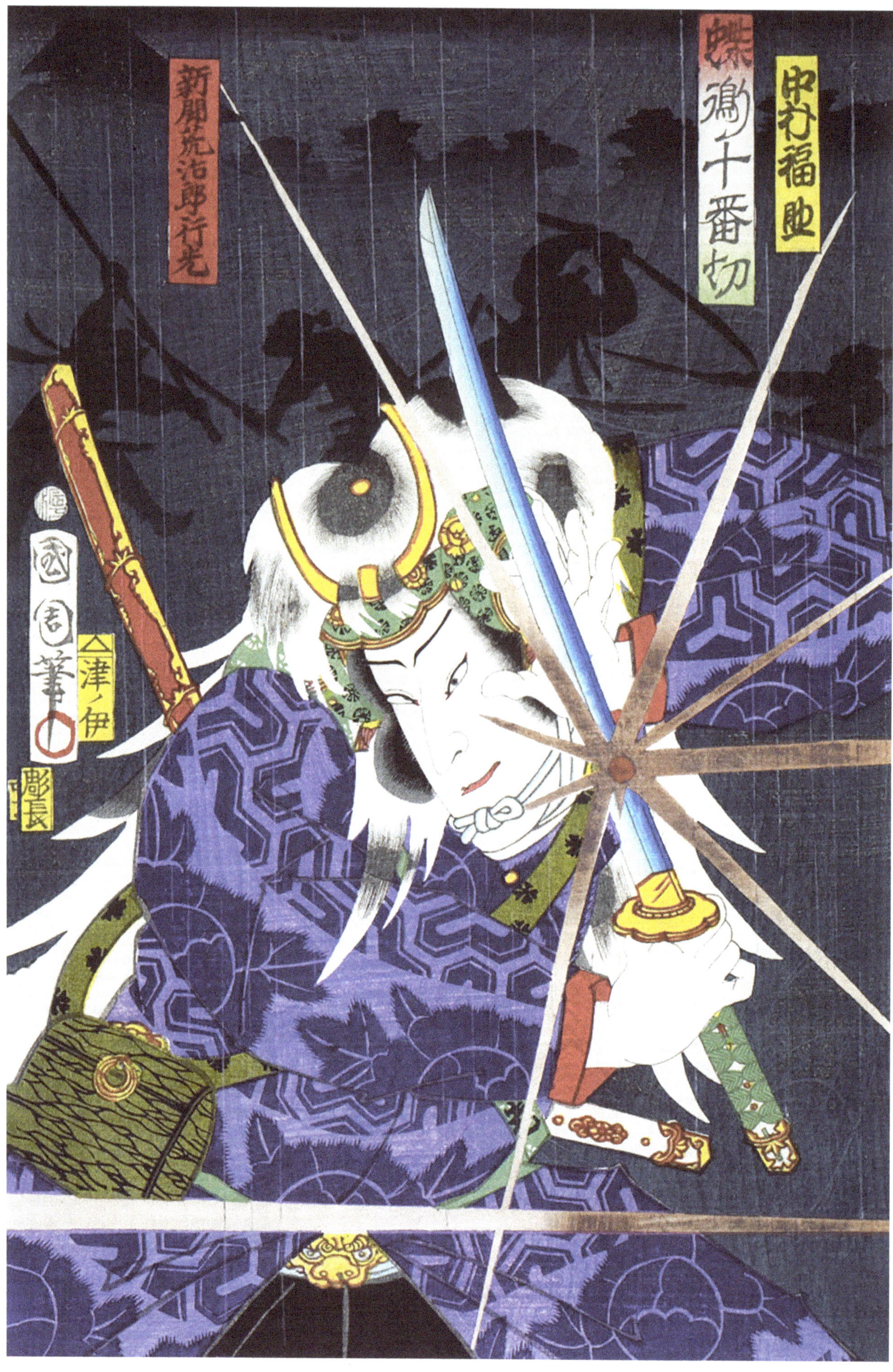
中村福助
蝶鵆十番切
新聞荒治郎行光
國周筆
會津ノ伊
彫長

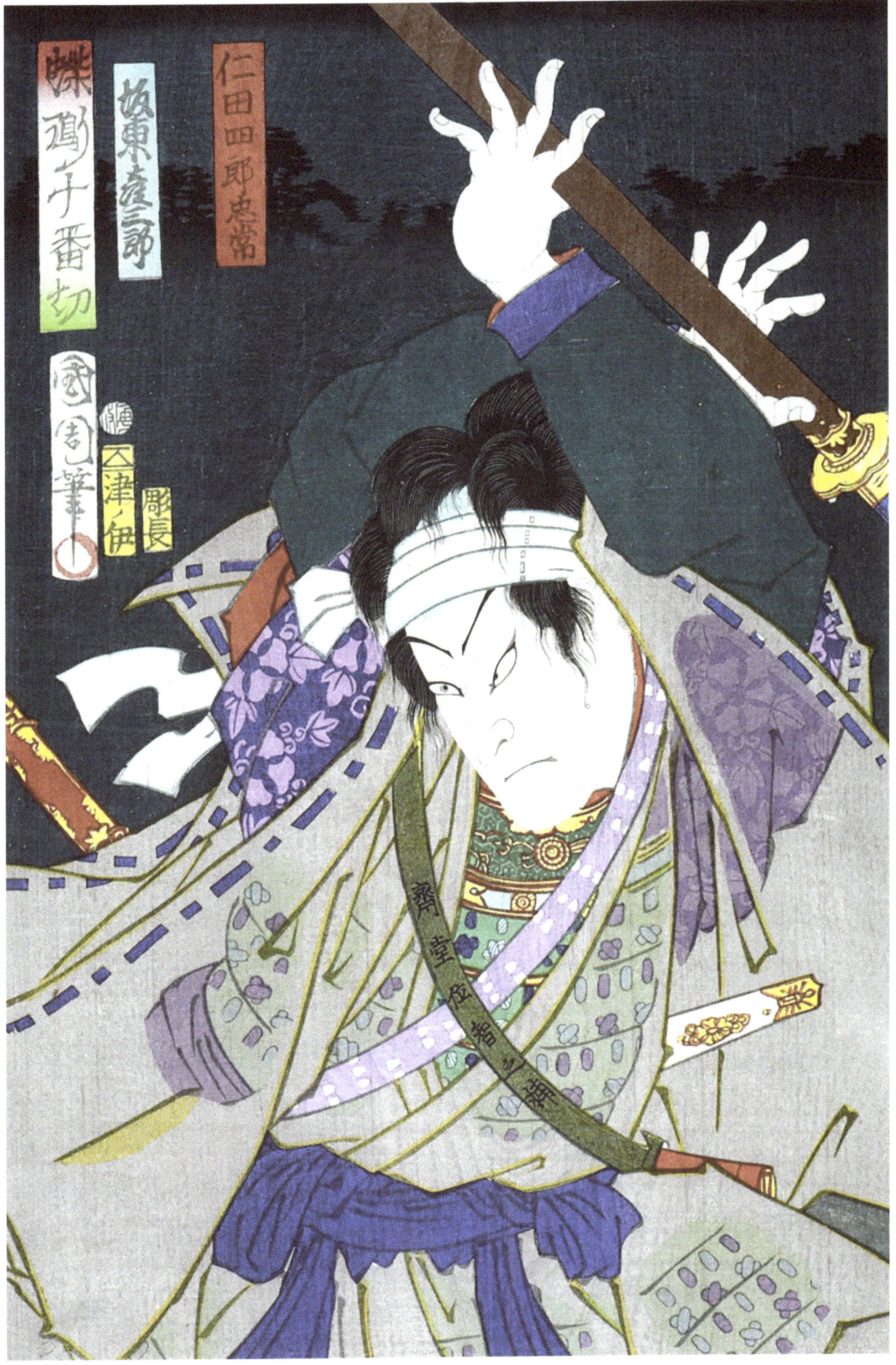
仁田四郎忠常
坂東彦三郎
蝶鵆子番切
國周筆
彫長
会津ノ伊

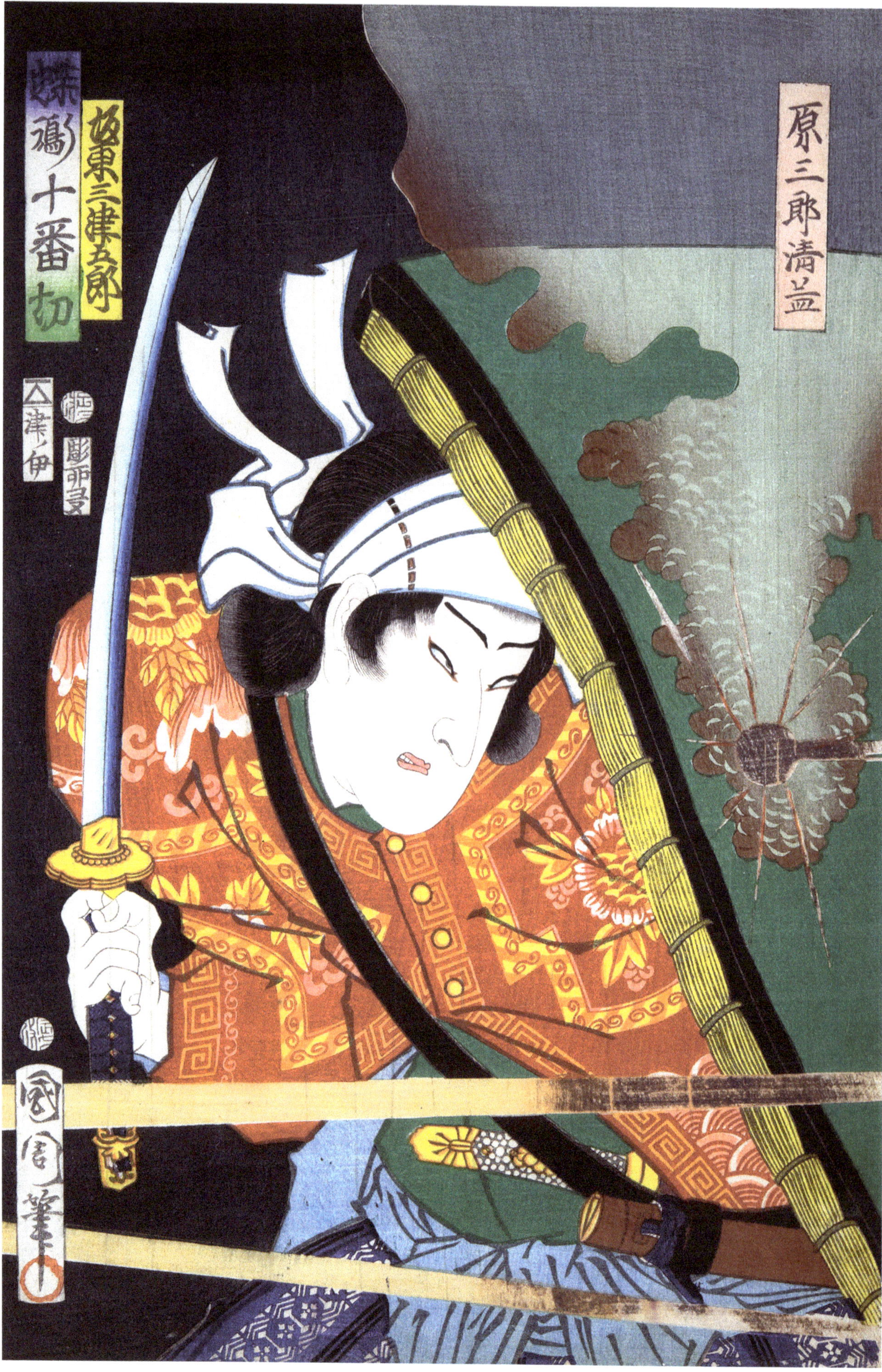
蝶飛十番切
坂東三津五郎
彫卯
大津ノ伊
國周筆
原三郎清盈

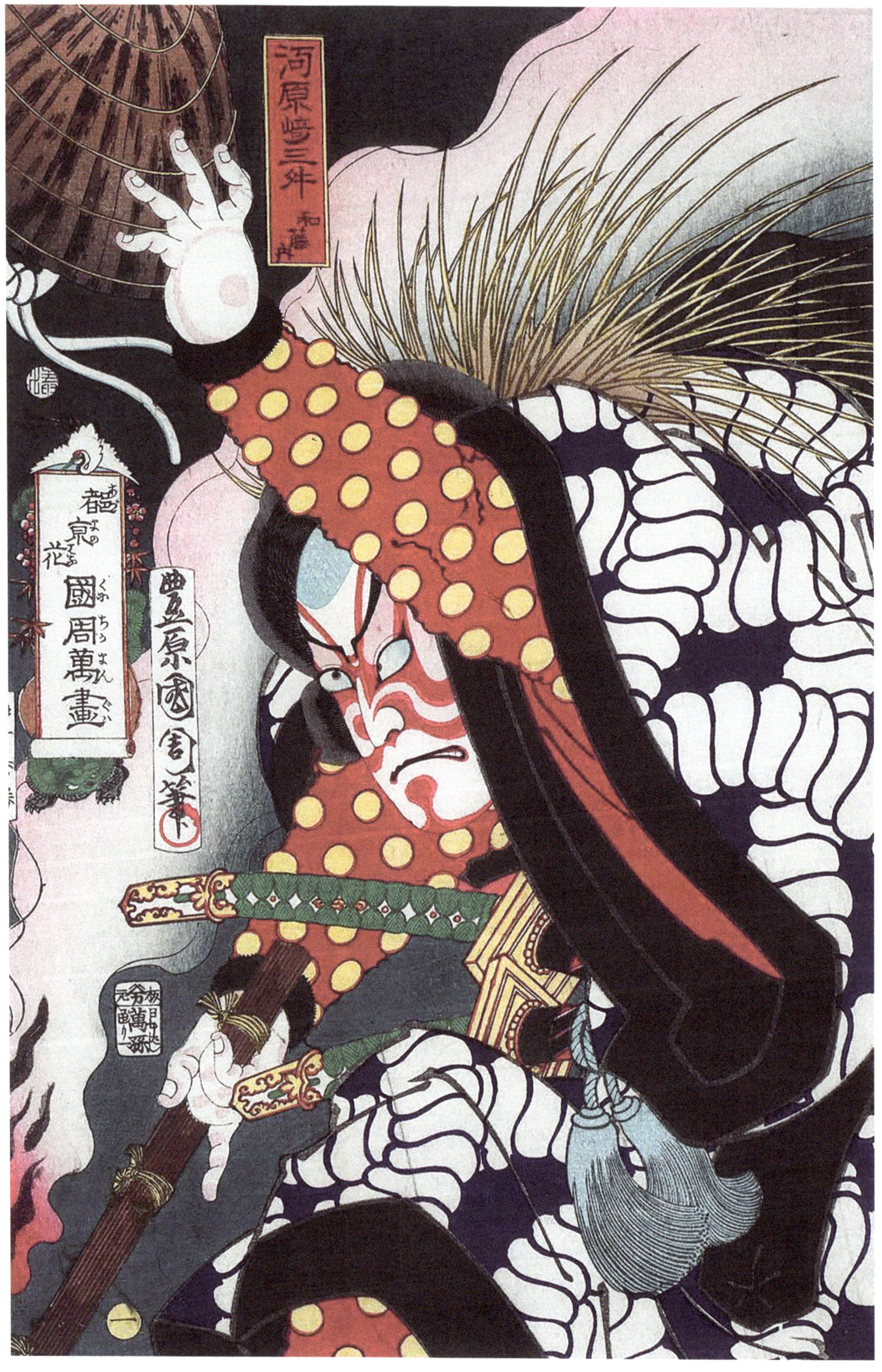

48

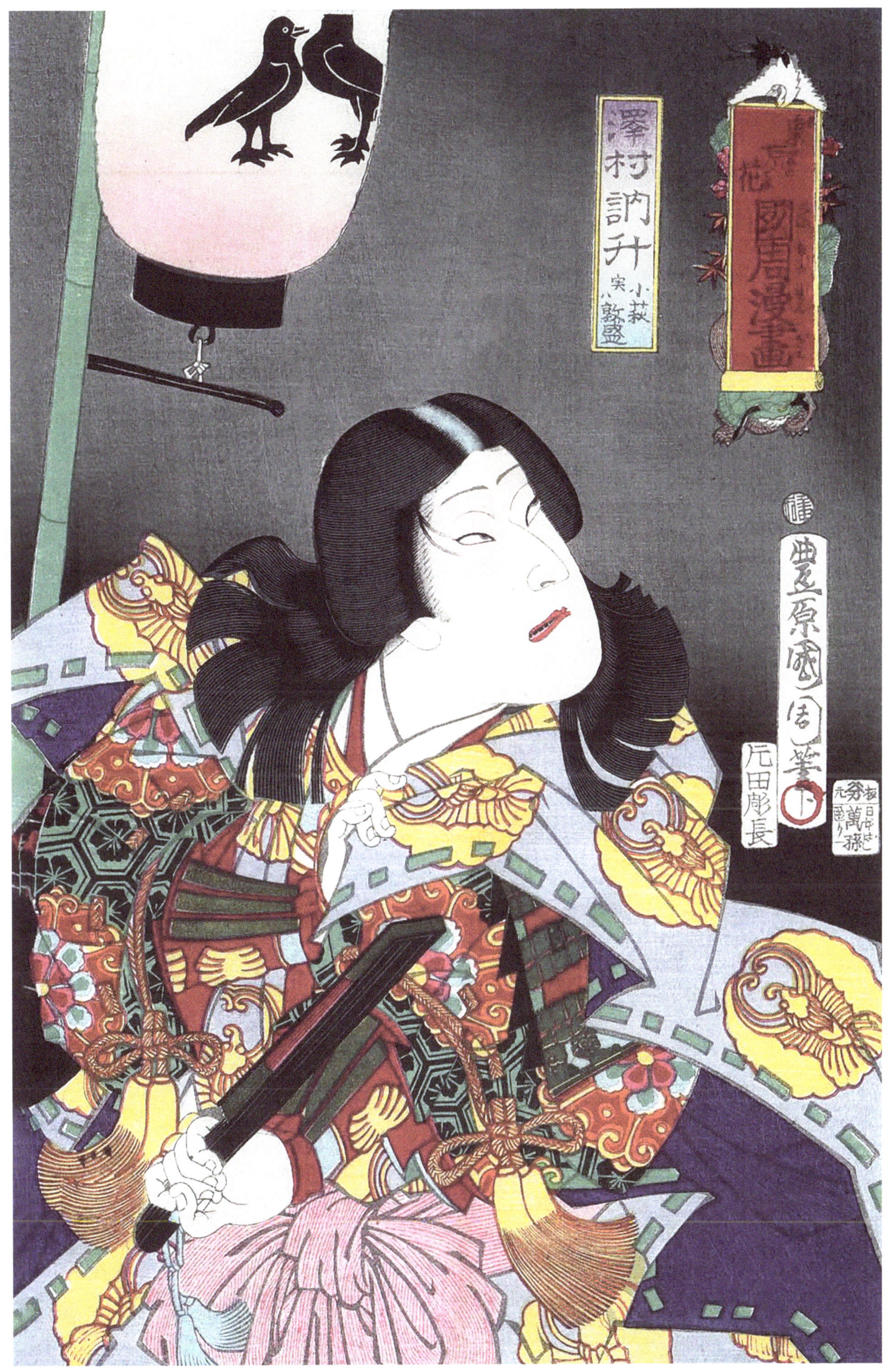
新古今國周漫畫
峯村訥升
小萩
実八盛盛
豊原國周筆
厄田彫長

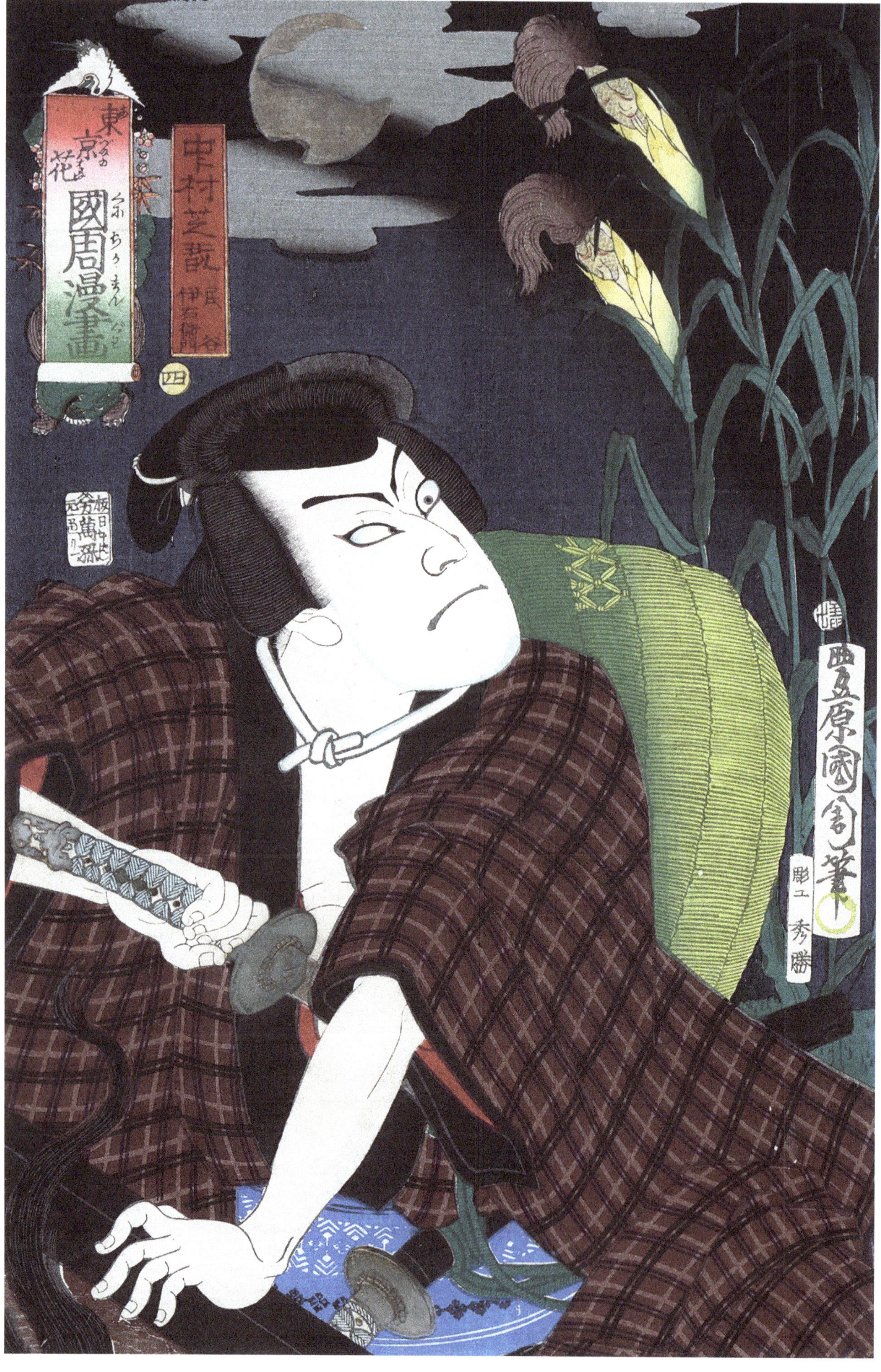

東京花
國周漫画
中村芝翫
民谷伊右衛門
豊原國周筆
彫工 秀勝

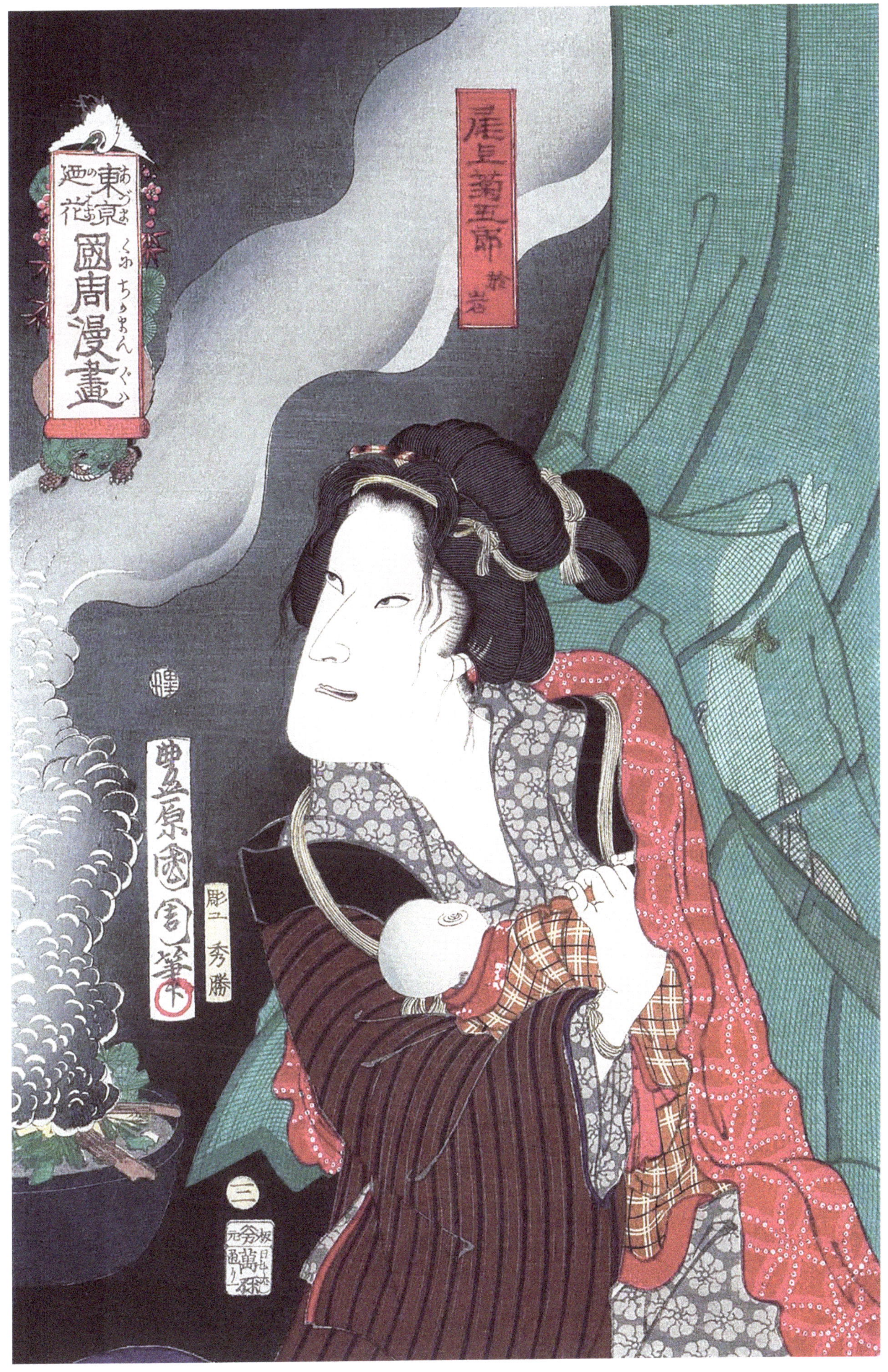
尾上菊五郎
拾岩

東京
迺花
國周漫畫

豊原國周筆
應ニ 秀勝

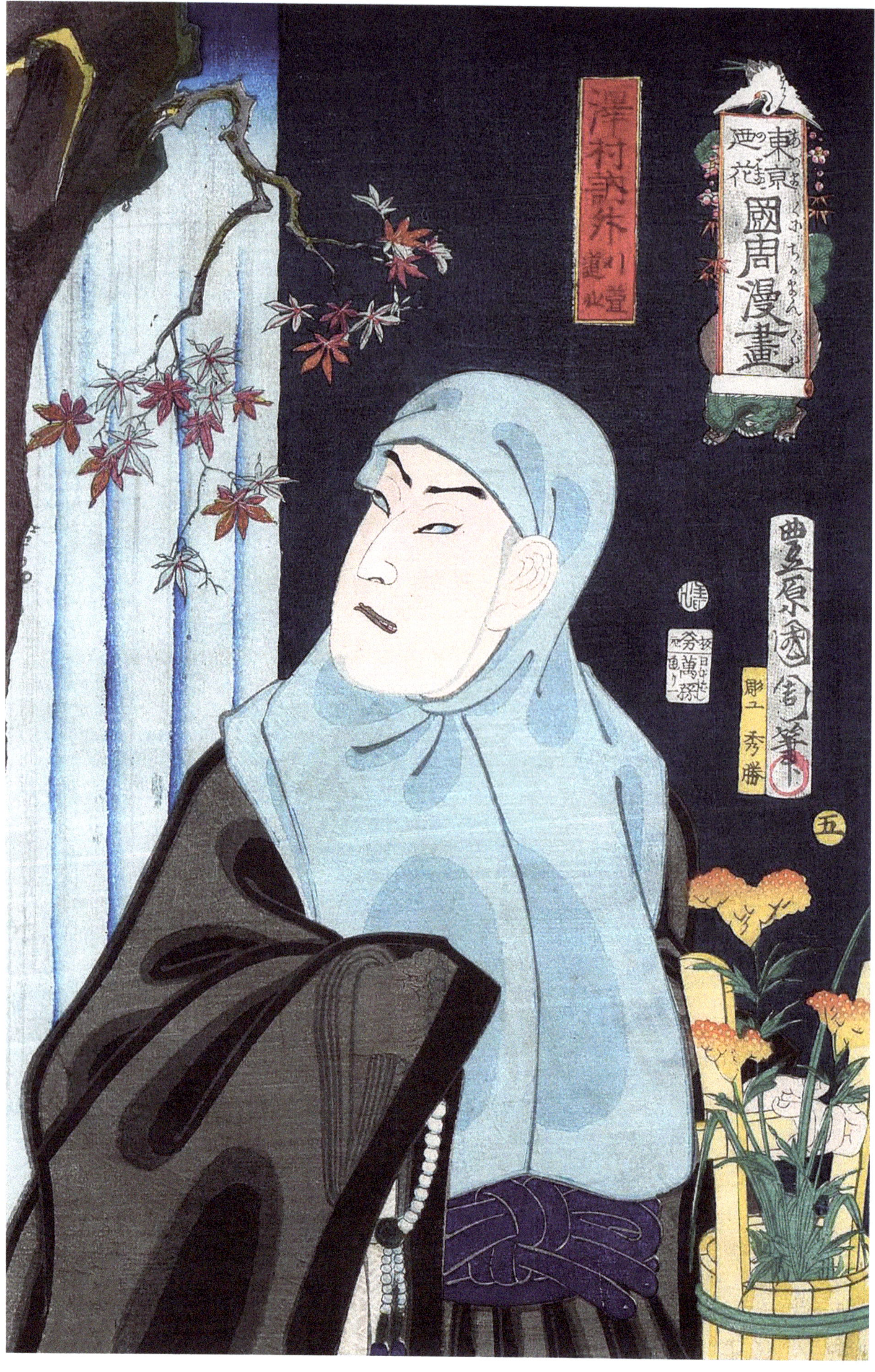
東京の悪の花
國周漫畫
豊原國周筆
澤村訥升
彫工 秀勝

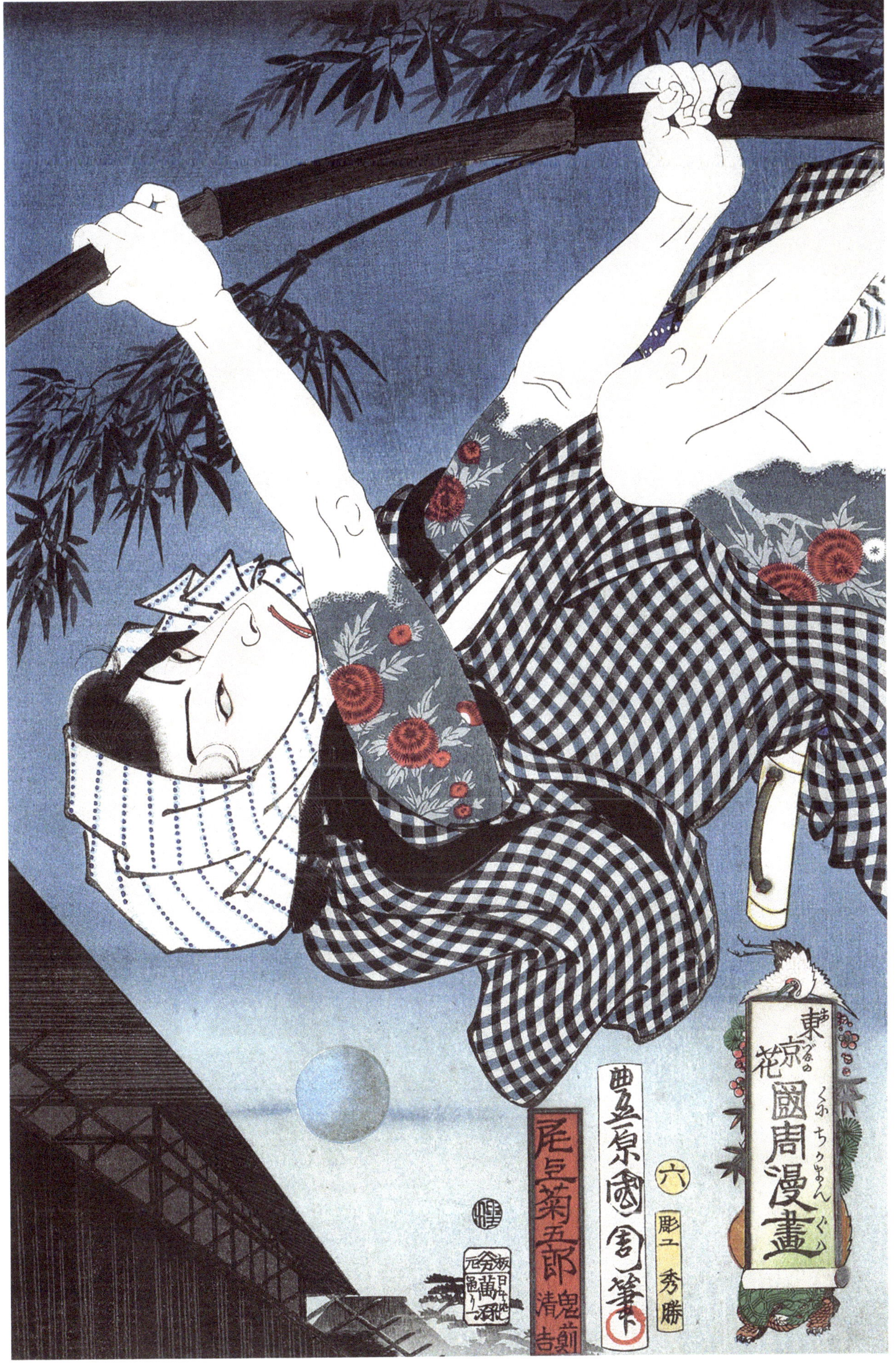

東京の花
國周漫畫
くふちうきやんぐ
豊五原國周筆
六 彫工 秀勝
尾上菊五郎
鬼剪
清吉

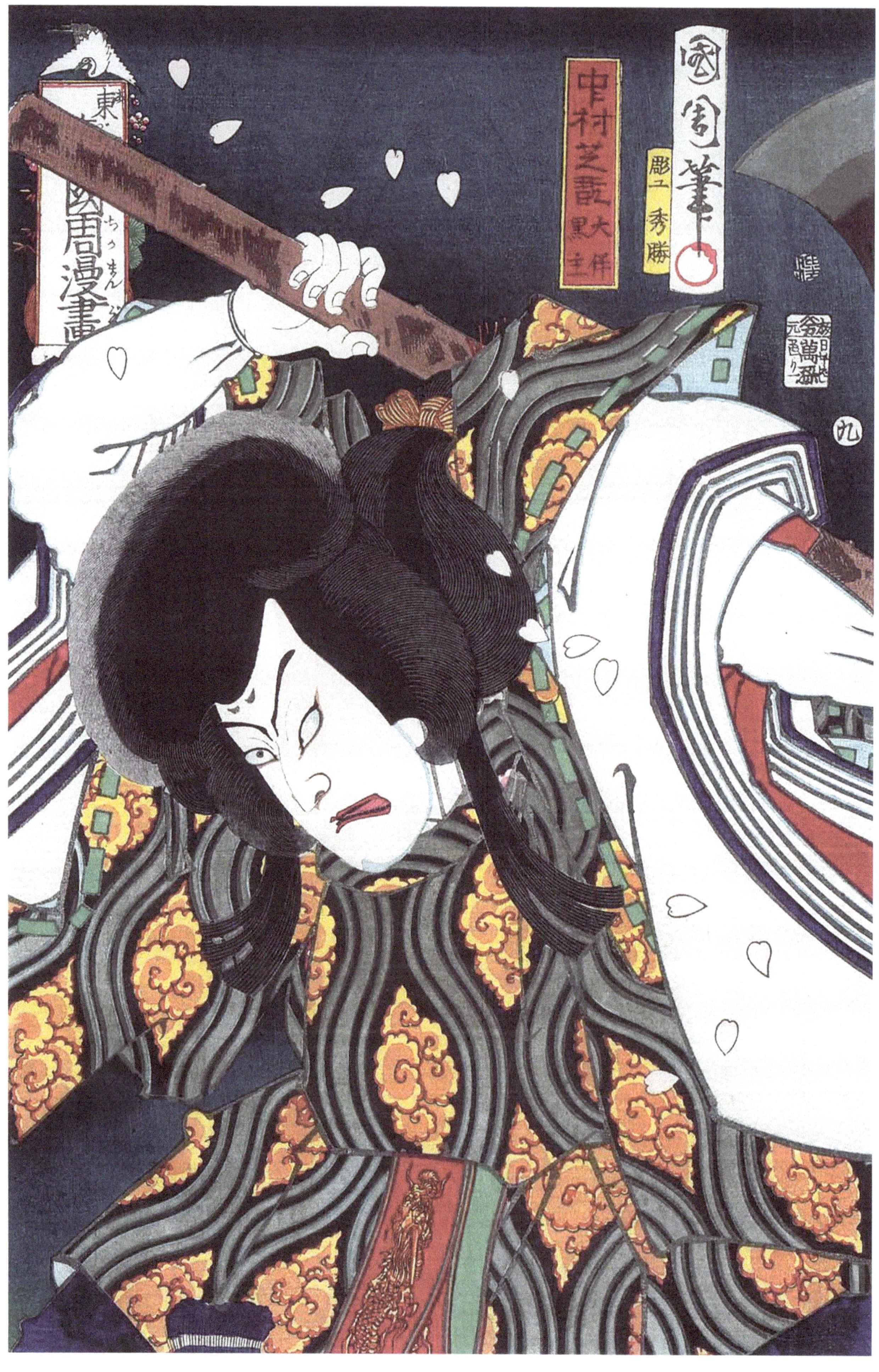
東
国周漫畫
ちゆまん

中村芝翫
大伴
黒主

國周筆
彫工 秀勝

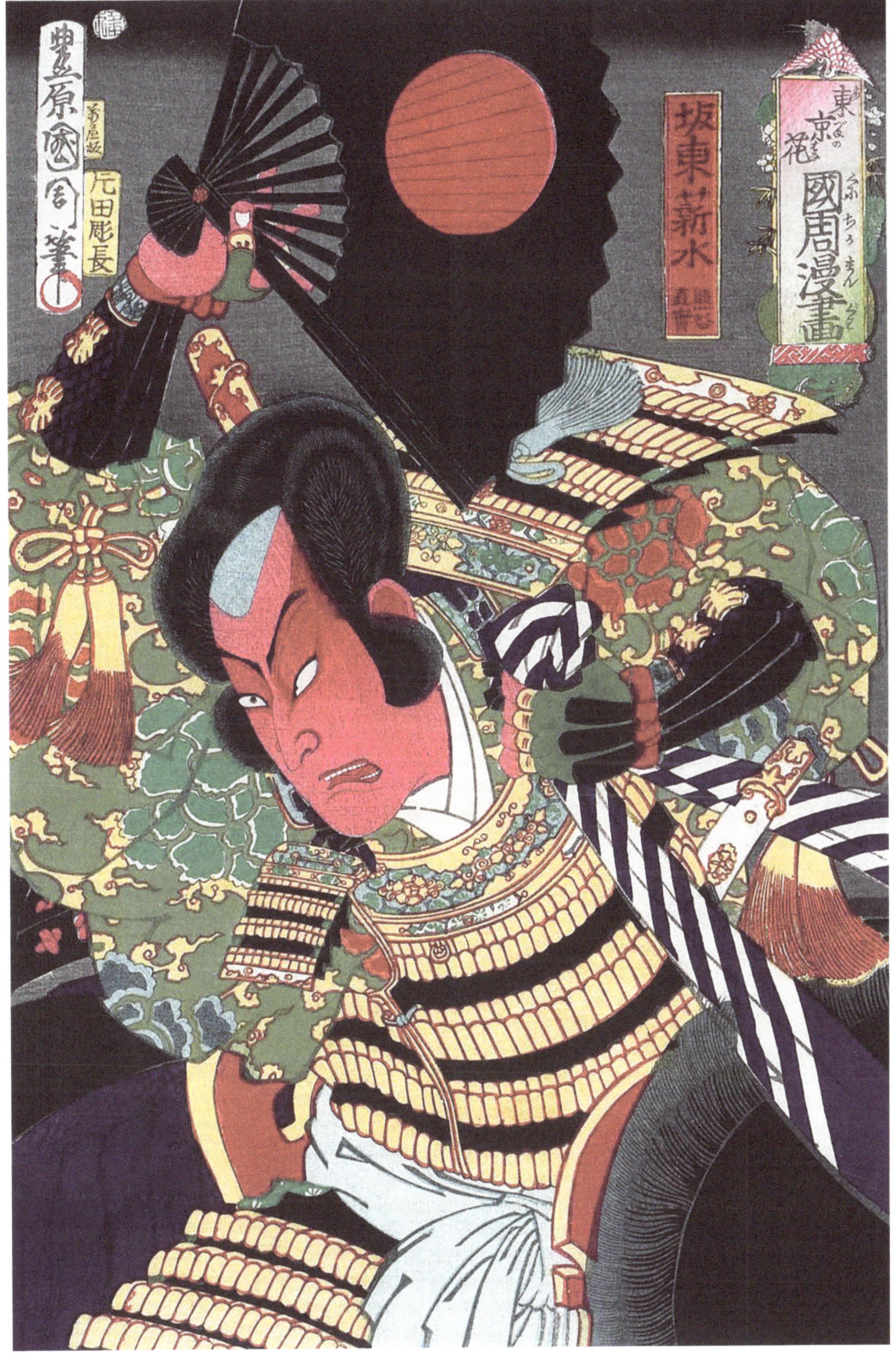
豊原國周筆
片田彫長
東京の花
國周漫畫
坂東薪水

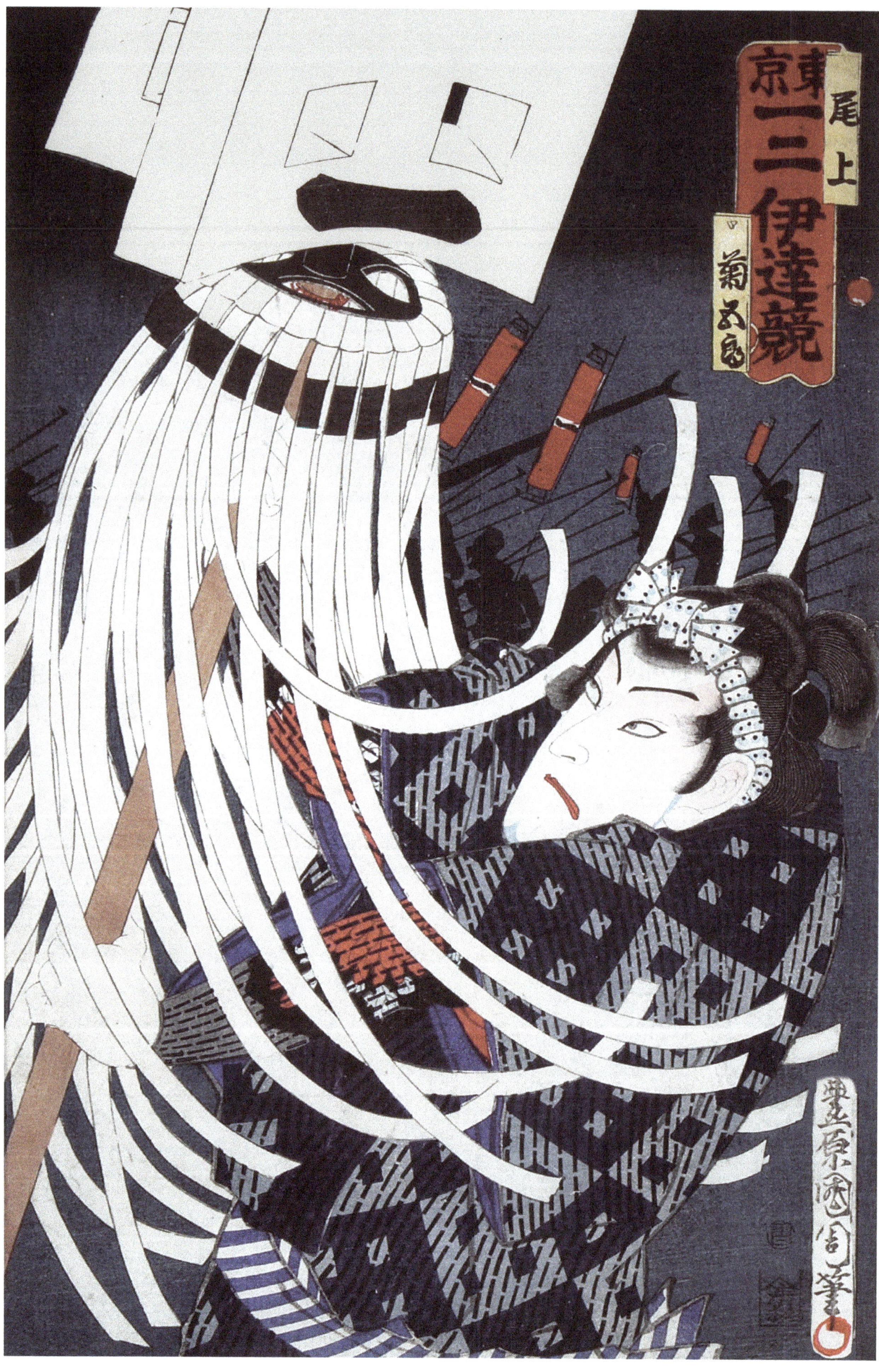

尾上
東京三十二伊達競
菊五郎
豊原國周筆

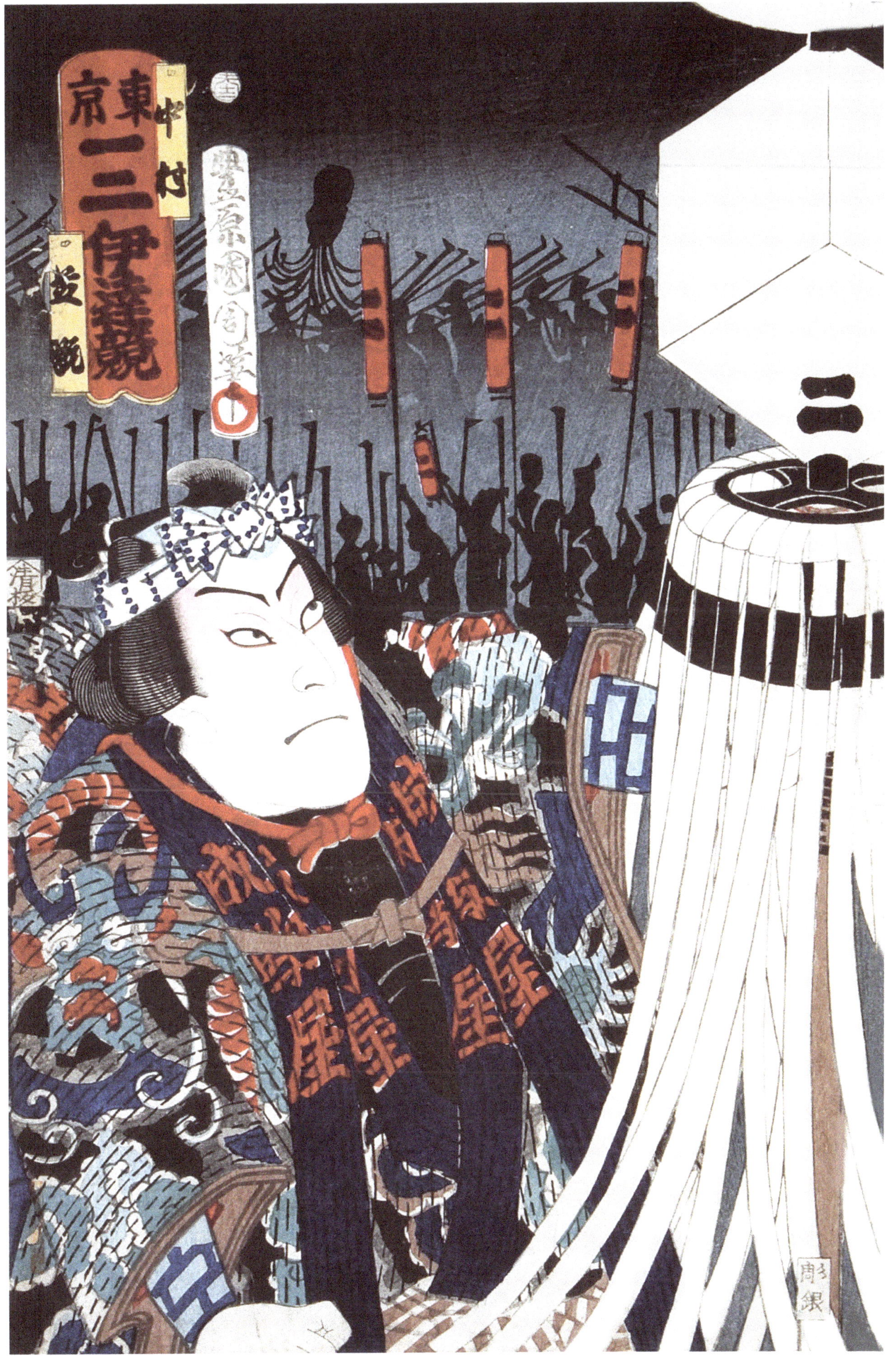
中村
東京
二三
伊達競
中村
後暁
豊原国周画
清揚
彫銀

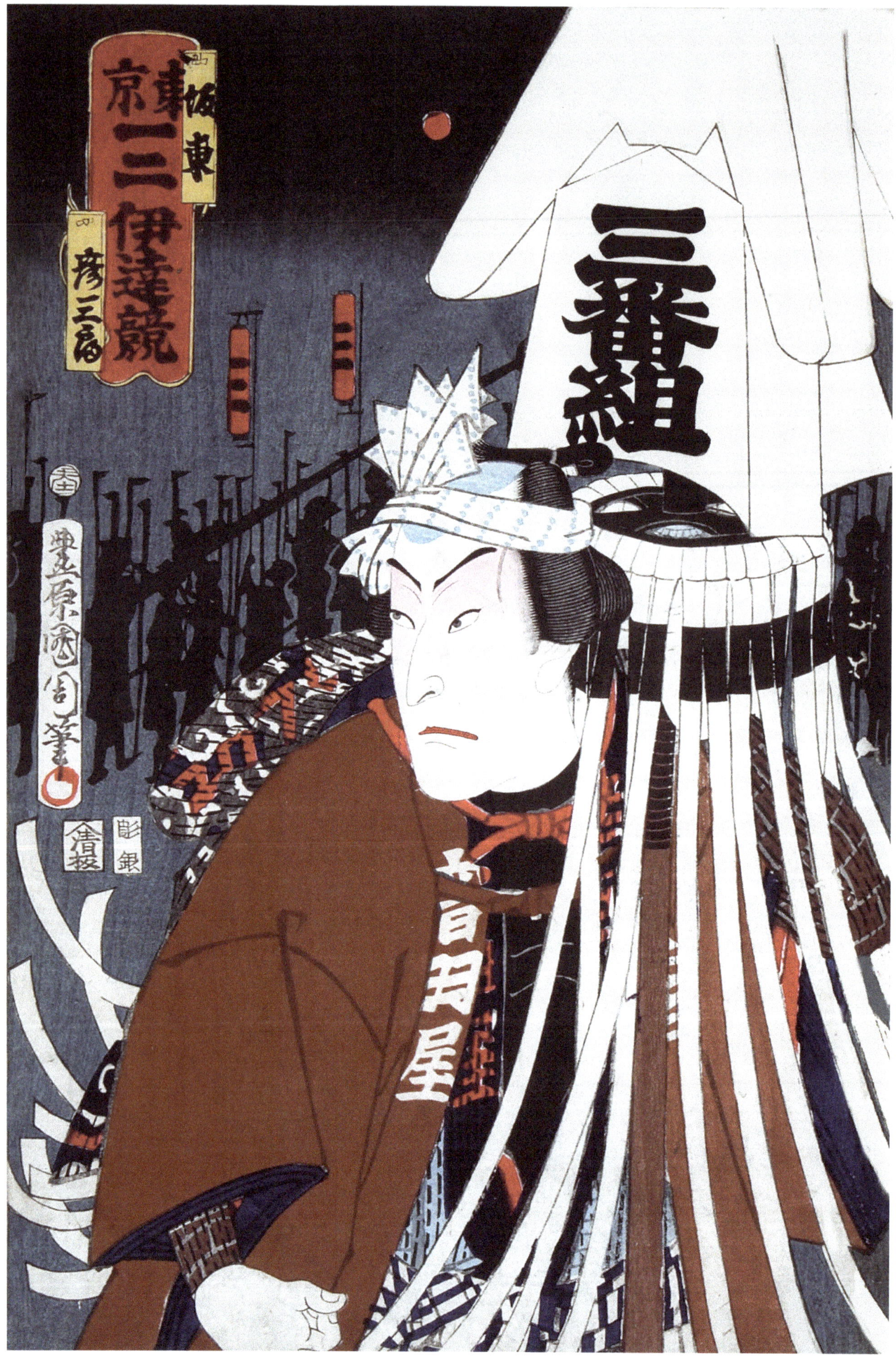

東
坂東
京三
伊達競
彦三店
三番組
豊原国周筆
彫銀
倉彫
百日屋

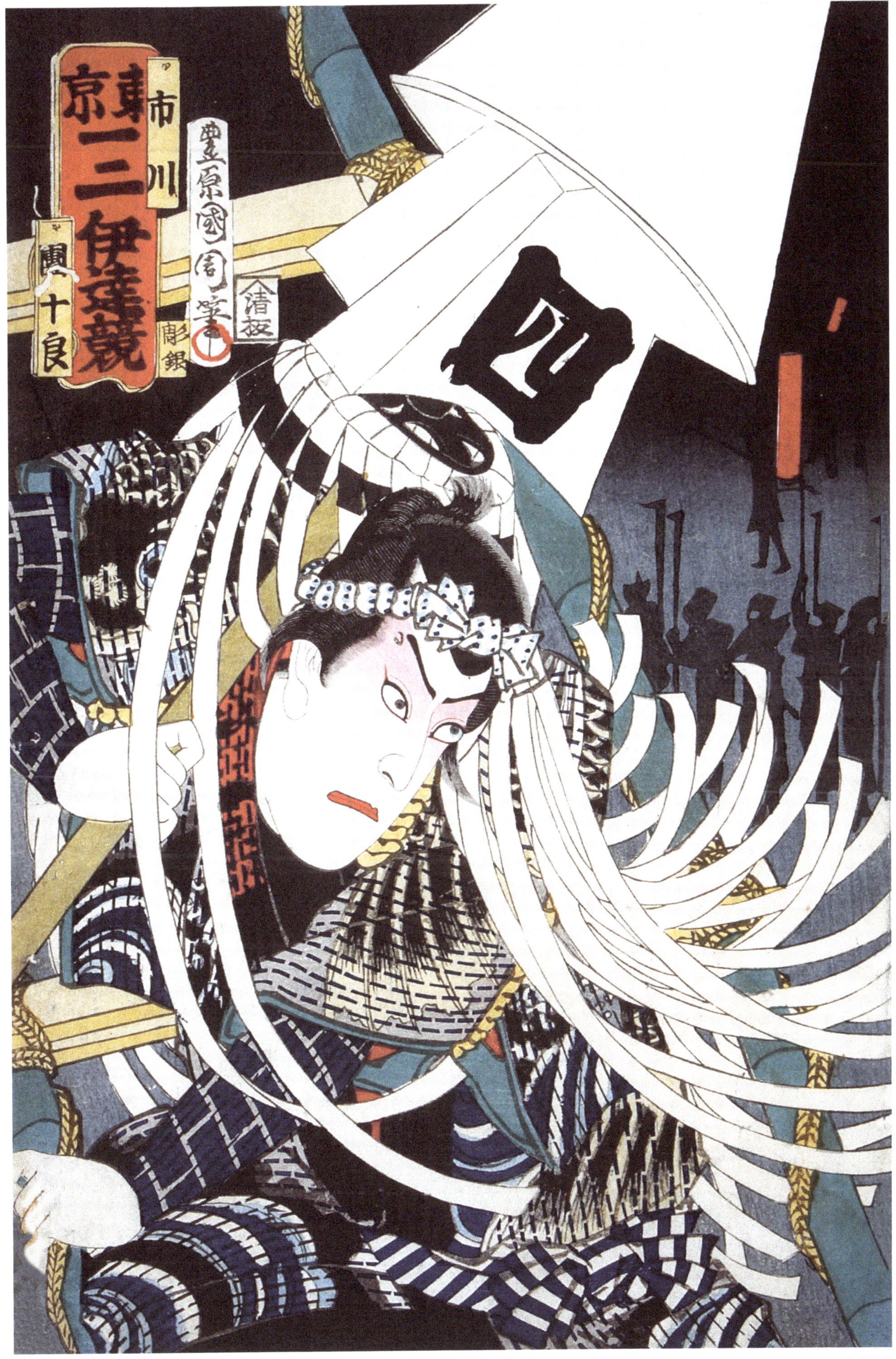

東京二　伊達競
市川
團十良
豊原國周筆
彫銀
清搨
四

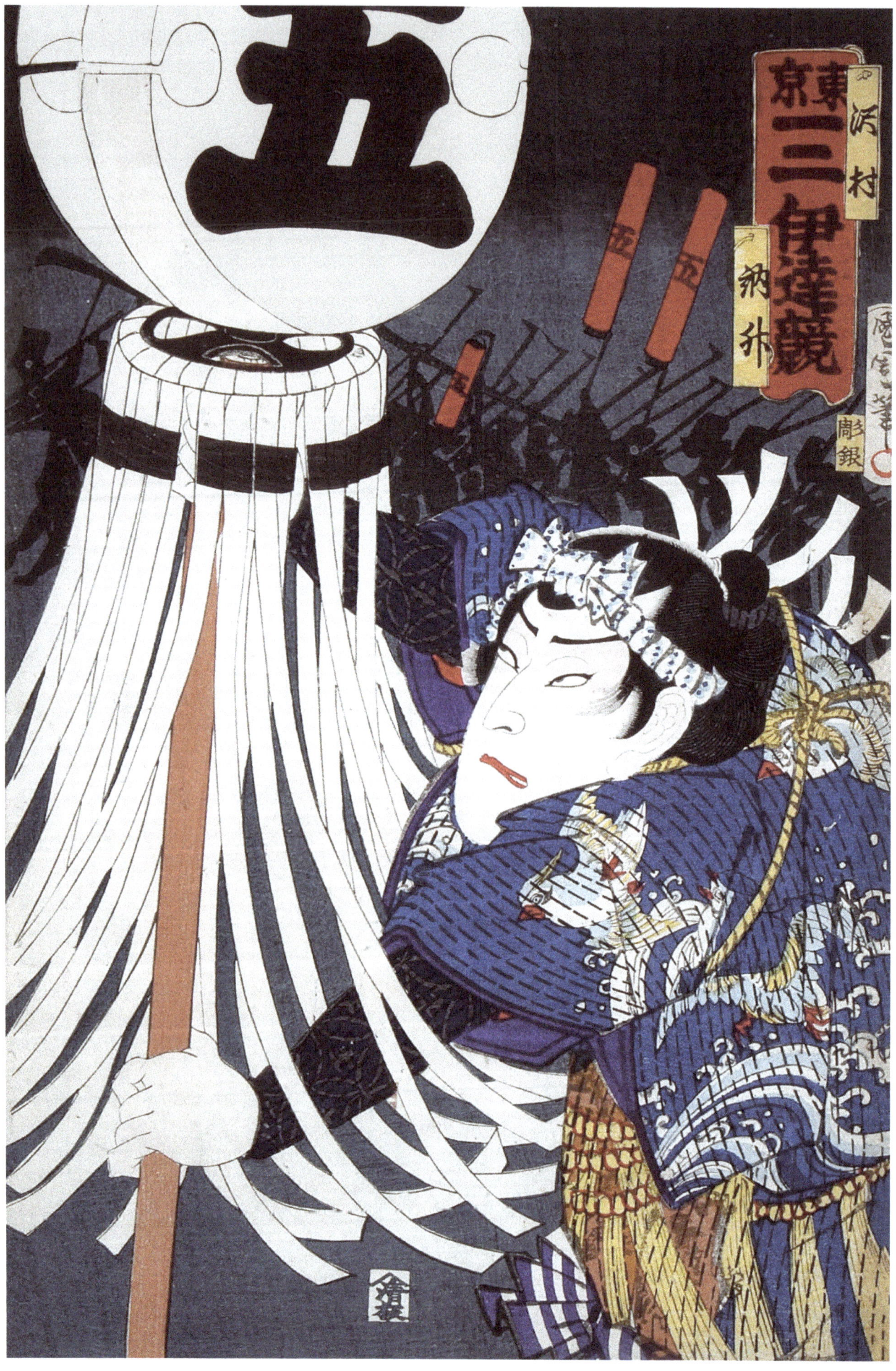
東京三伊達競
沢村
納升
彫銀

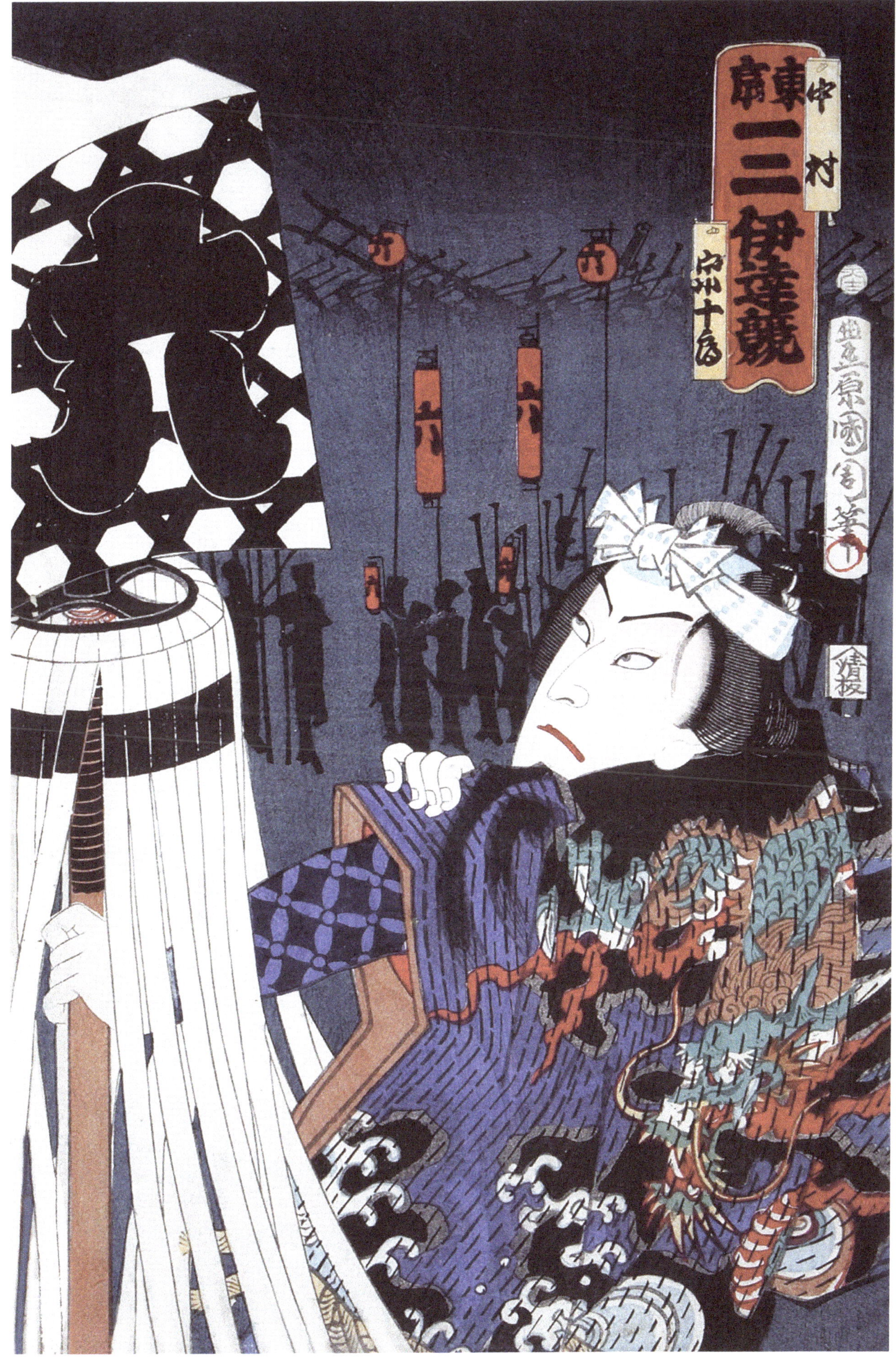
中村
東三
房伊達競
市十
郎
立応斎国周筆
清板

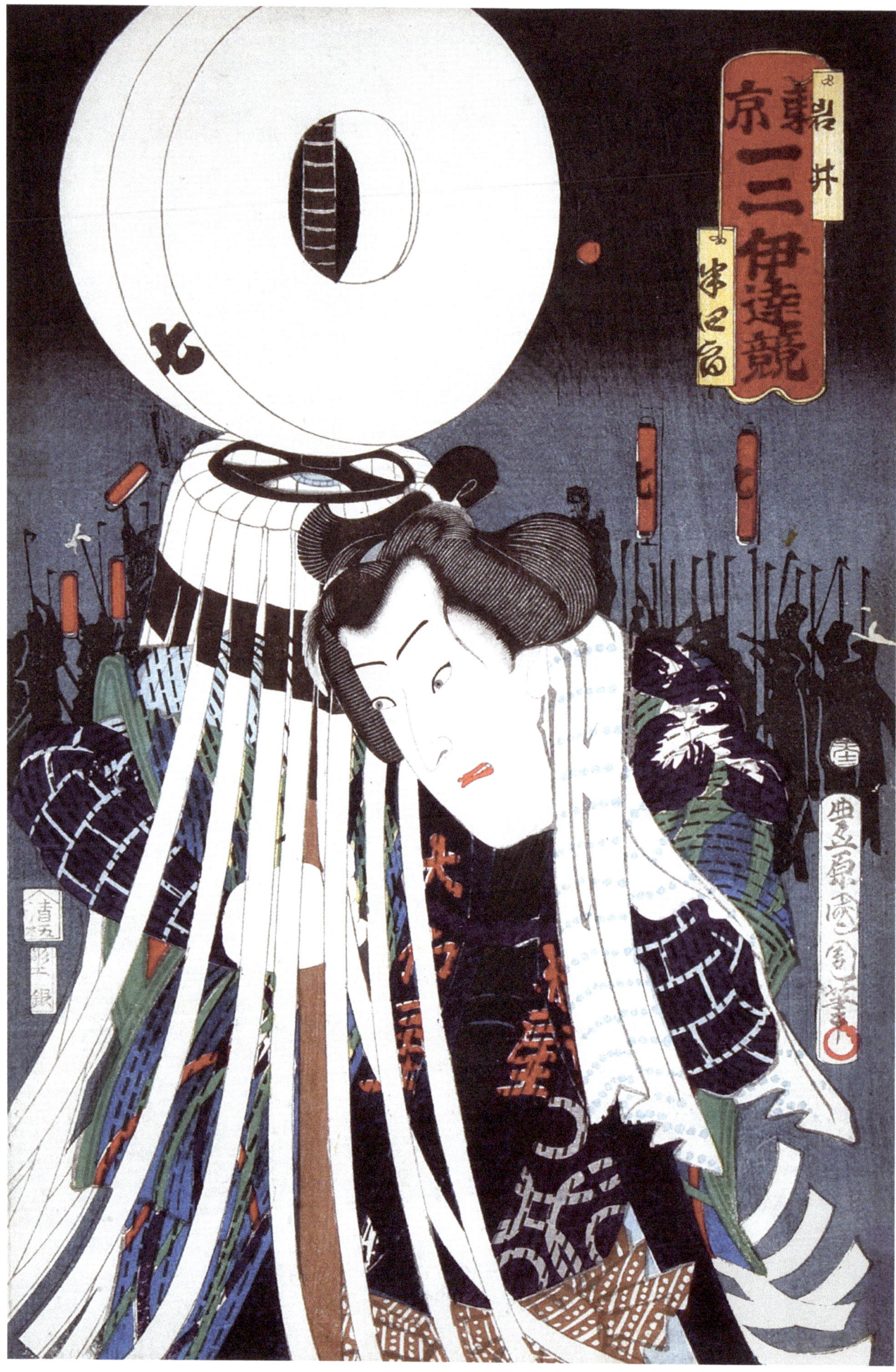

東京
三伊達競

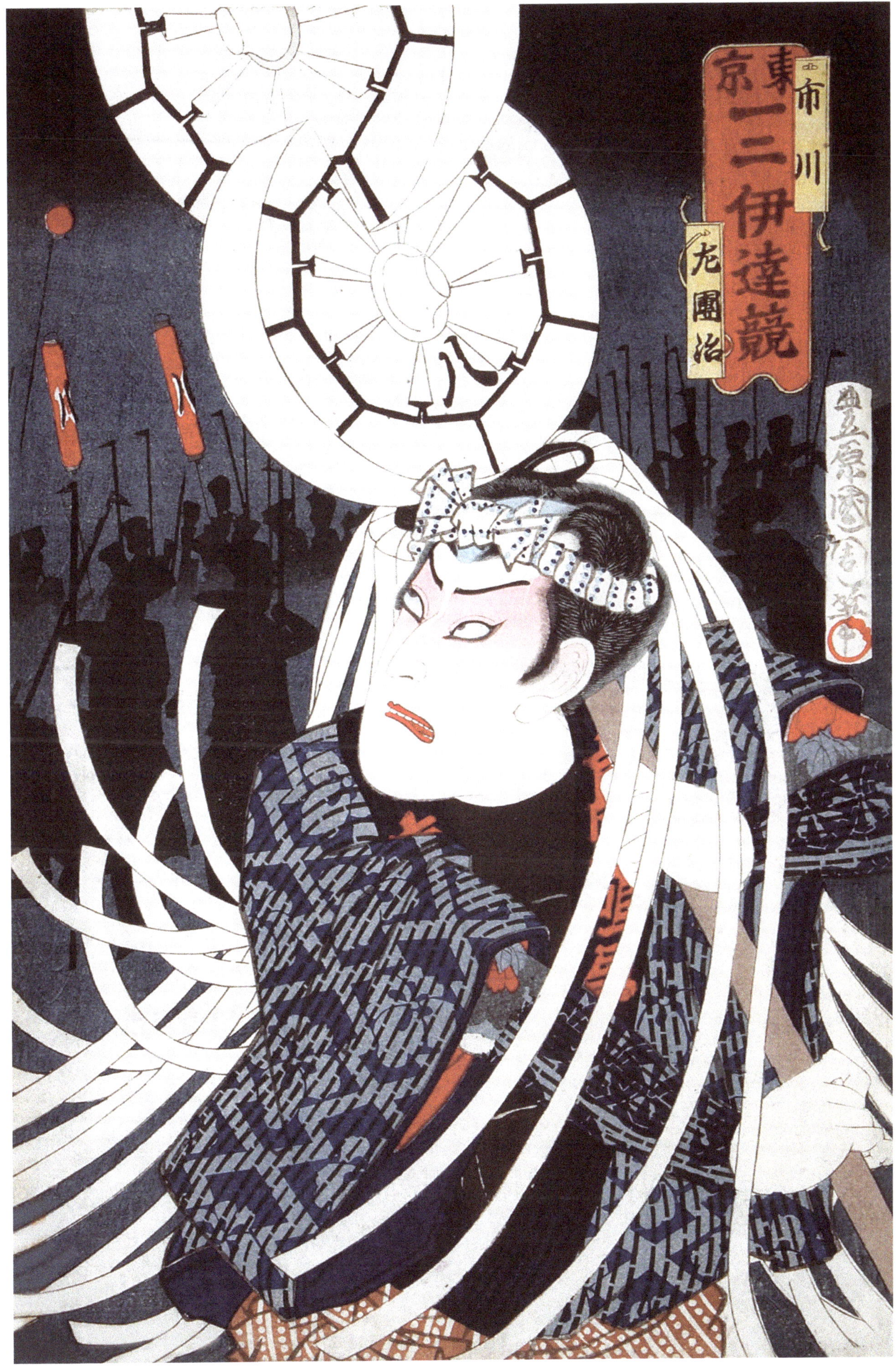

市川
東京一二伊達競
龍圓治
應需五原國鶴戯画

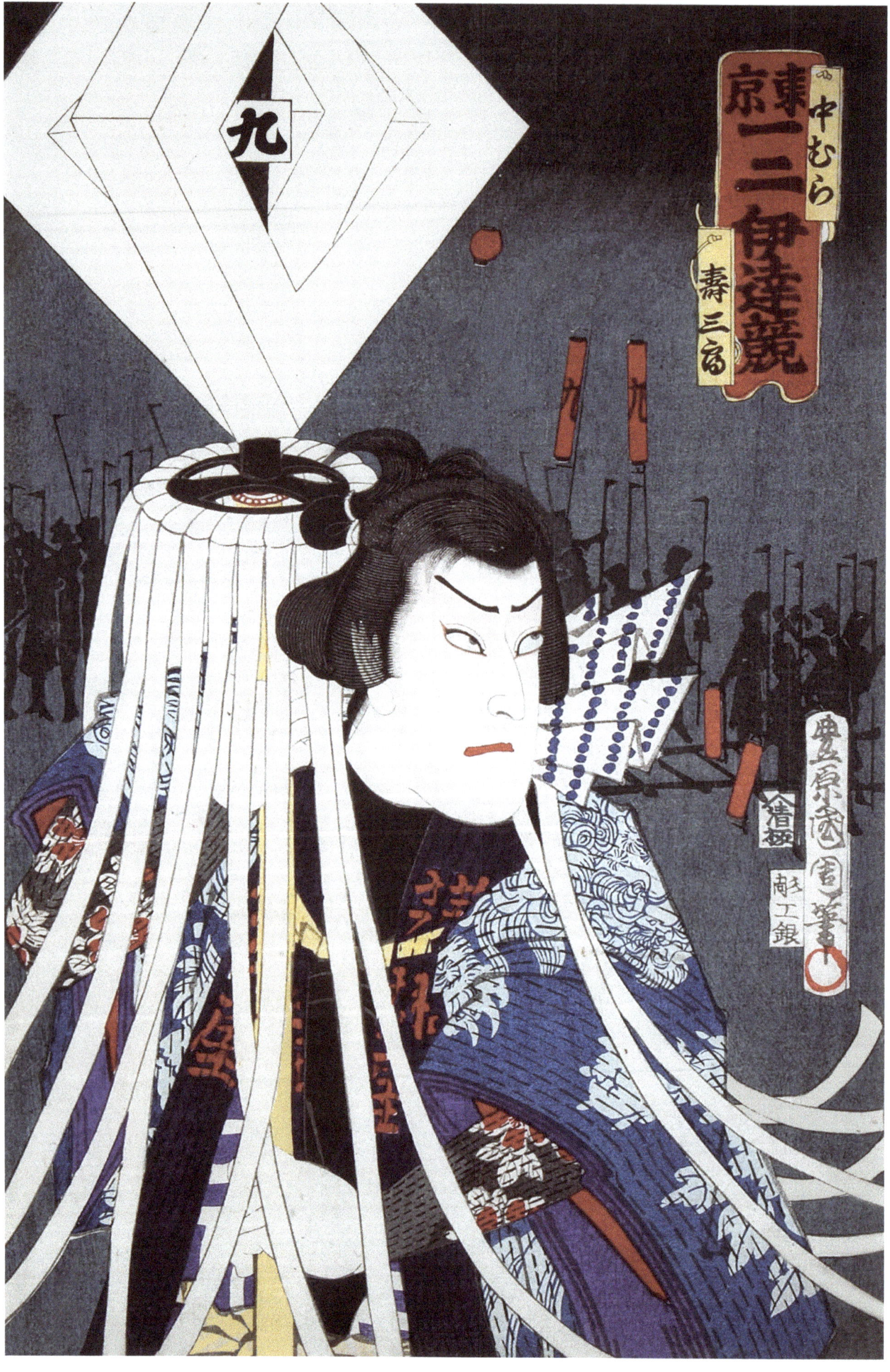

東京
三二伊達競
中むら
壽三宮
豊原國周畫筆
改印
彫工銀
九

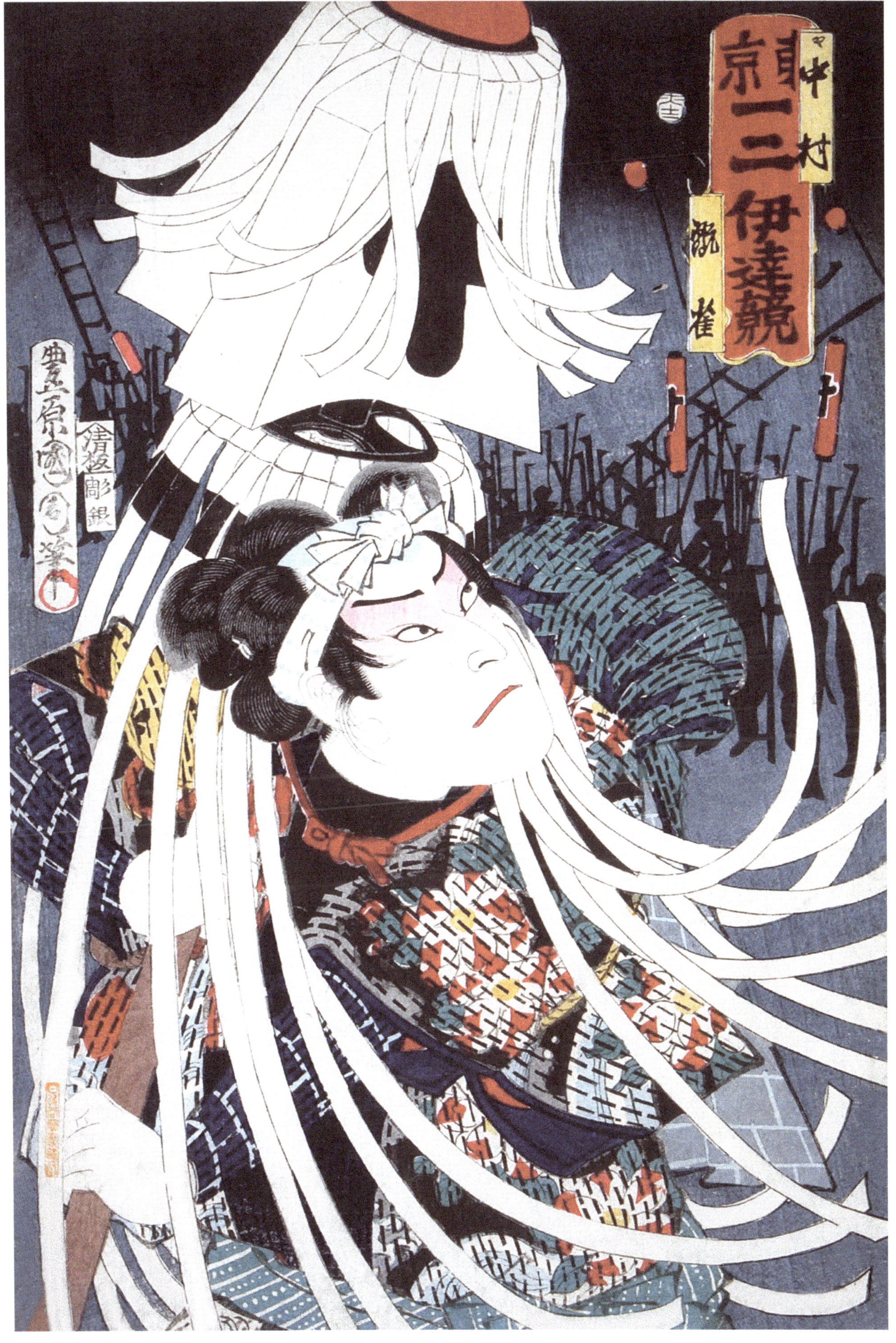
中村
京二三伊達競
鷲
豊原國周筆
清親彫銀

KIJUTSU JUNISHI NO UCHI

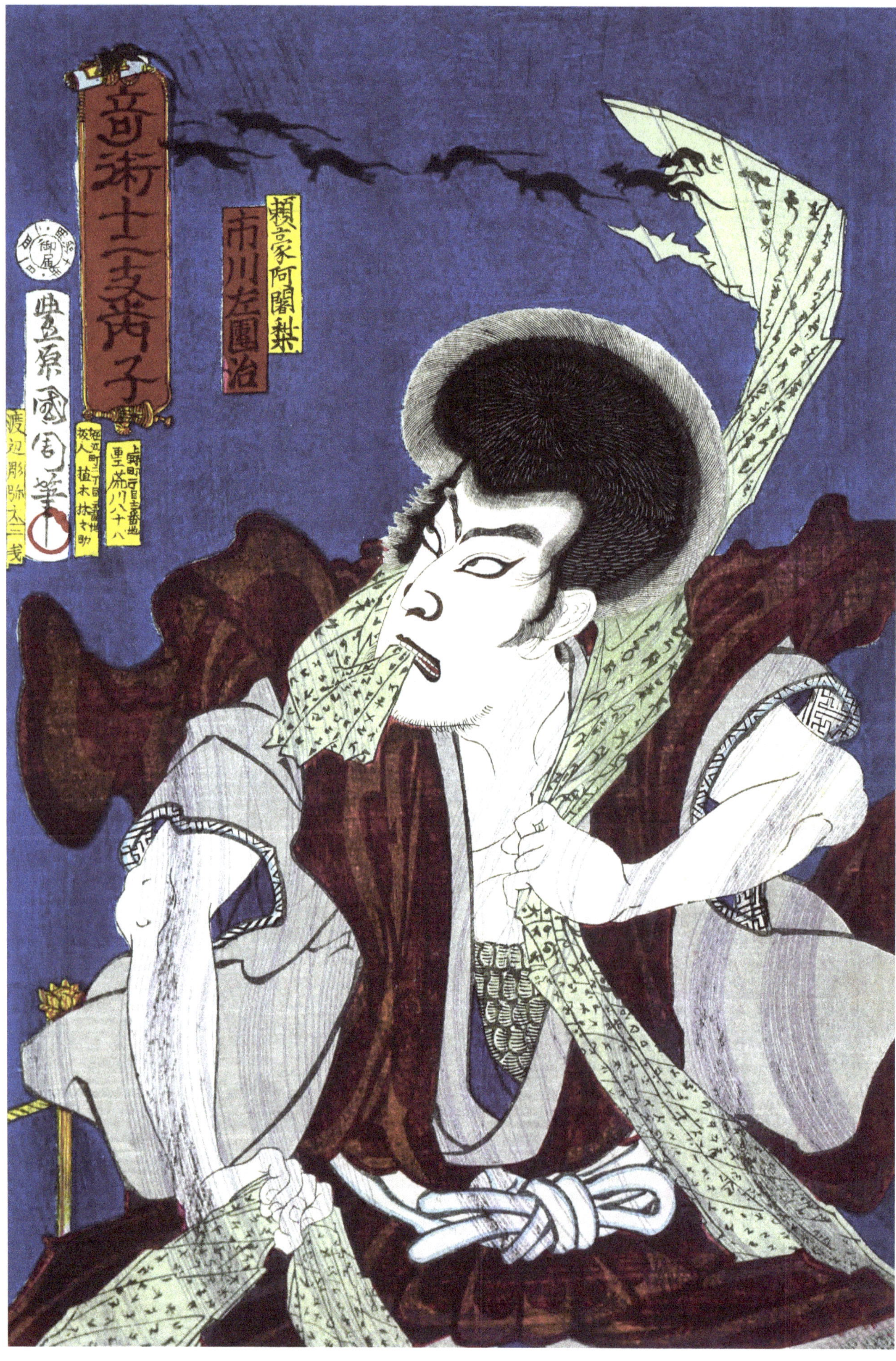
音羽十二支芽子
頼豪家阿闍梨
市川左團治
豐原國周筆
渡辺彫弥太二彫

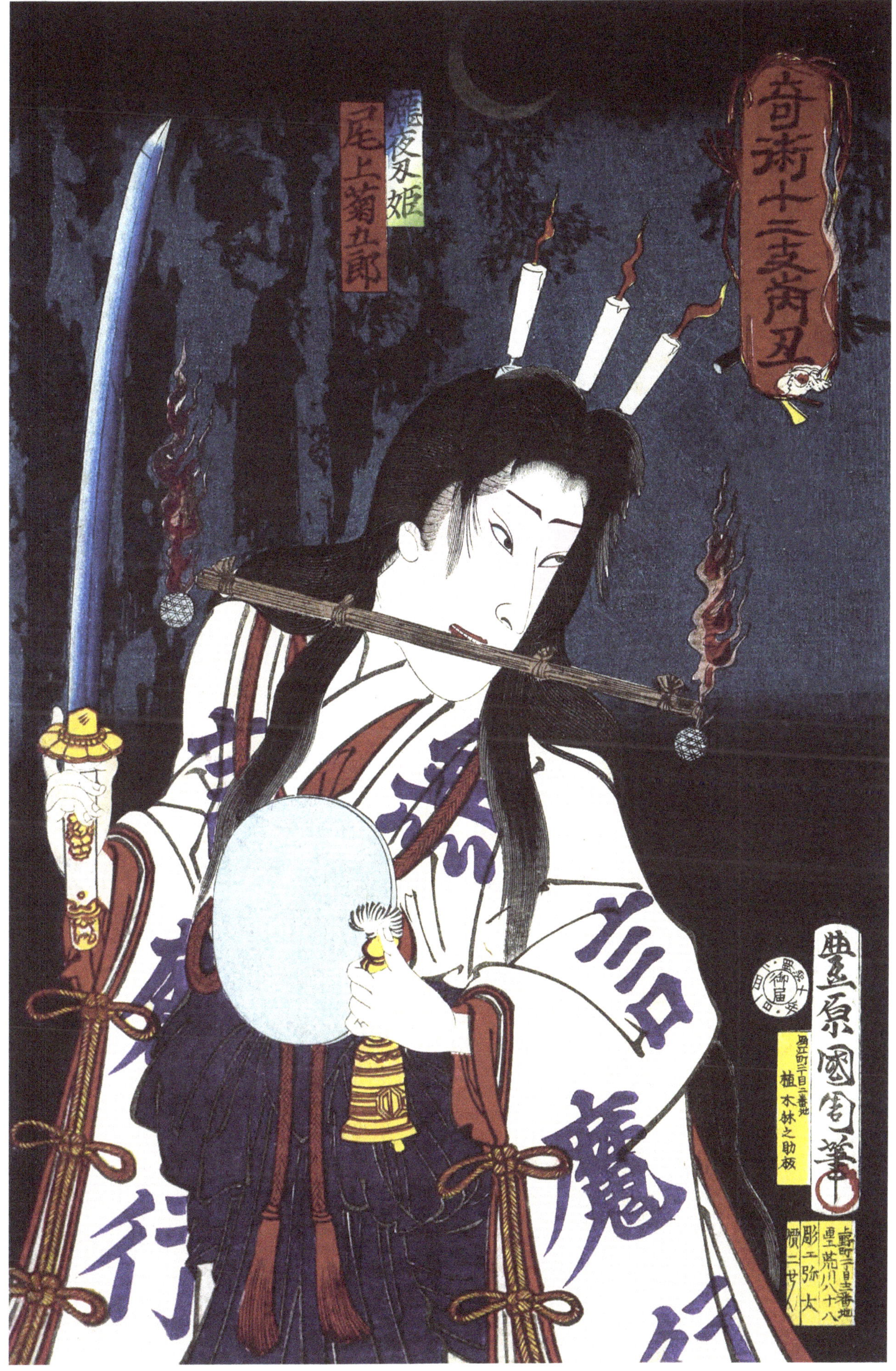
奇術十二支尚天
羅夜叉姫
尾上菊五郎
豊原國周筆
上野町二丁目二番地
彫工弥太
植木妹之助板

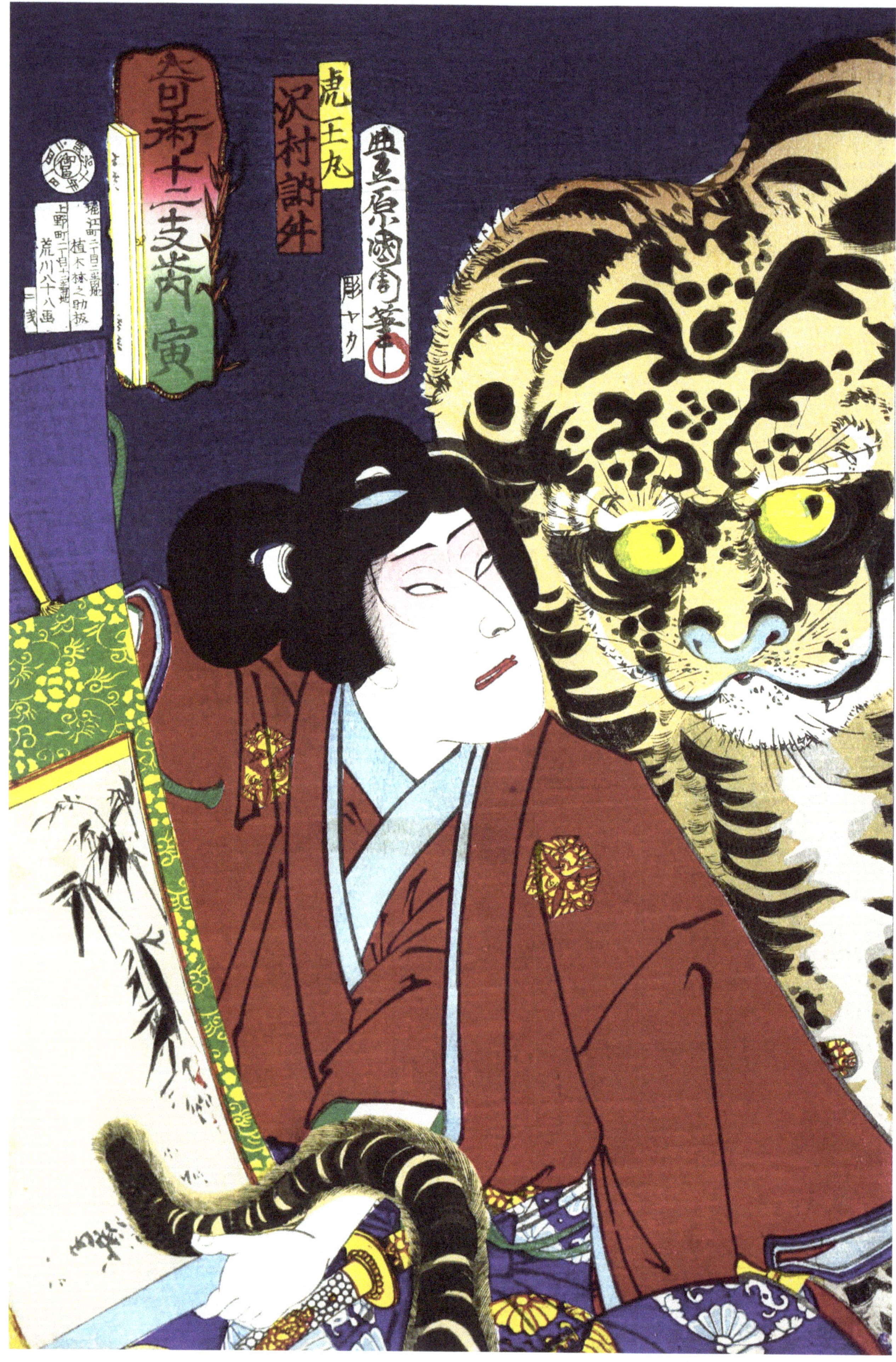
奇術十二支内 寅
虎王丸
沢村訥升
豊原國周筆
彫ヤク
堀江町二丁目三番地
植木林之助板
上野町二丁目十三番地
荒川八十八画
弐

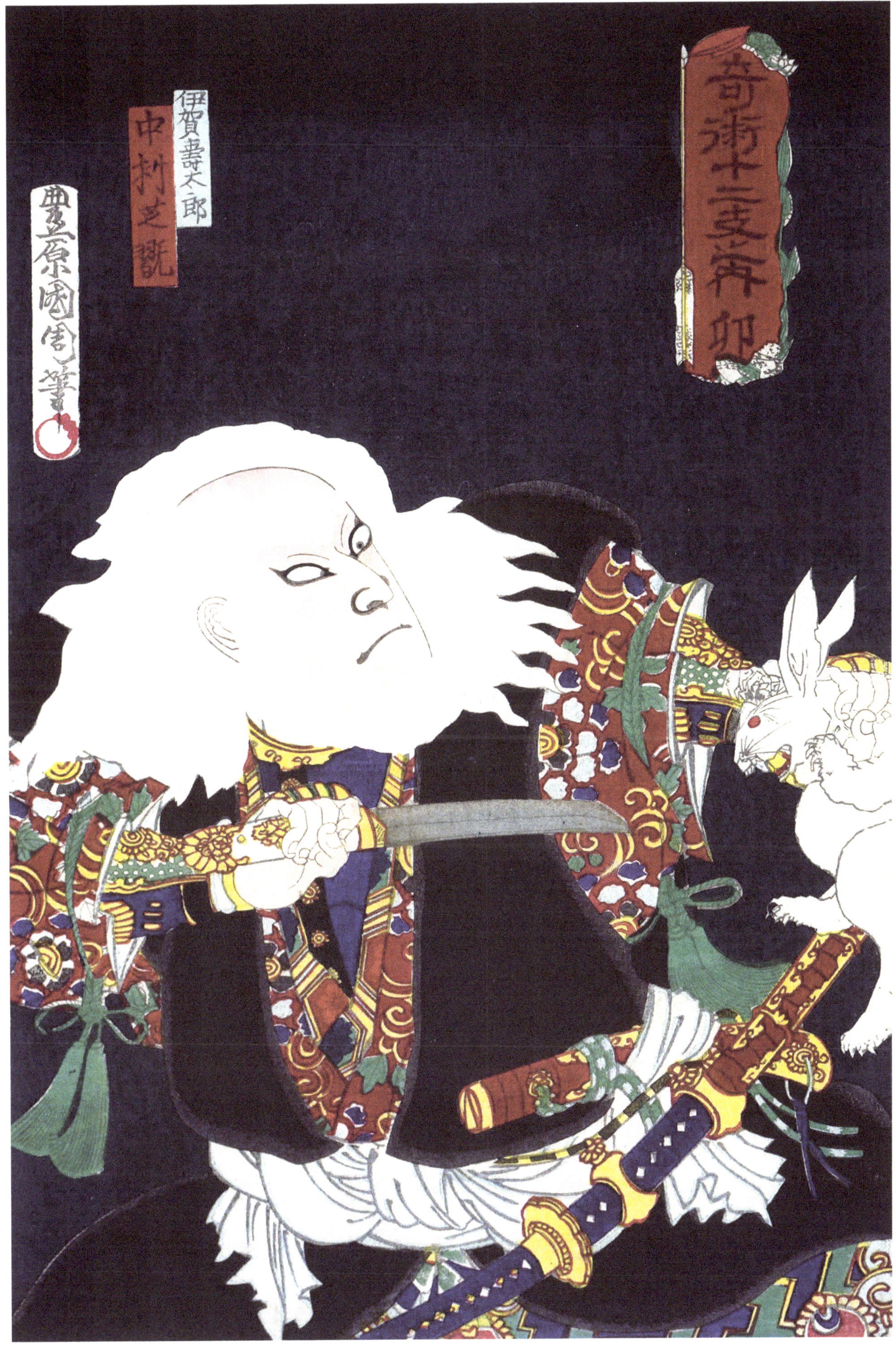

奇術十二支帚ノ内
伊賀壽太郎
中村芝翫
豊原國周筆

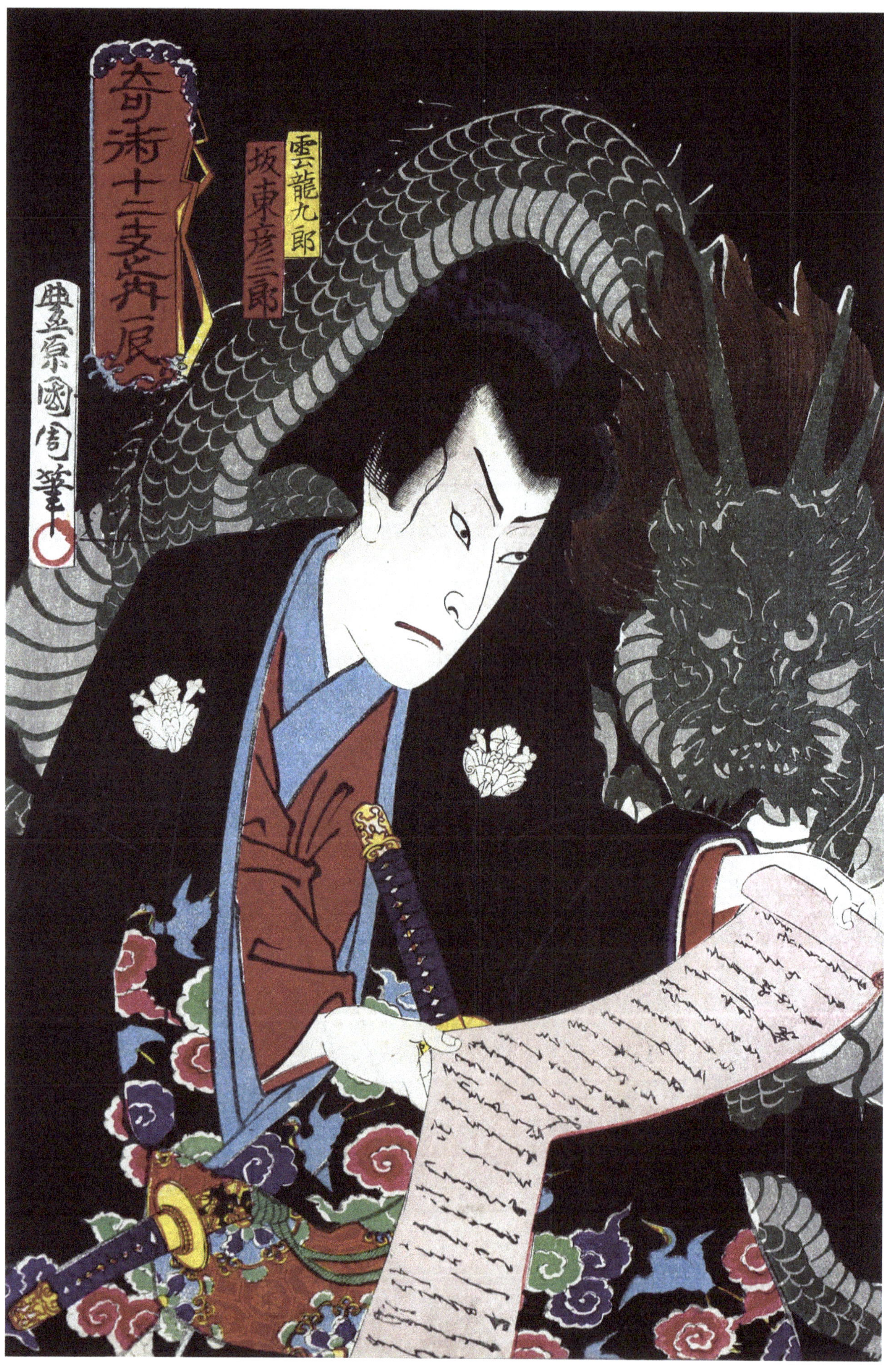
奇術十二支之内
雲龍九郎
坂東彦三郎
豊原國周筆

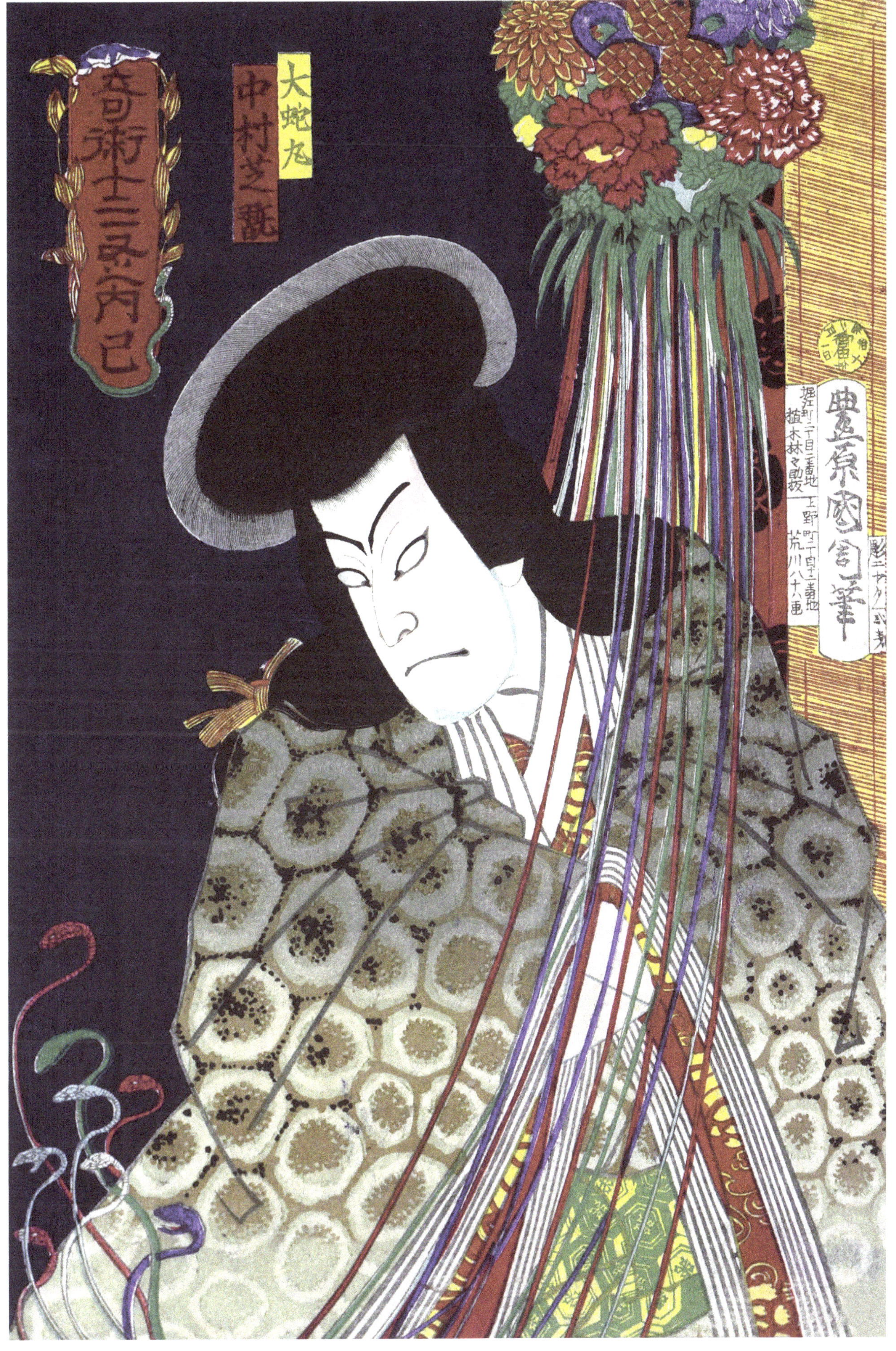
奇術十三ケ月之内
巳
大蛇丸
中村芝翫
豊原國周筆
堀江町二丁目二番地
上野町一丁目二番地
植木林々助板
荒川八十重

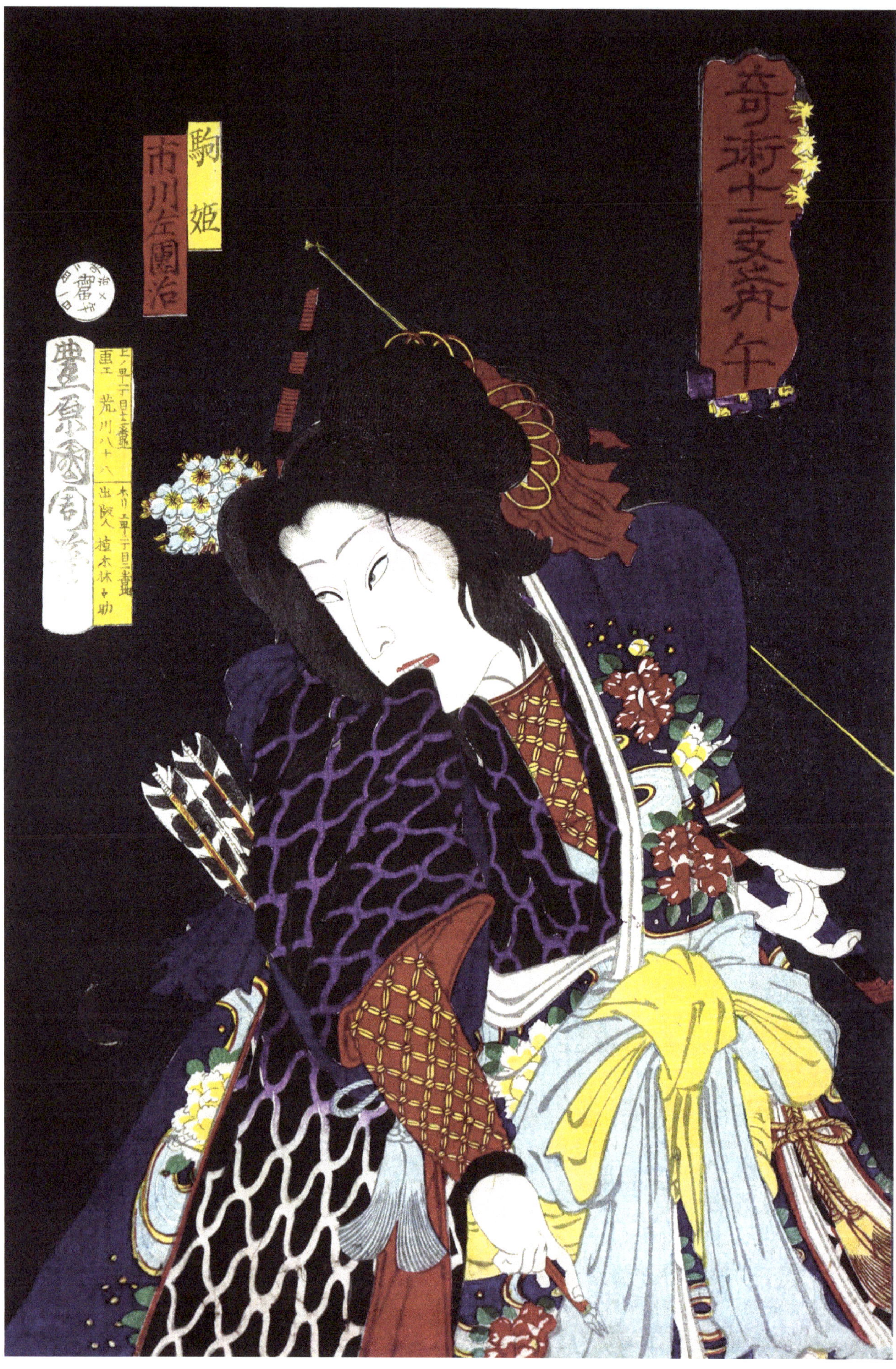

奇術十二支弄午
駒姫
市川左團治
豊原國周筆

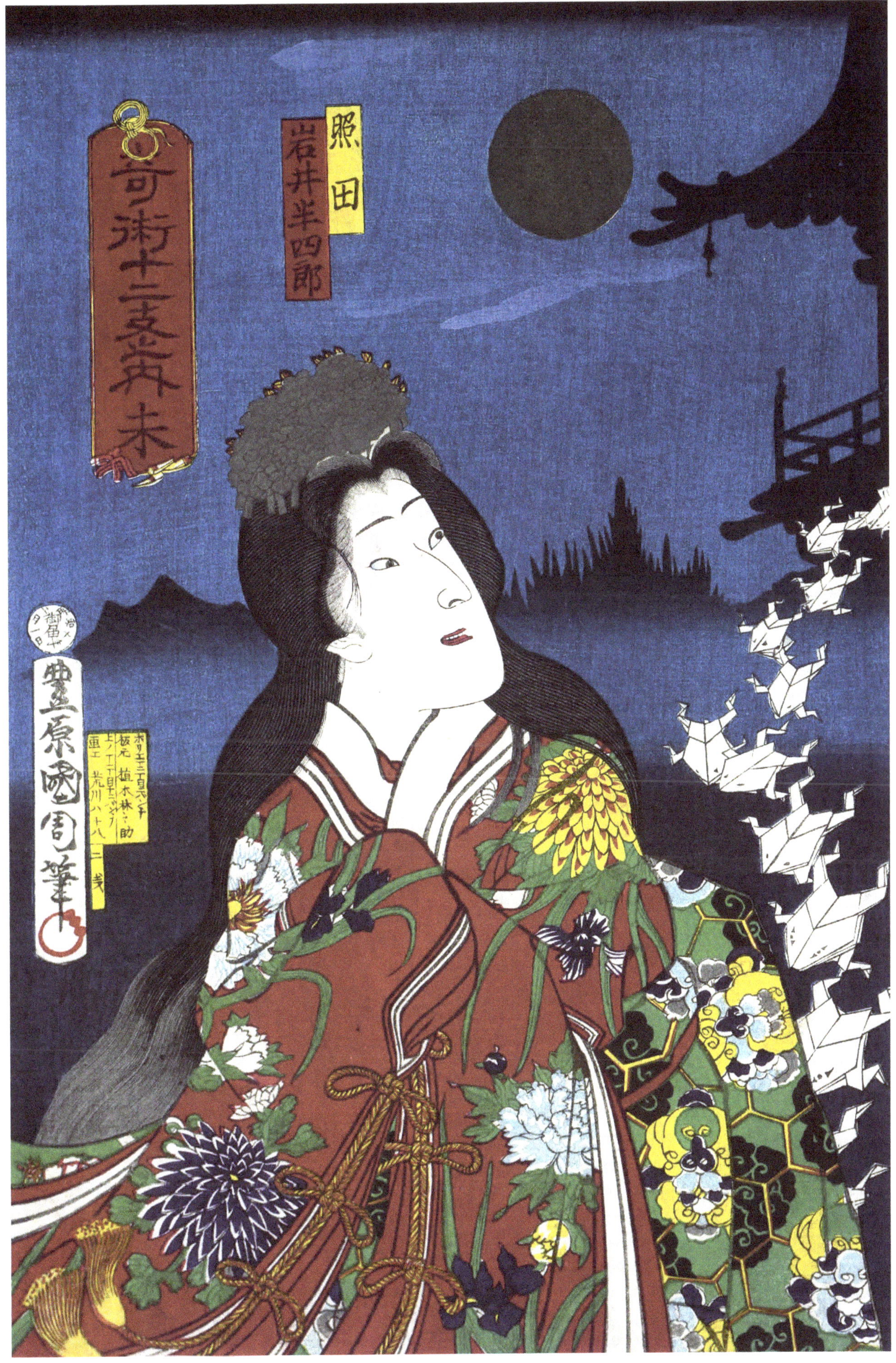
奇術十二支内　未
照田
岩井半四郎
豊原國周筆

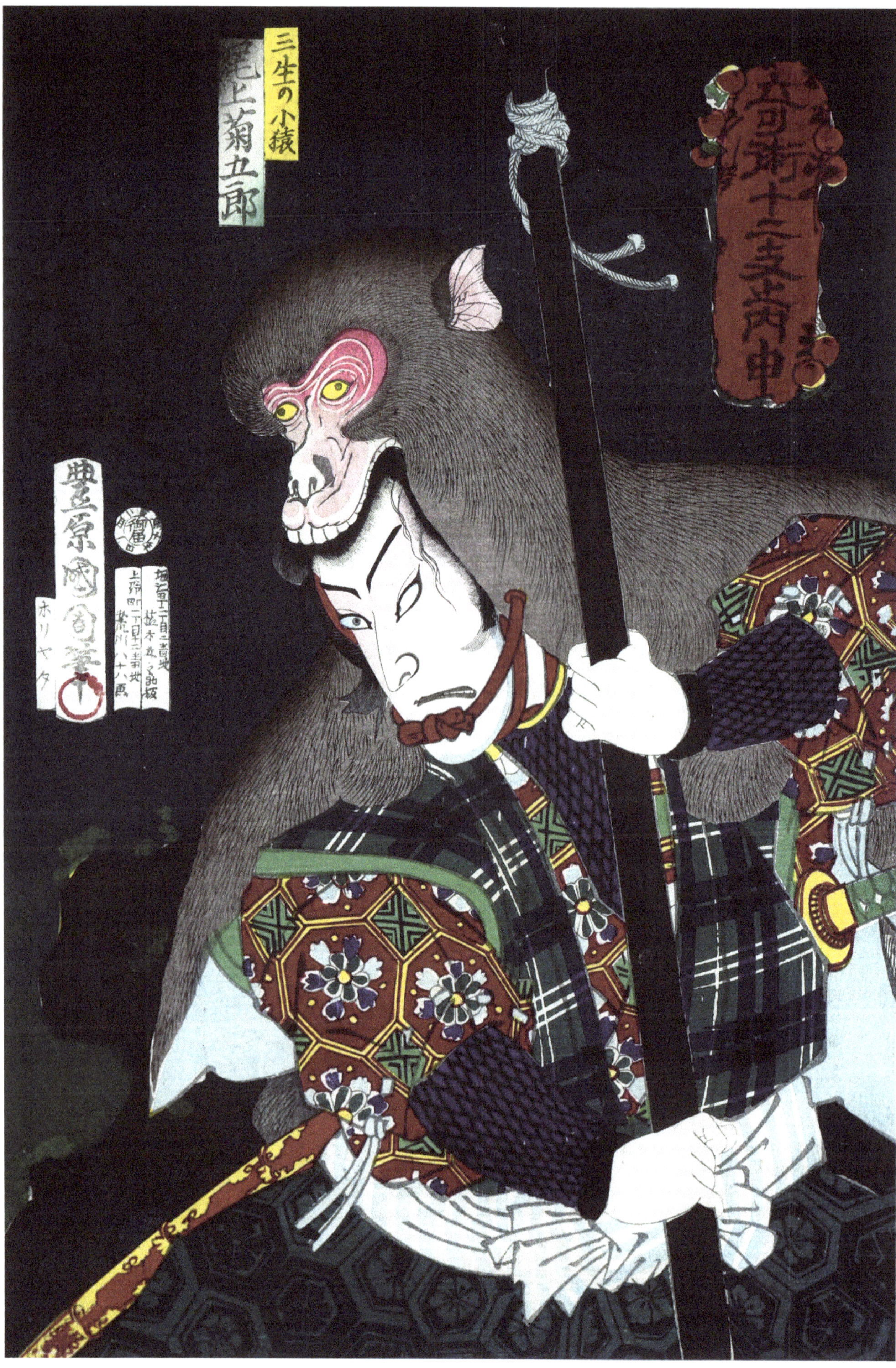
三生の小猿
尾上菊五郎
當時十二支丼申
豊原國周筆
ホリヤタ

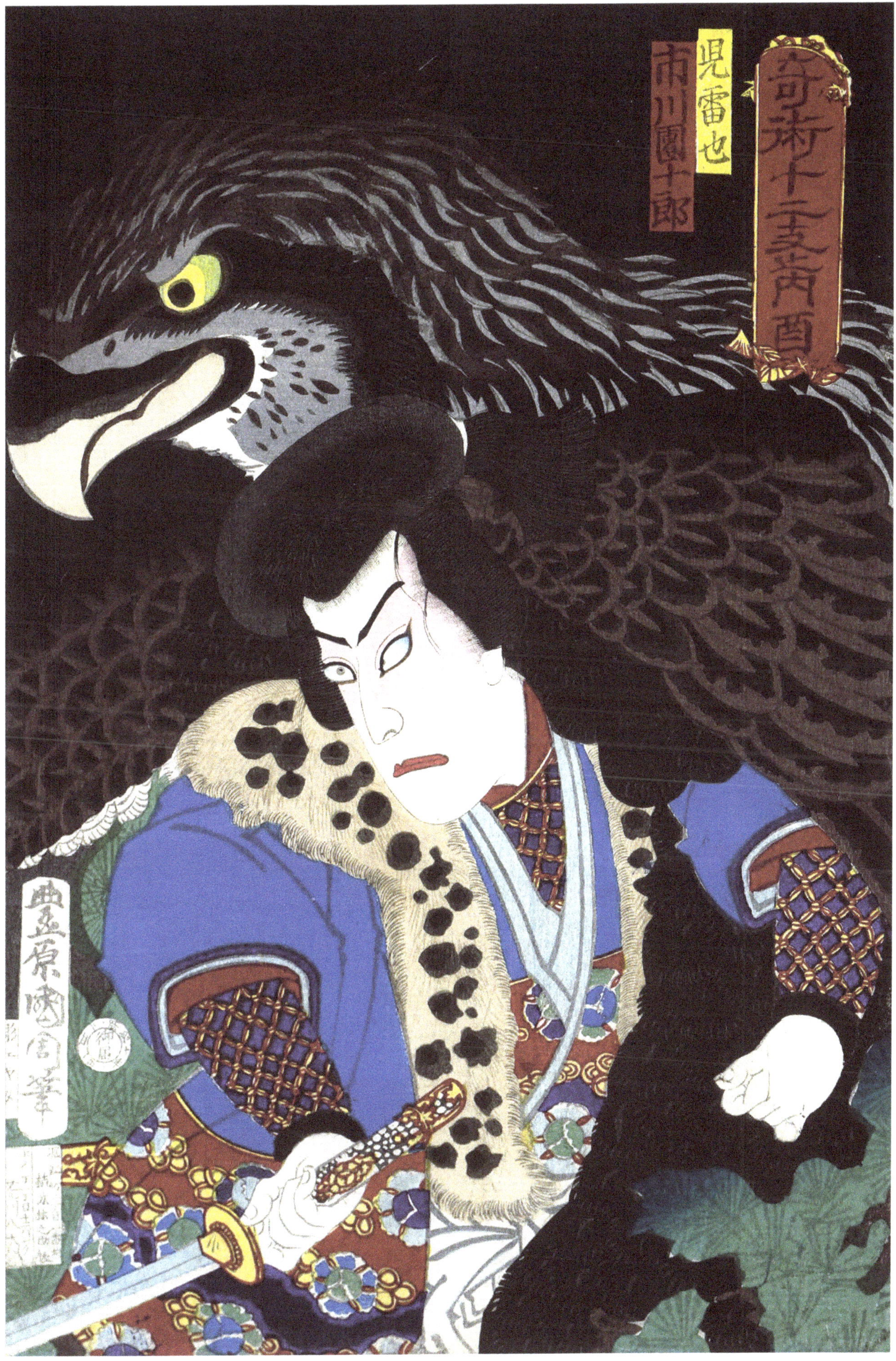
奇術十二支内 酉
児雷也
市川團十郎
豊原國周筆

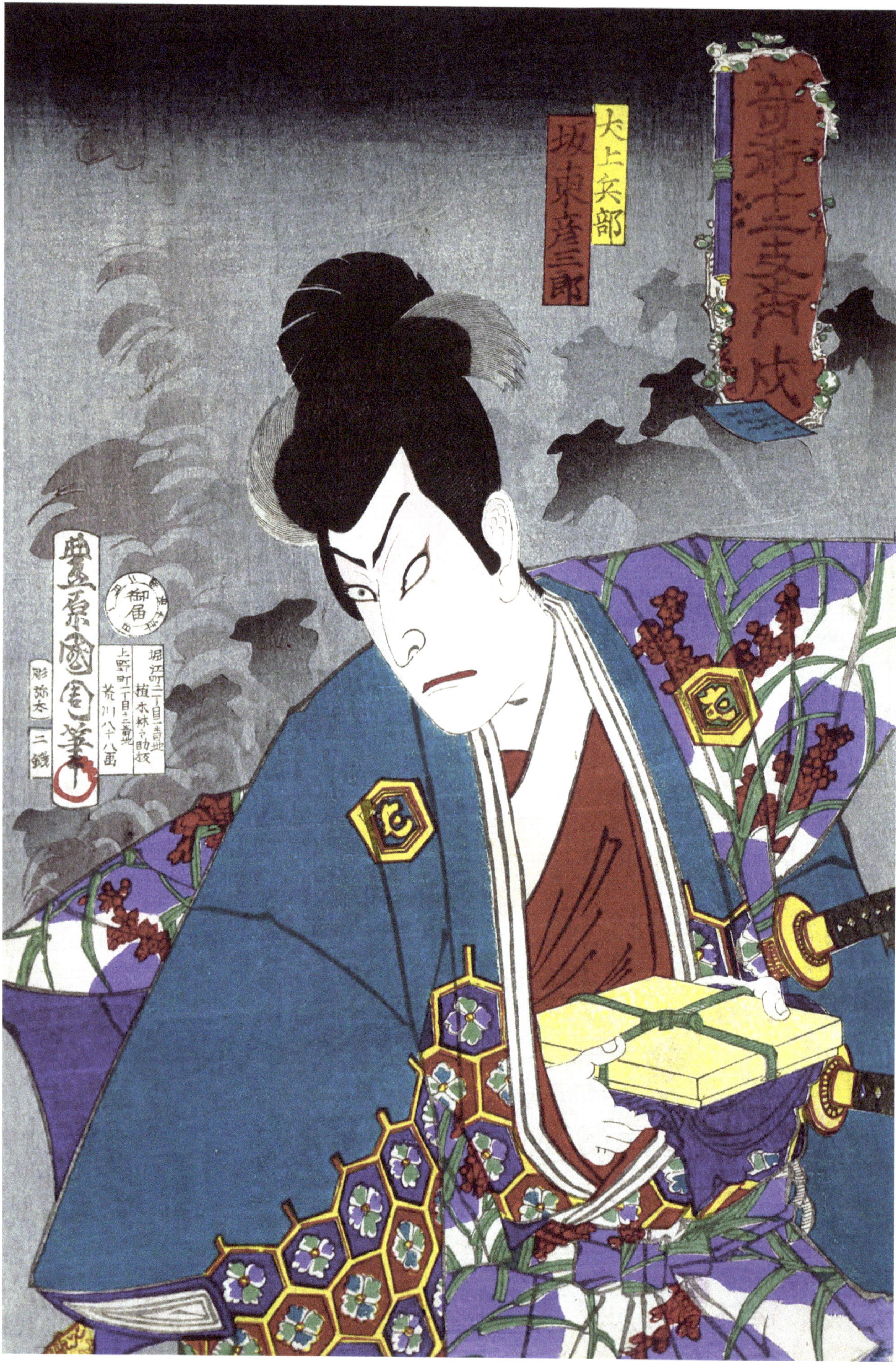
荷神十二支画成

大上矢部
坂東彦三郎

豊原國周筆

彫弥太
二鐡

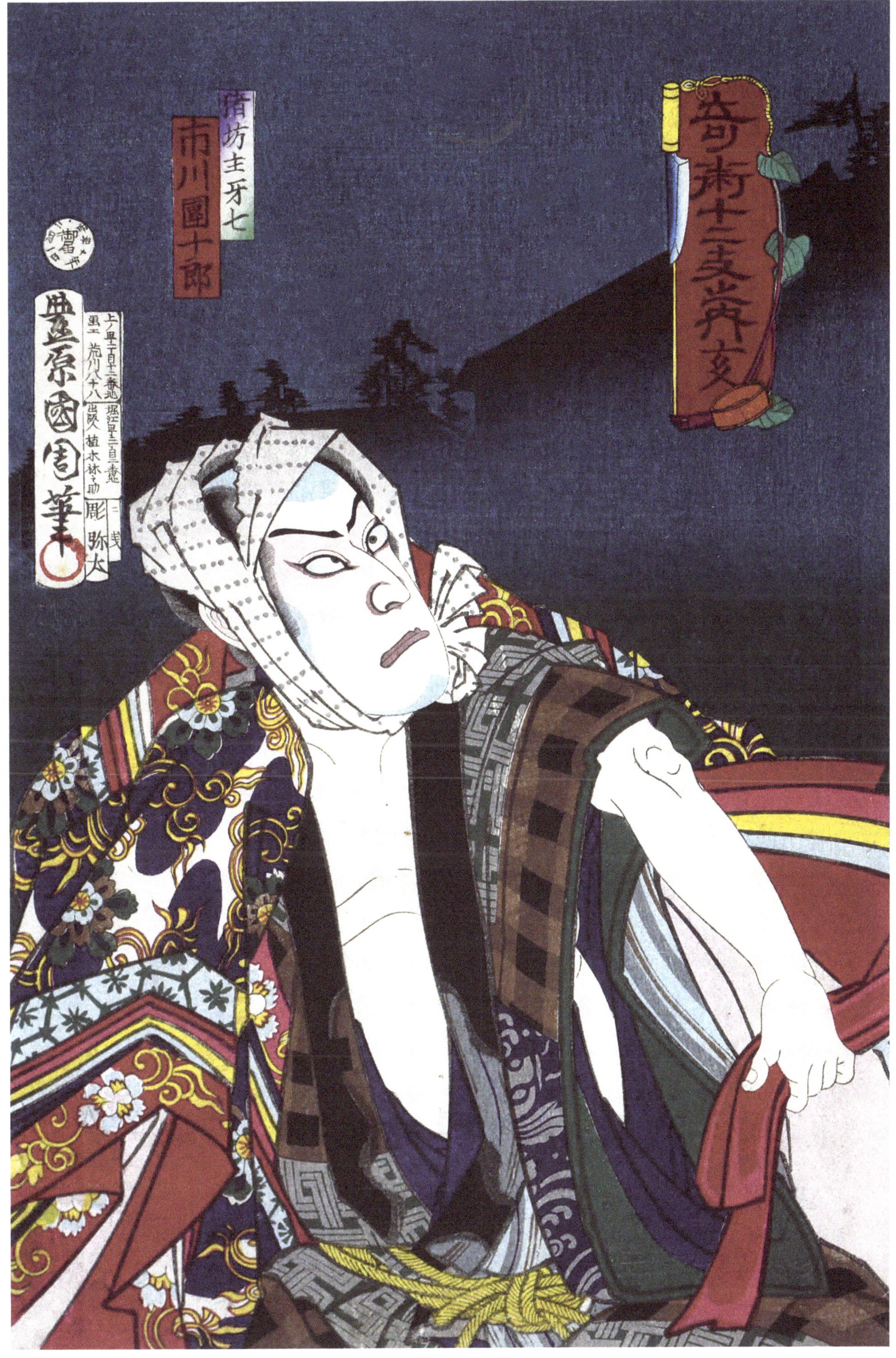
奇術十二支当亥

宿坊主牙七
市川團十郎

豊原國周筆

上ル二丁目十二番地　堀江里三丁目　應
里ニ　荒川八十八出版　植木林之助　彫　弥太

CHIMEI JUNIKAGETSU NO UCHI

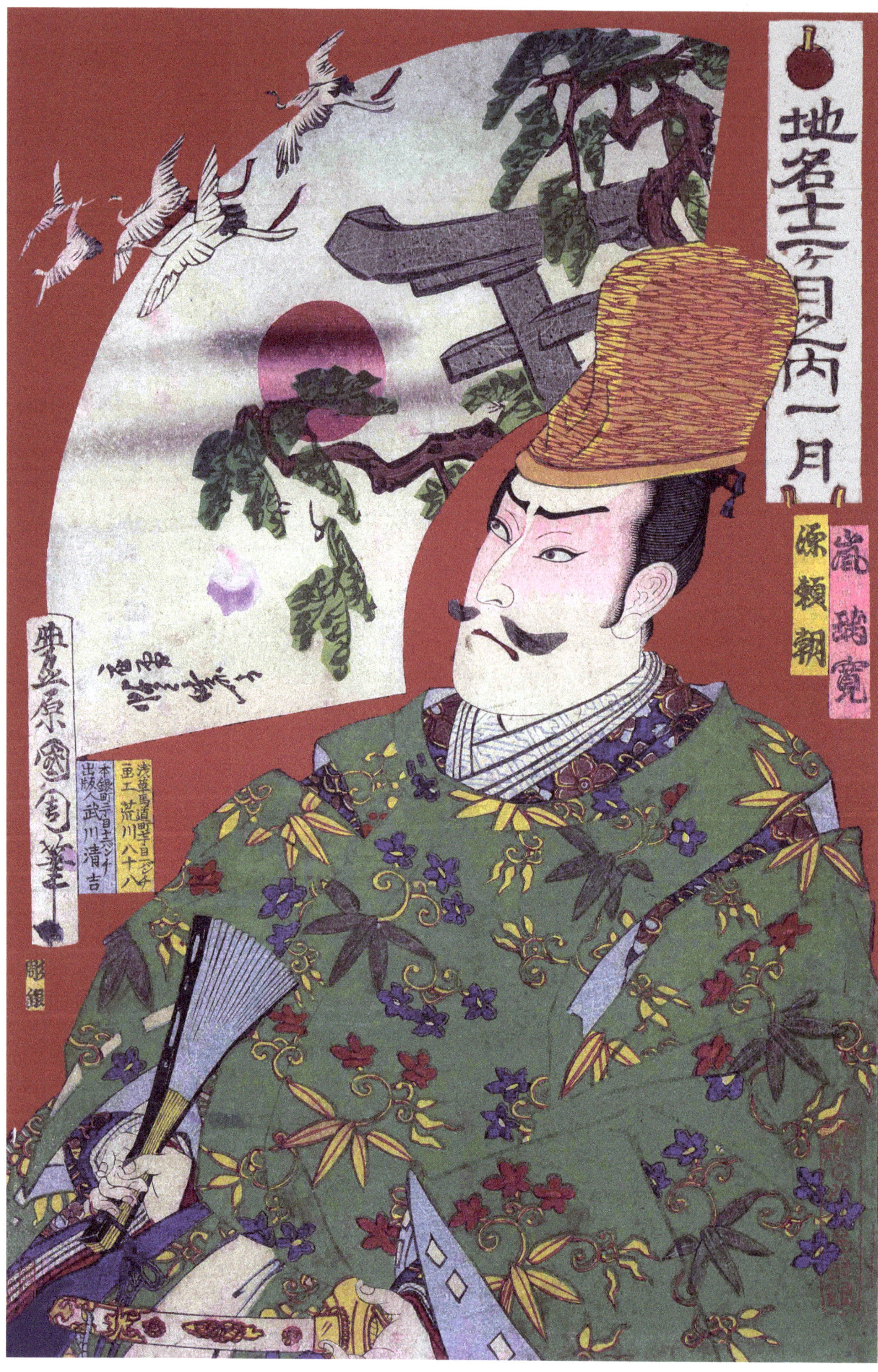

地名十二ヶ月之内一月
源頼朝
嵐璃寛
豊原国周筆
浅草馬道四丁目ニシテ
彫工 荒川八十八
本銀町三丁目ニシテ
出版人 武川清吉

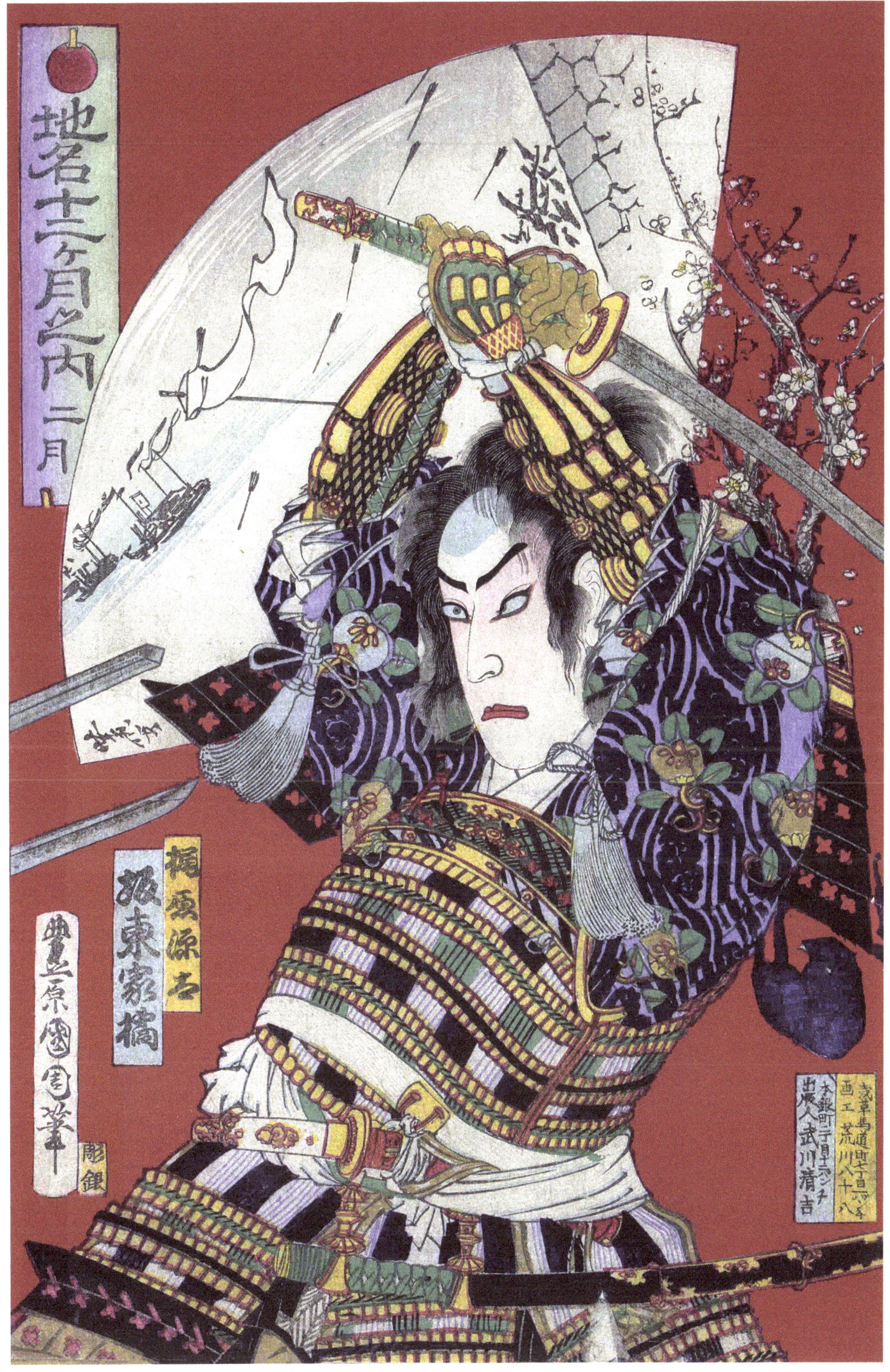
地名十二ヶ月之内　二月
梶原源太
坂東家橘
豊原國周筆
彫銀
浅草馬道　□□□□□□
画工　荒川八十八
出版人　武川清吉

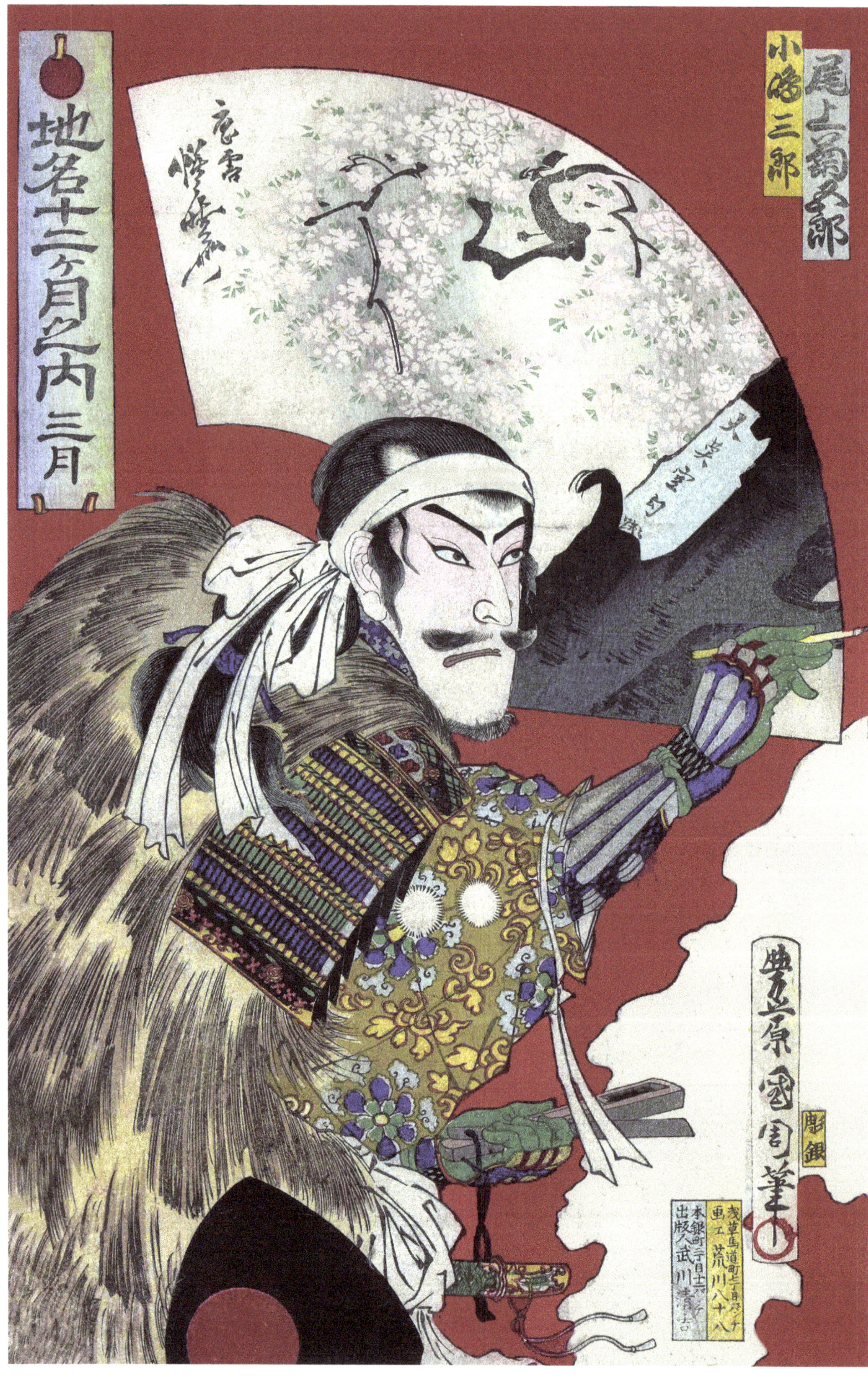
尾上菊五郎
小鴨三郎
地名十二ヶ月之内 三月
豊原國周筆
彫銀

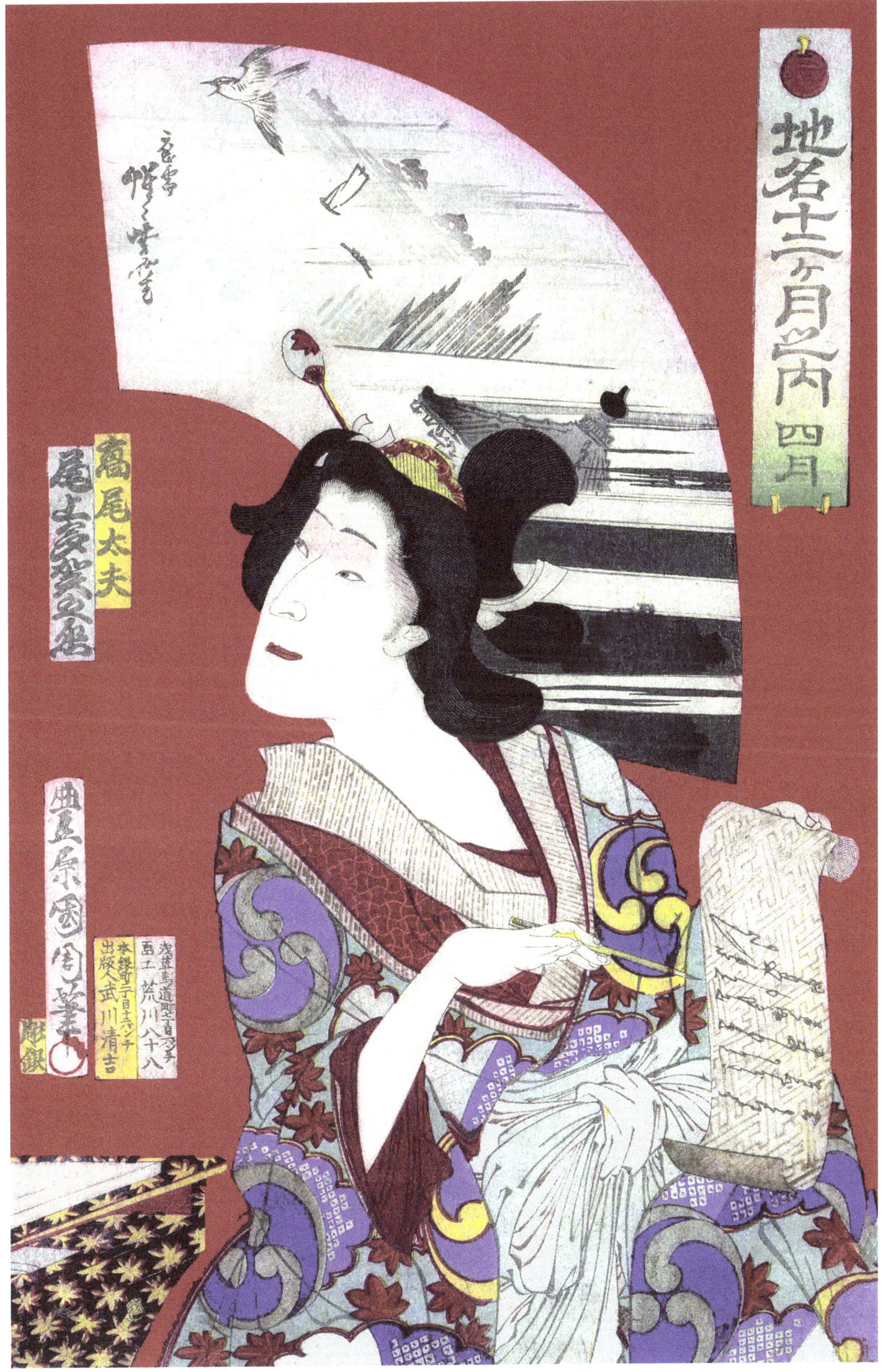
地名十二ヶ月之内
四月
高尾太夫
尾上多賀之丞
応需豊原国周筆
彫銀

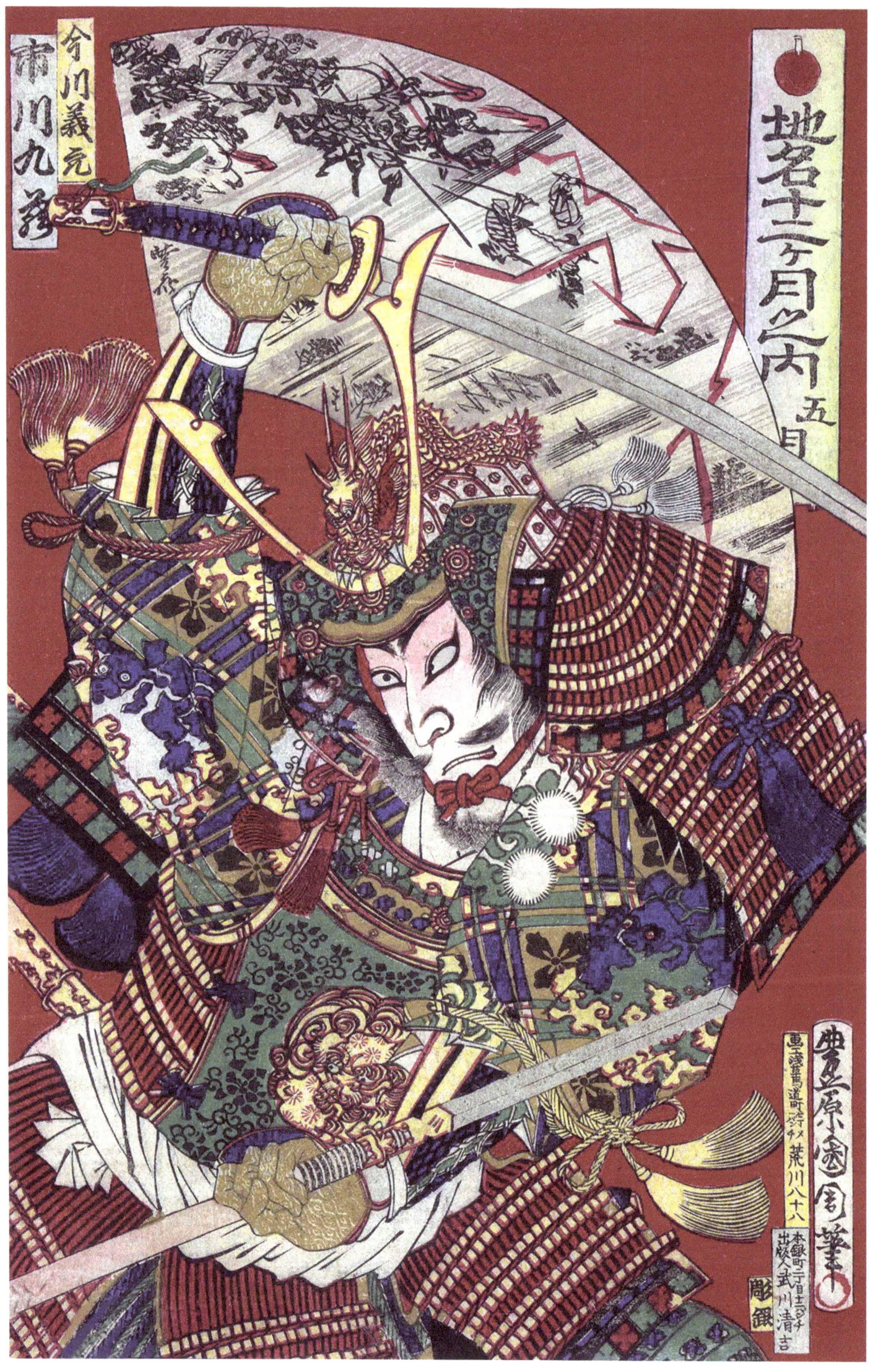

今川義元
市川九蔵
地名十二ヶ月之内
五月
豊原小國周筆
荒川八十八
彫銀

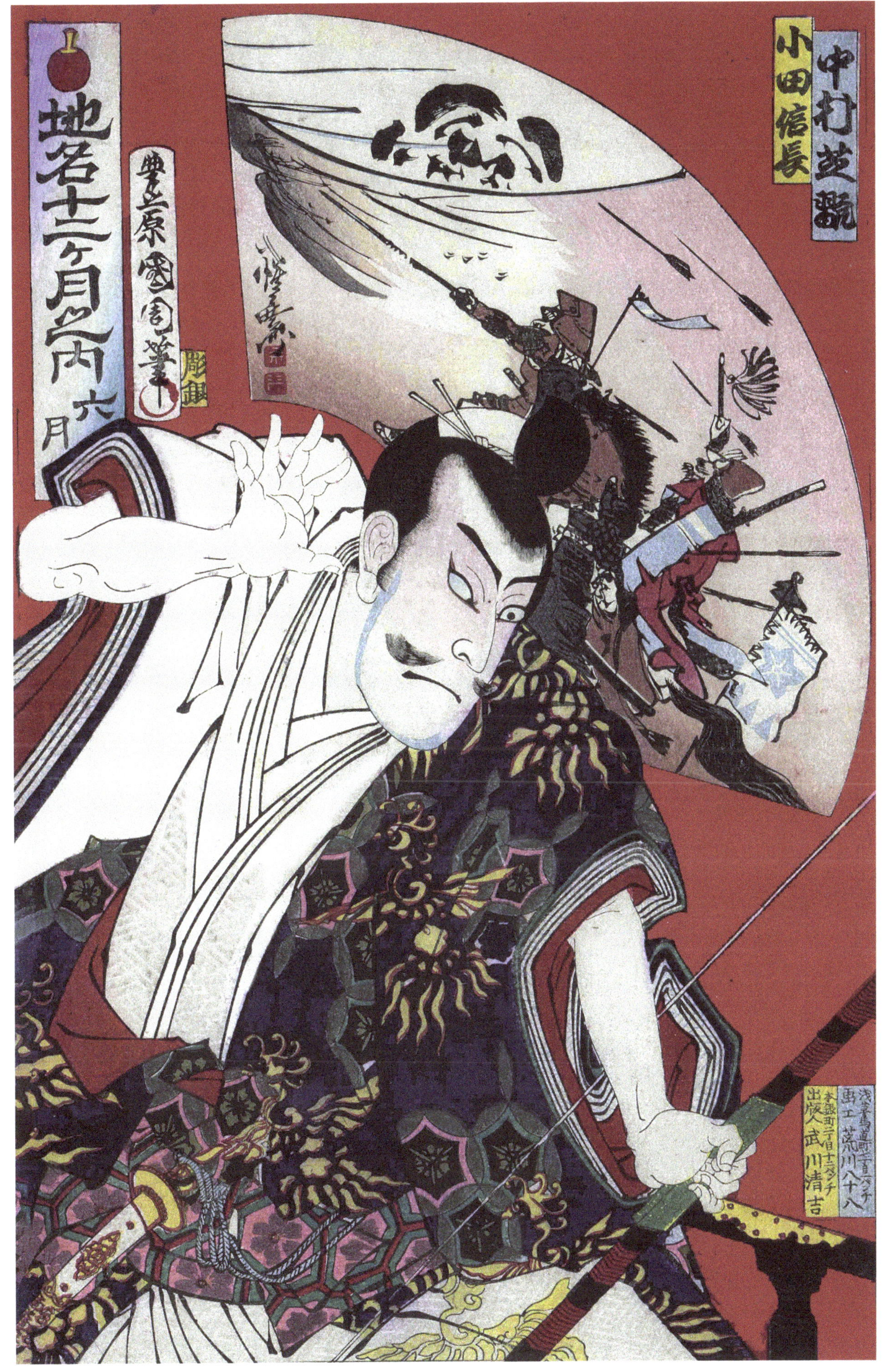
地名十二ヶ月之内 六月
豊原國周筆
彫録
中村芝翫
小田信長
浅草馬道町二丁目三バンチ
画工 荒川八十八
出版人 武川清吉

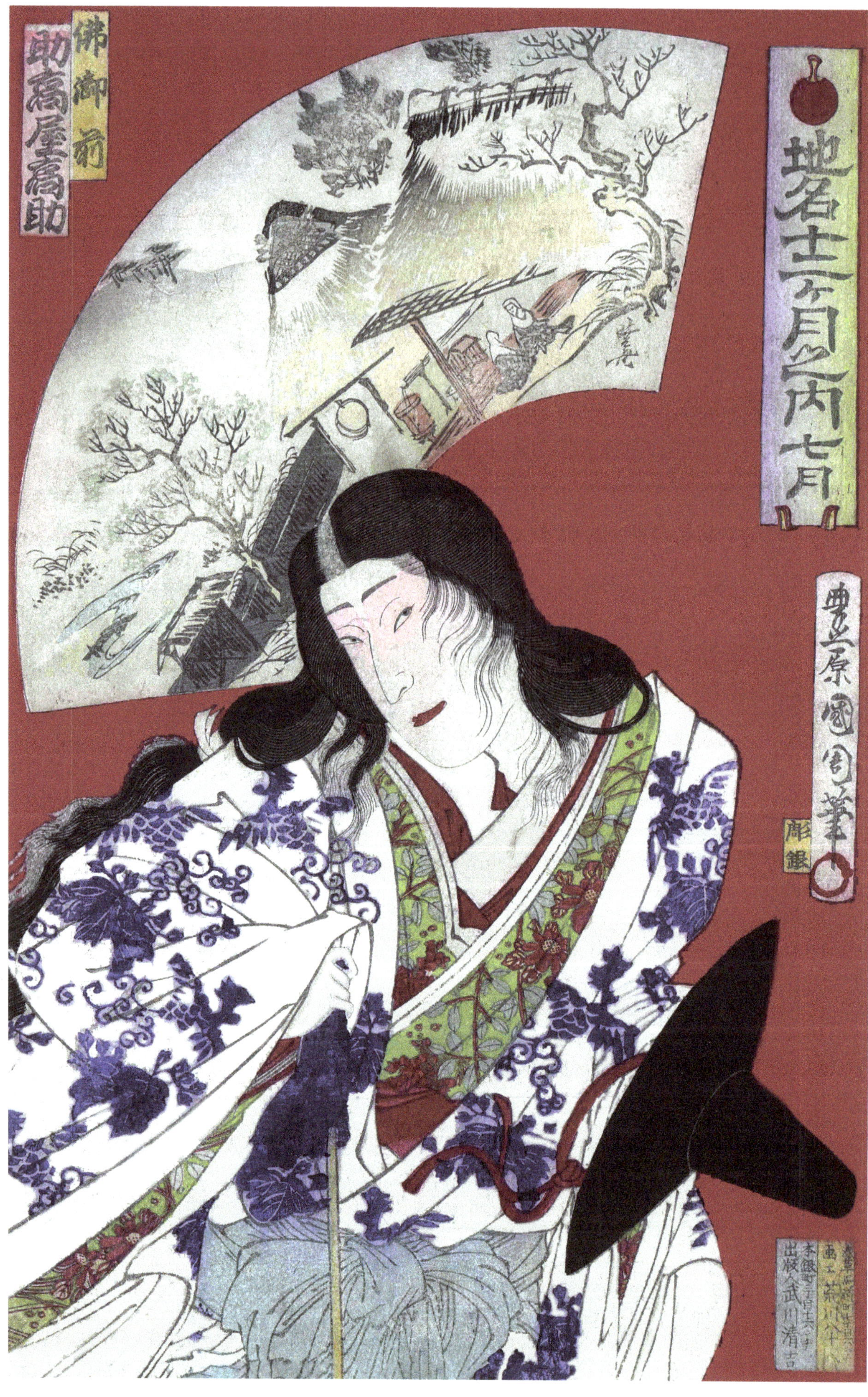

佛御前
助高屋高助
地名十二ヶ月之内七月
豊原國周筆
彫銀
本銀町三丁目十六バ
出版人武川清吉

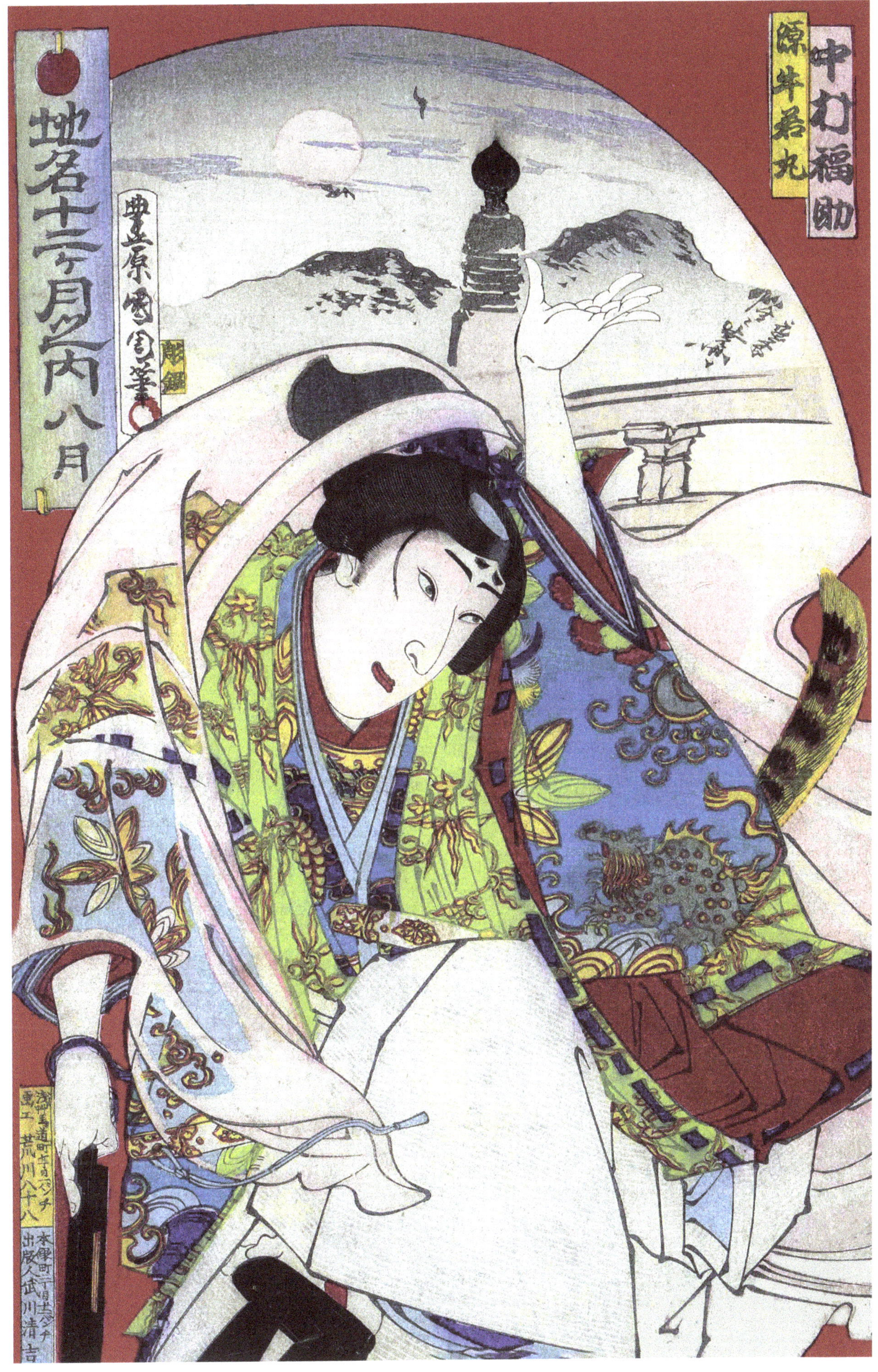
中村福助
源牛若丸
地名十二ヶ月之内　八月
豊工原国周筆
彫鐵
浅草田原町二丁目二バンチ
画工　荒川八十八
本銀町二丁目二バンチ
出版人　武川清吉

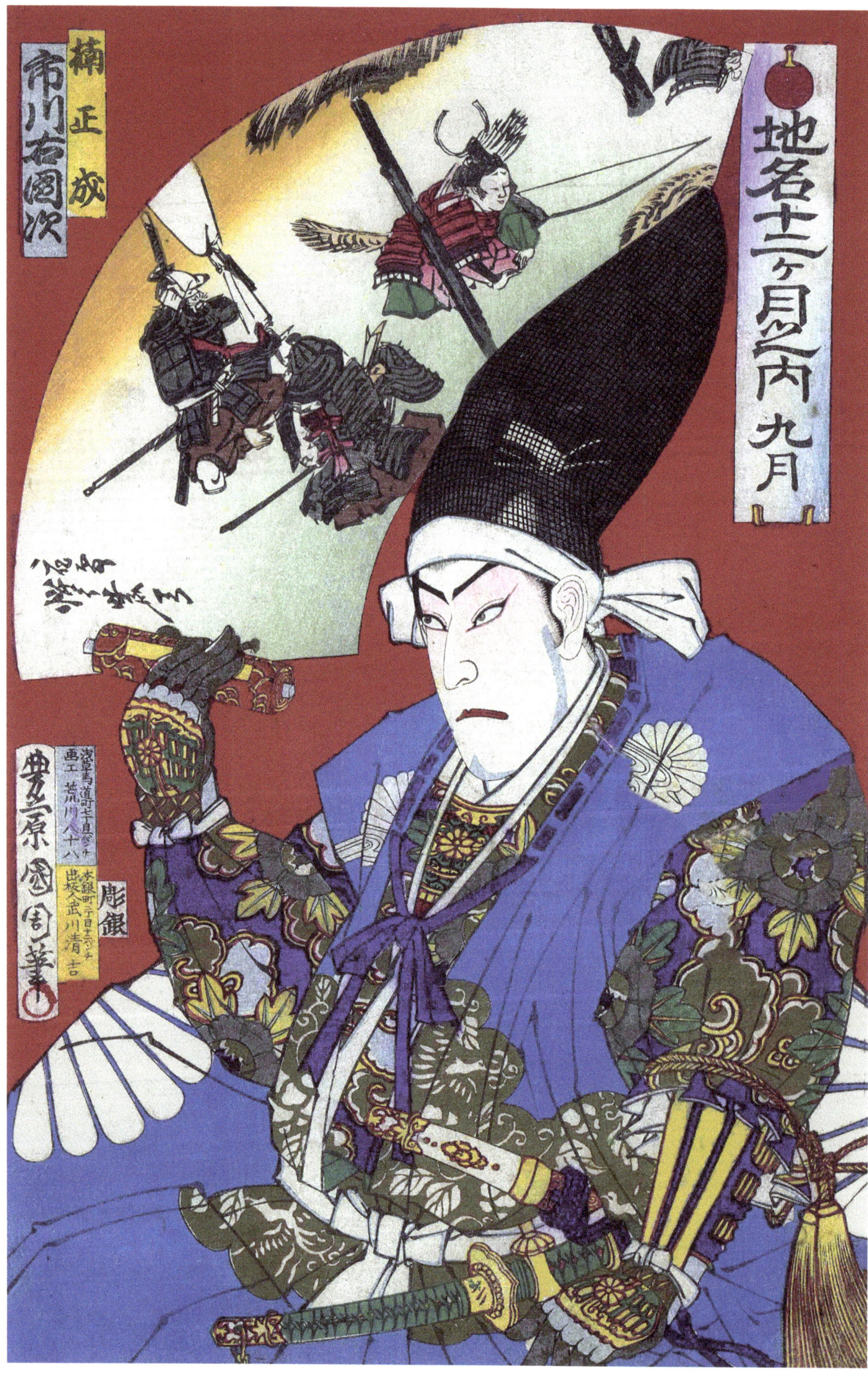

楠 正成
市川右團次
地名十二ヶ月ノ内 九月
彫銀
豊原國周筆

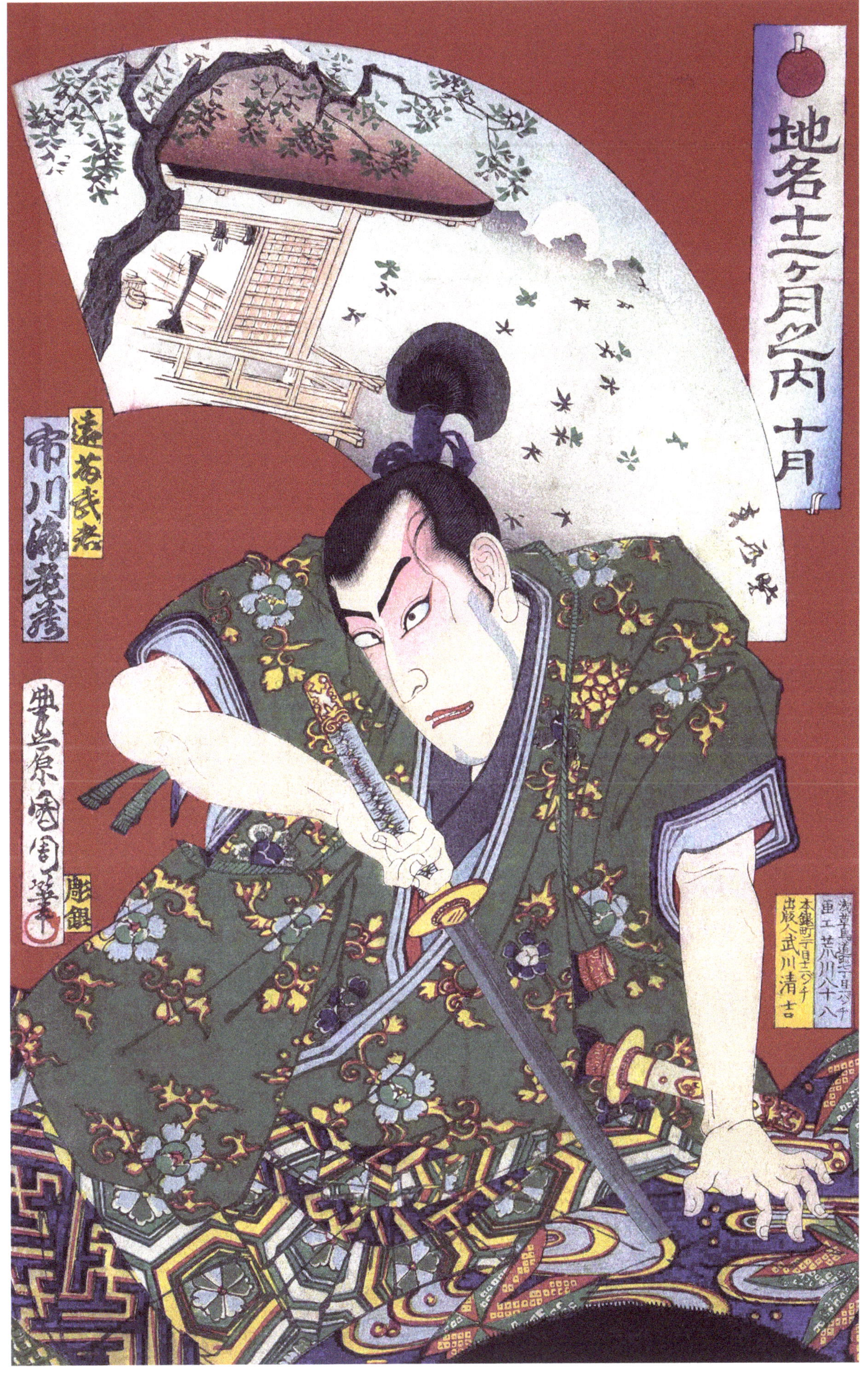

地名十二ヶ月之内 十月
遠荷武君
市川海老蔵
豊原國周筆
彫銀
浅草馬道元三丁目バンチ
重工 荒川八十八
出版人 武川清吉

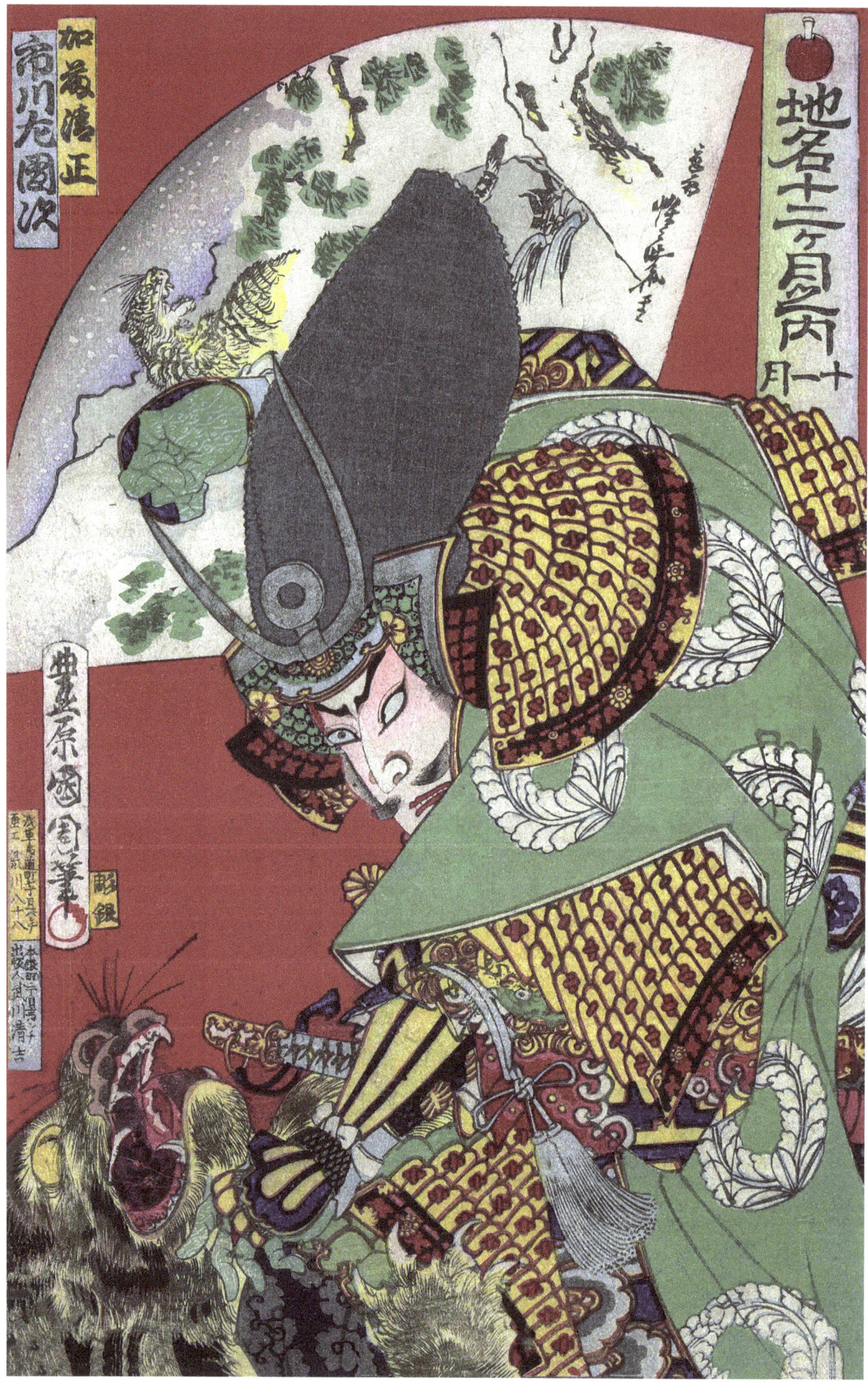
加藤清正
市川左團次

地名十二ヶ月之内
十一月

豊原國周筆

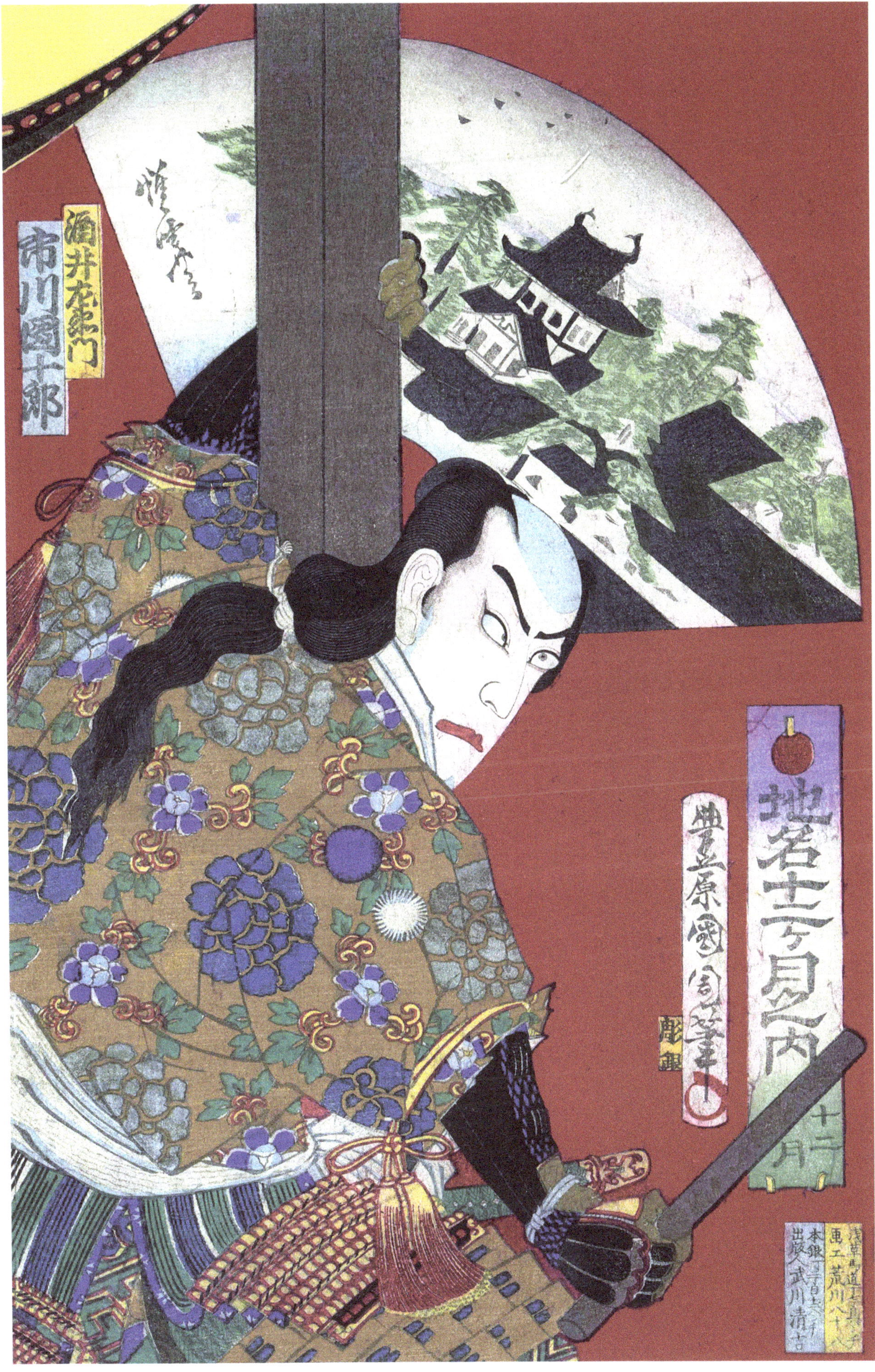
酒井左衛門
市川團十郎
地名十二ヶ月ノ内
豊原國周筆
彫銀
十二月
本銀二丁目土行
浅草東道玉具
車工荒川へ十八
出版人武川清吉

MITATE HAKKENDEN NO UCHI

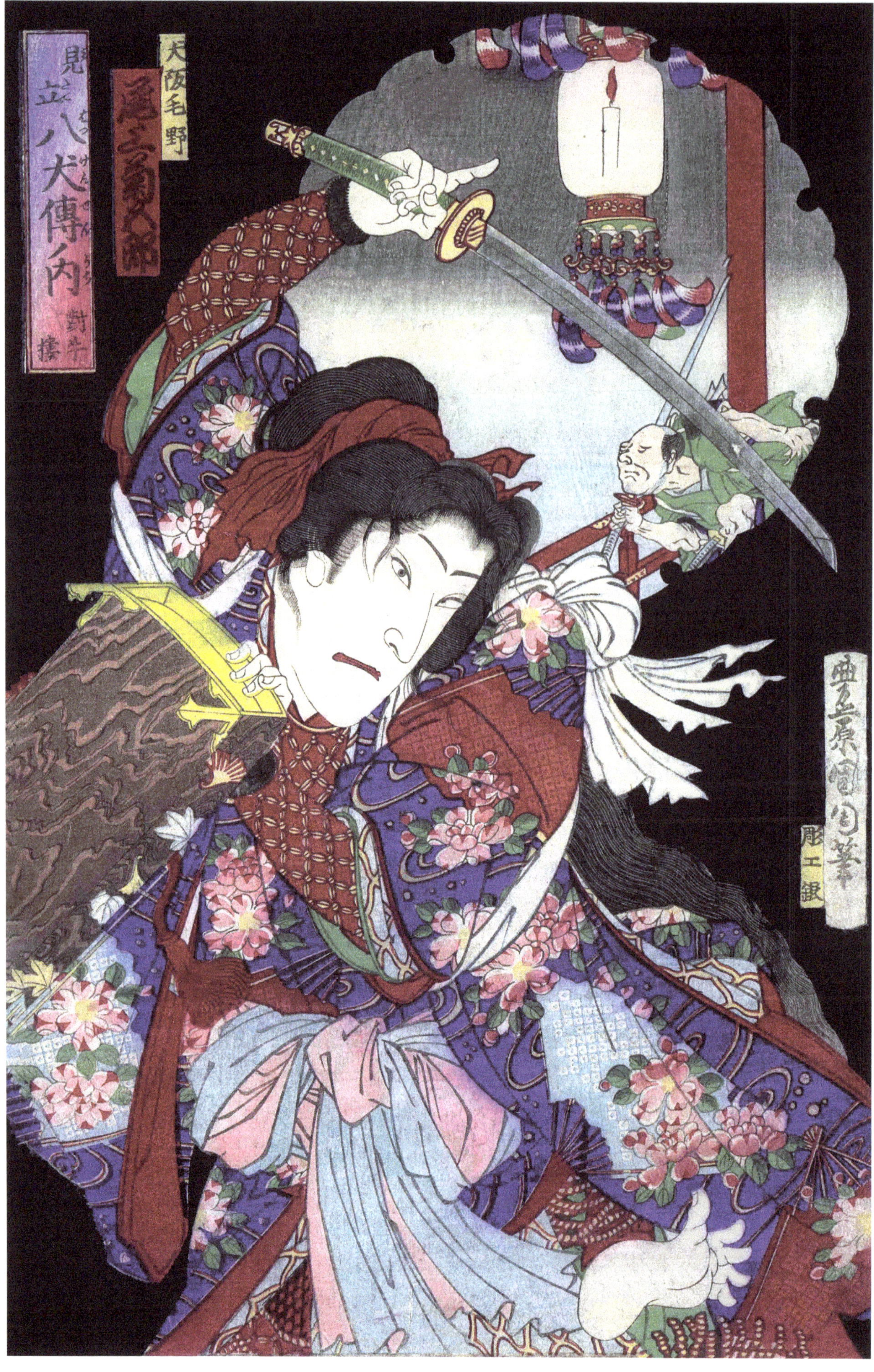
大阪毛野
嵐三五郎

魁立
八犬傳ノ内

豊原國周筆

彫工銀

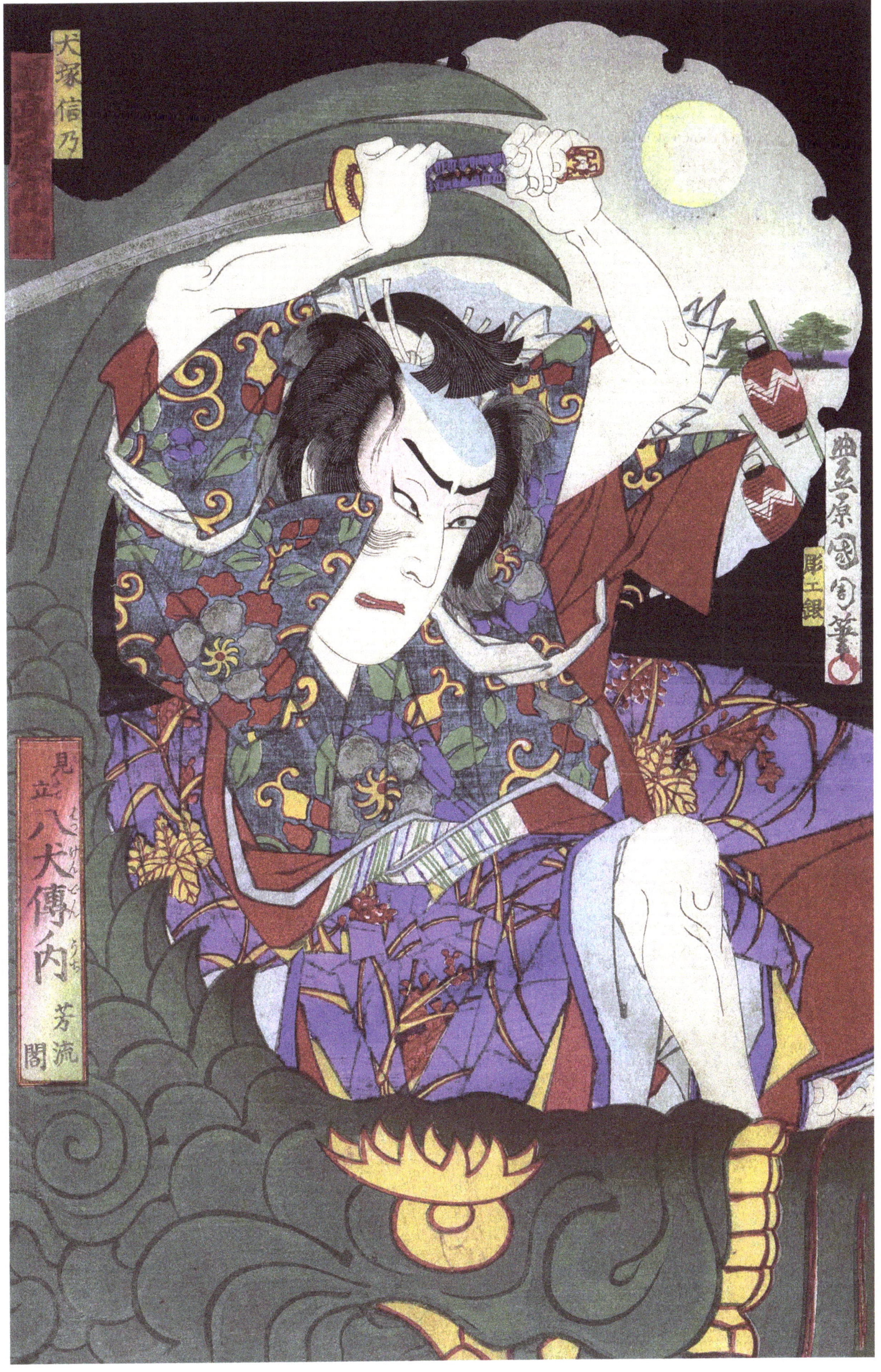
犬塚信乃
見立八犬傳内
芳流閣
豊原國周筆
彫工銀

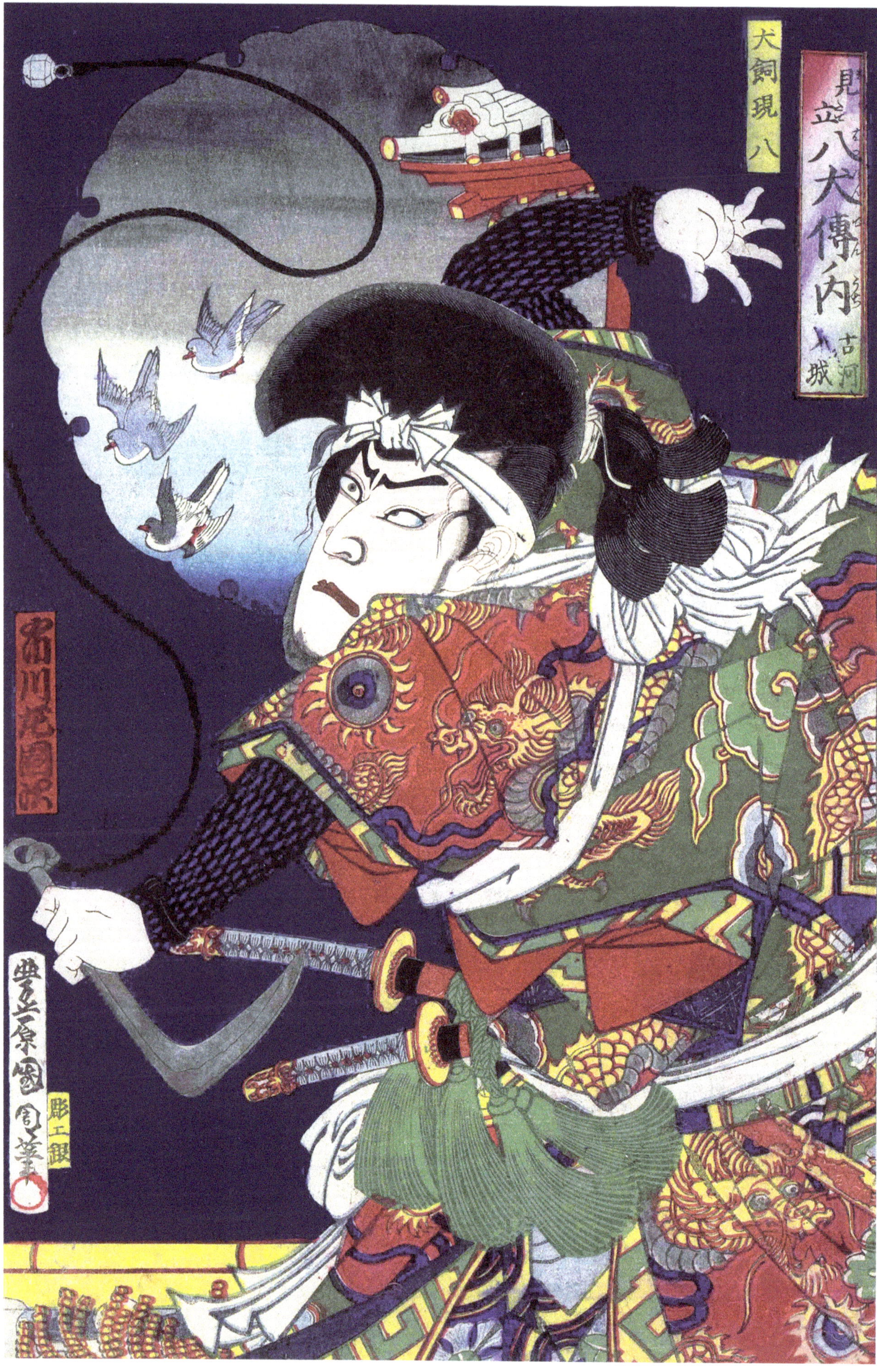
犬飼現八

見立八犬傳ノ内

市川元圖㦮

豐原國周筆
彫工銀

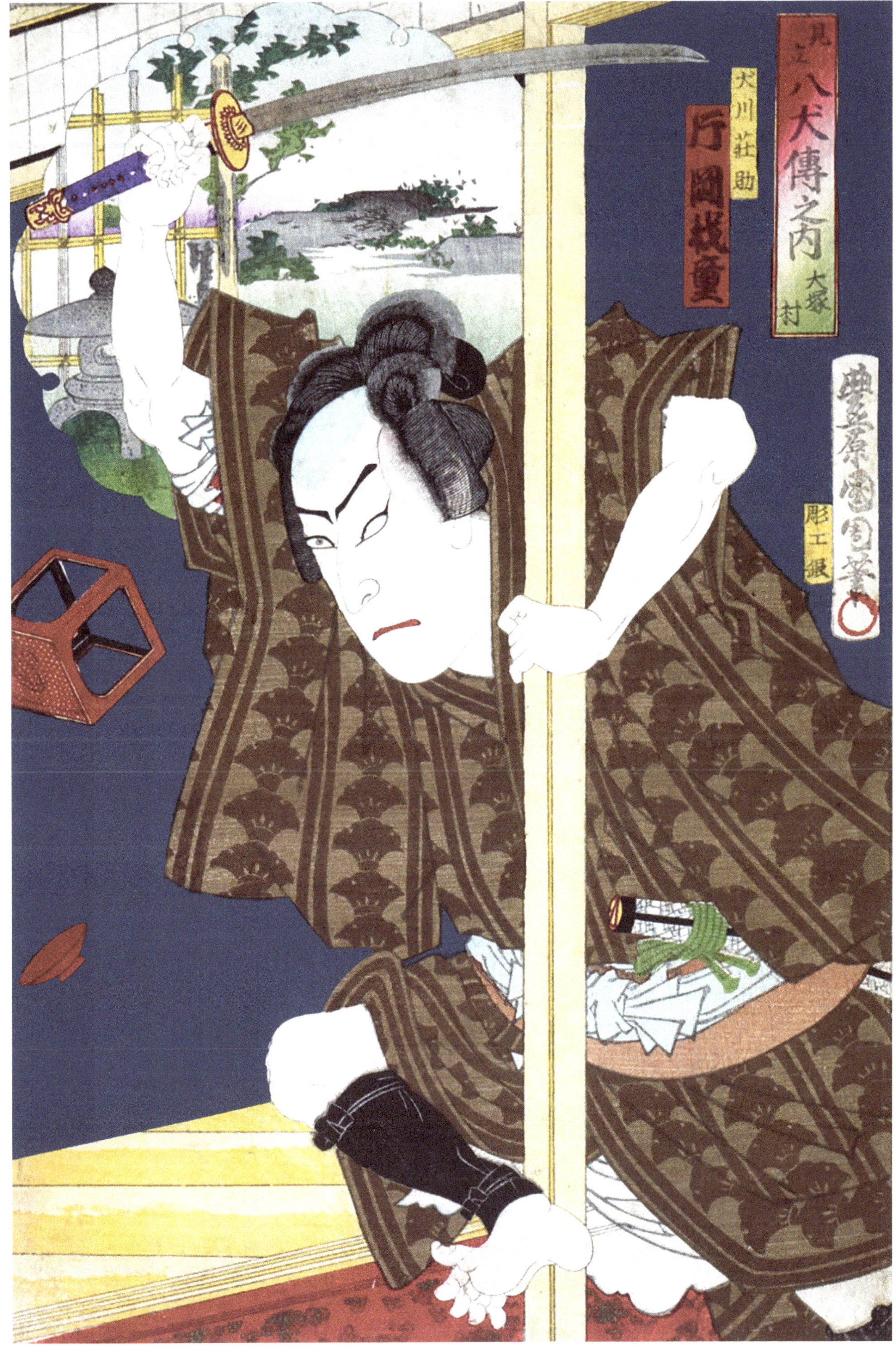

見立八犬傳之内
犬川莊助
片岡枝重
大塚村
豊原國周筆
彫工藏

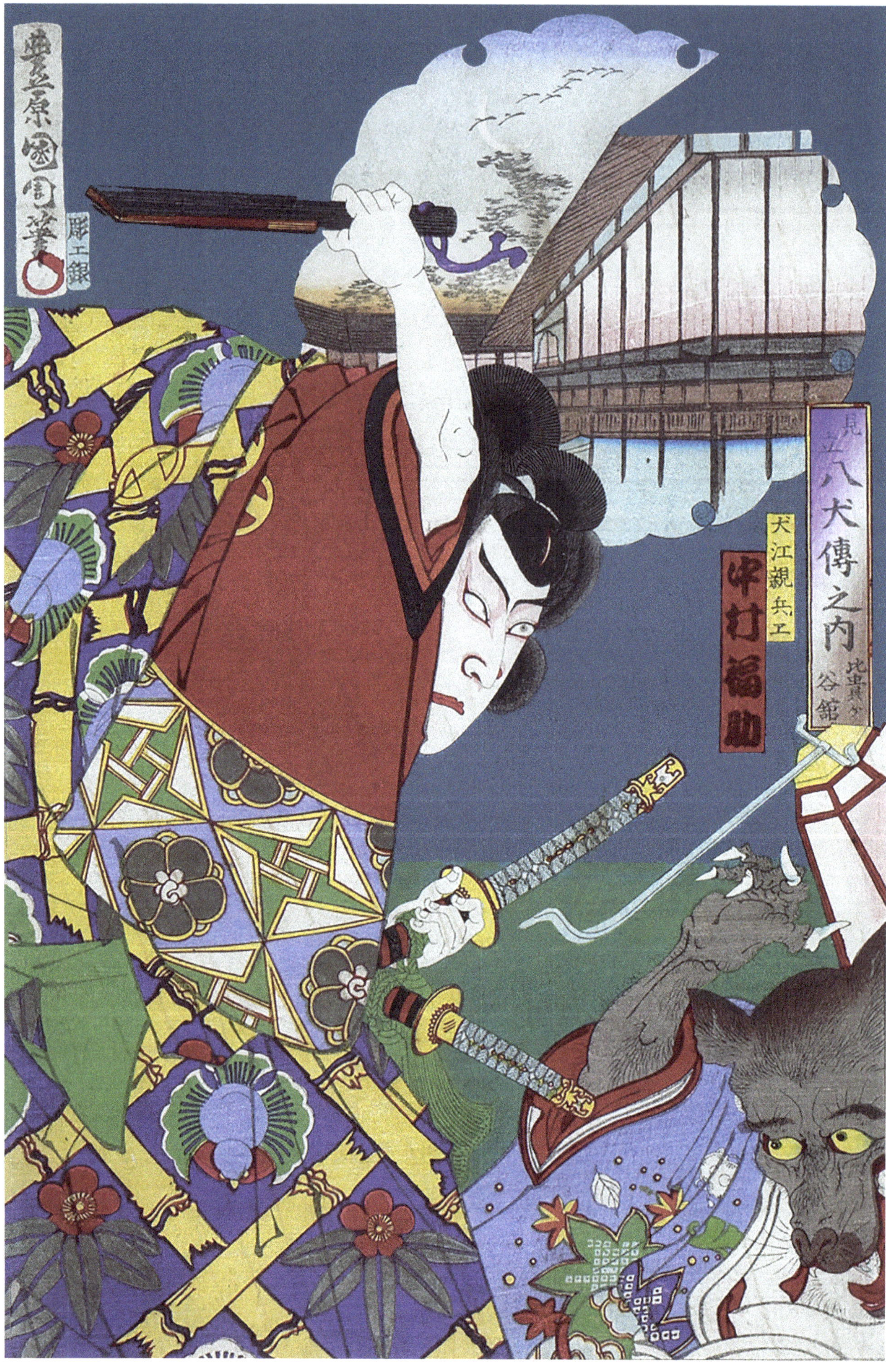
豊原國周筆
彫工銀
見立八犬傳之内
比志異タ
谷舘
犬江親兵エ
沖打福助

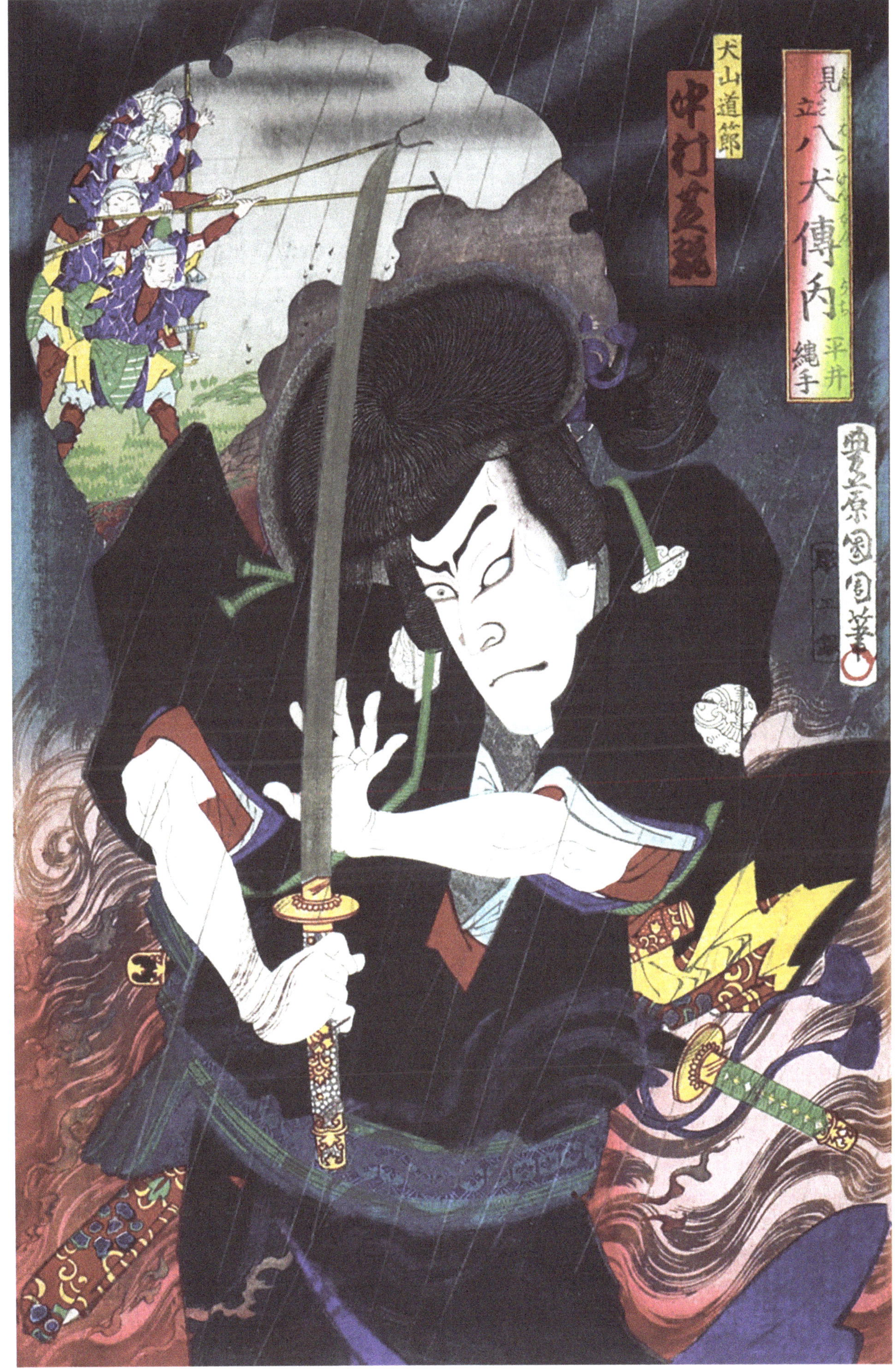
見立八犬傳內
平井
縄手
犬山道節
忠与五郎
豊原國周筆

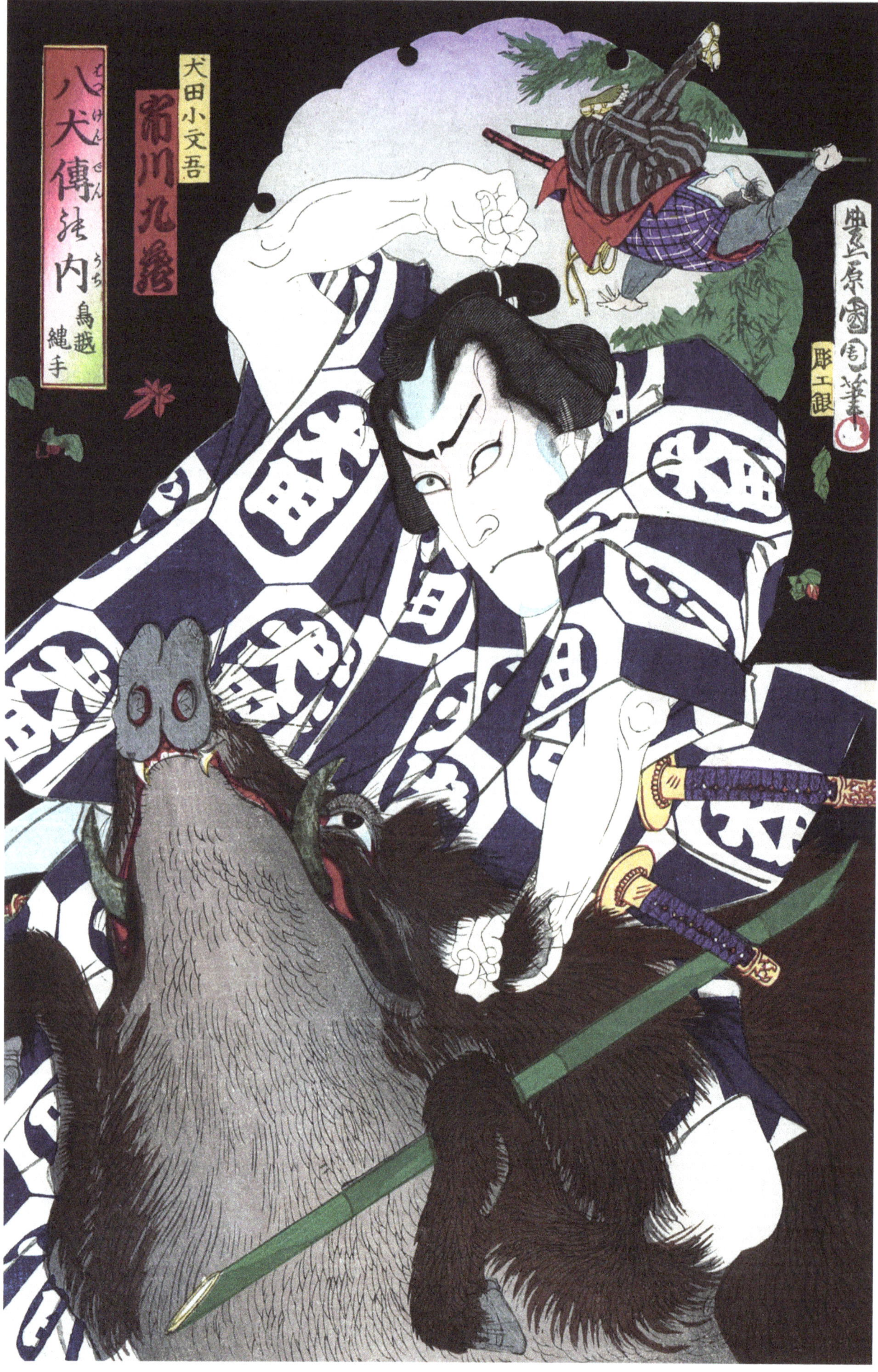
犬田小文吾
市川九蔵
八犬傳犬之内
鳥越
縄手
豊原國周筆
彫工銀

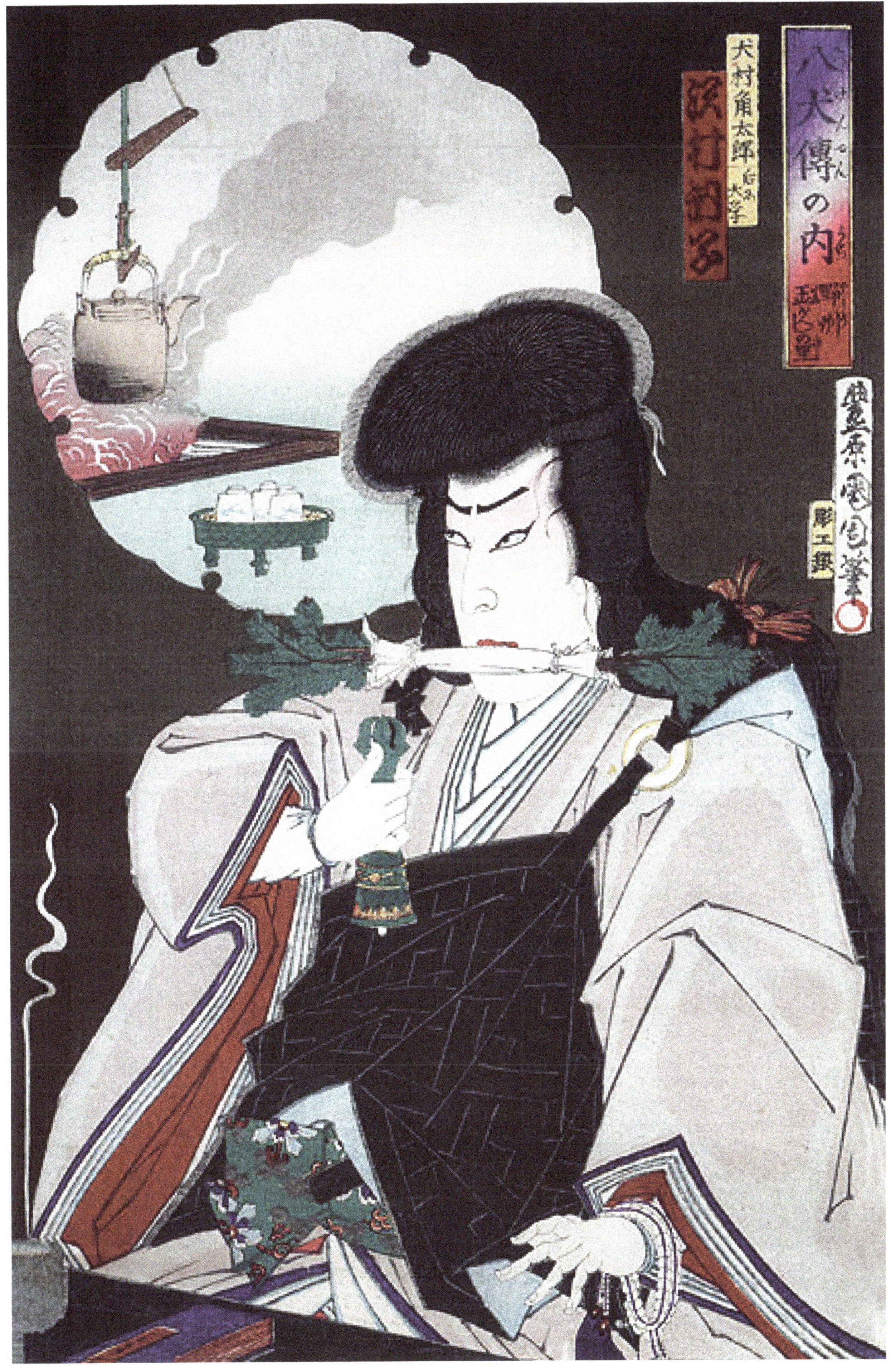
八犬傳の内
犬村角太郎
沢村訥子

GISHI MEIMEI-DEN

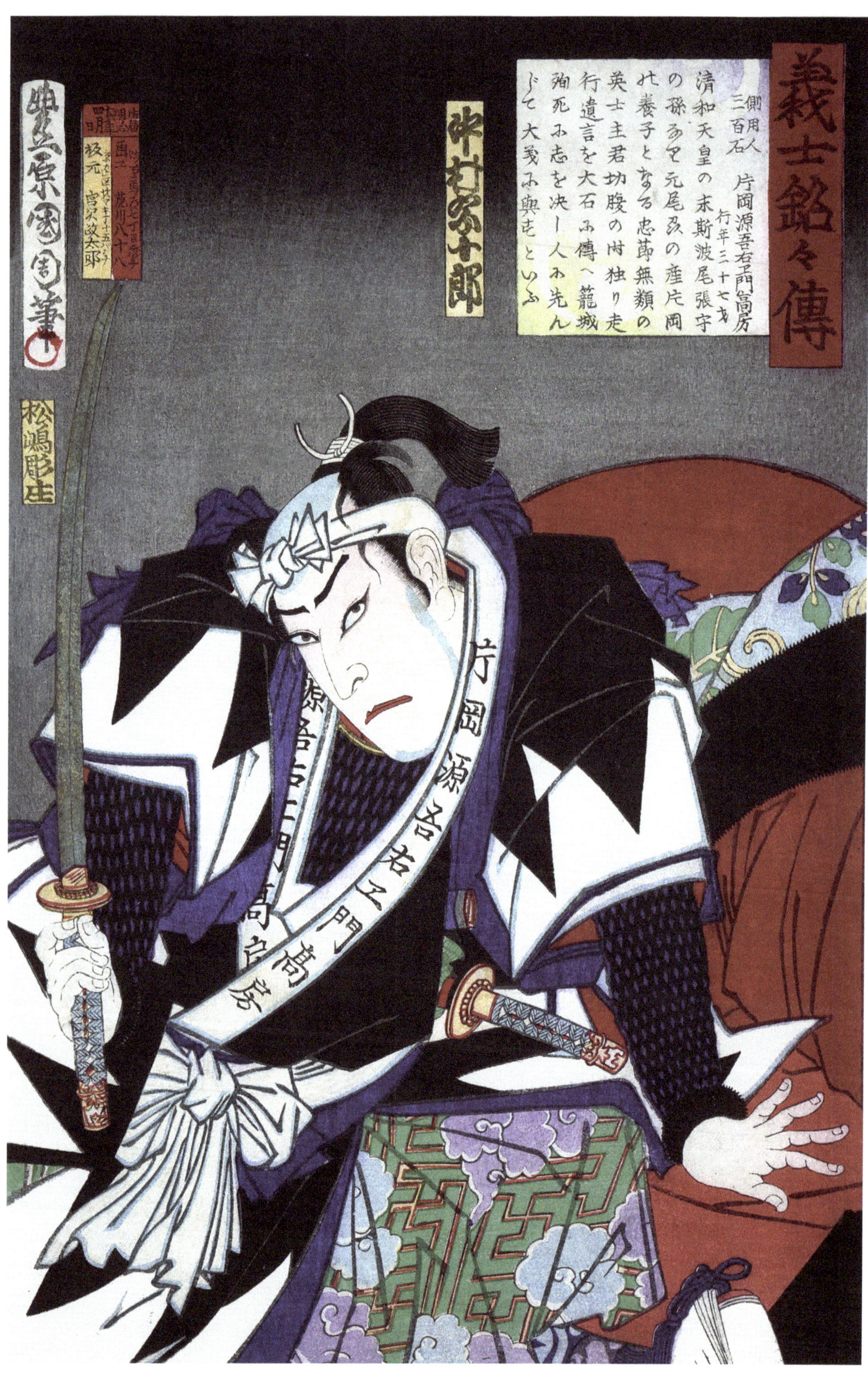

義士銘々傳
側用人　三百石　片岡源吾右門高房　行年三十七才
清和天皇の末斯波尾張守の孫ありて元尾及の産片岡此養子とする忠莭無類の英士主君切腹の耳独り走り行遺言を大石ふ傳へ籠城殉死ふ志を決し一人ふ先んじて大義ふ與をといふ
中村芝翫
豊原国周筆
松嶋彫庄
画工　荒川八十八
極元　宮次改太郎

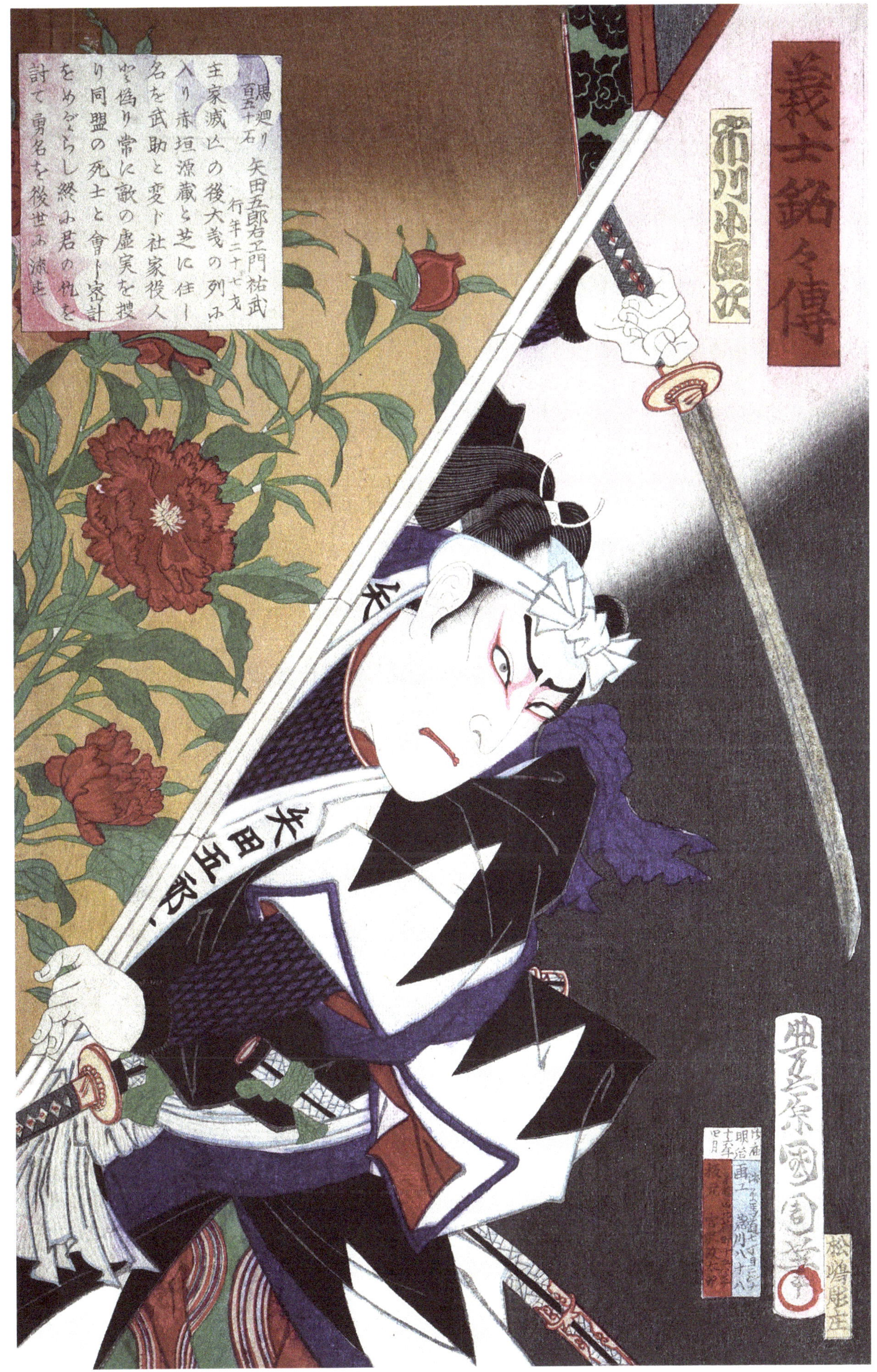

義士銘々傳
市川小團次
馬廻り
百五十石　矢田五郎右エ門祐武
行年二十七戈
主家滅亡の後大義の列み
入り赤垣源蔵と芝に住一
名を武助と変ト社家役人
空偽り常に敵の虚実を捜
り同盟の死士と會ト密計
をめぐらし終み君の杭を
討て勇名を後世み流ы
豊原國周筆
松嶋邑正
明治十六年四月

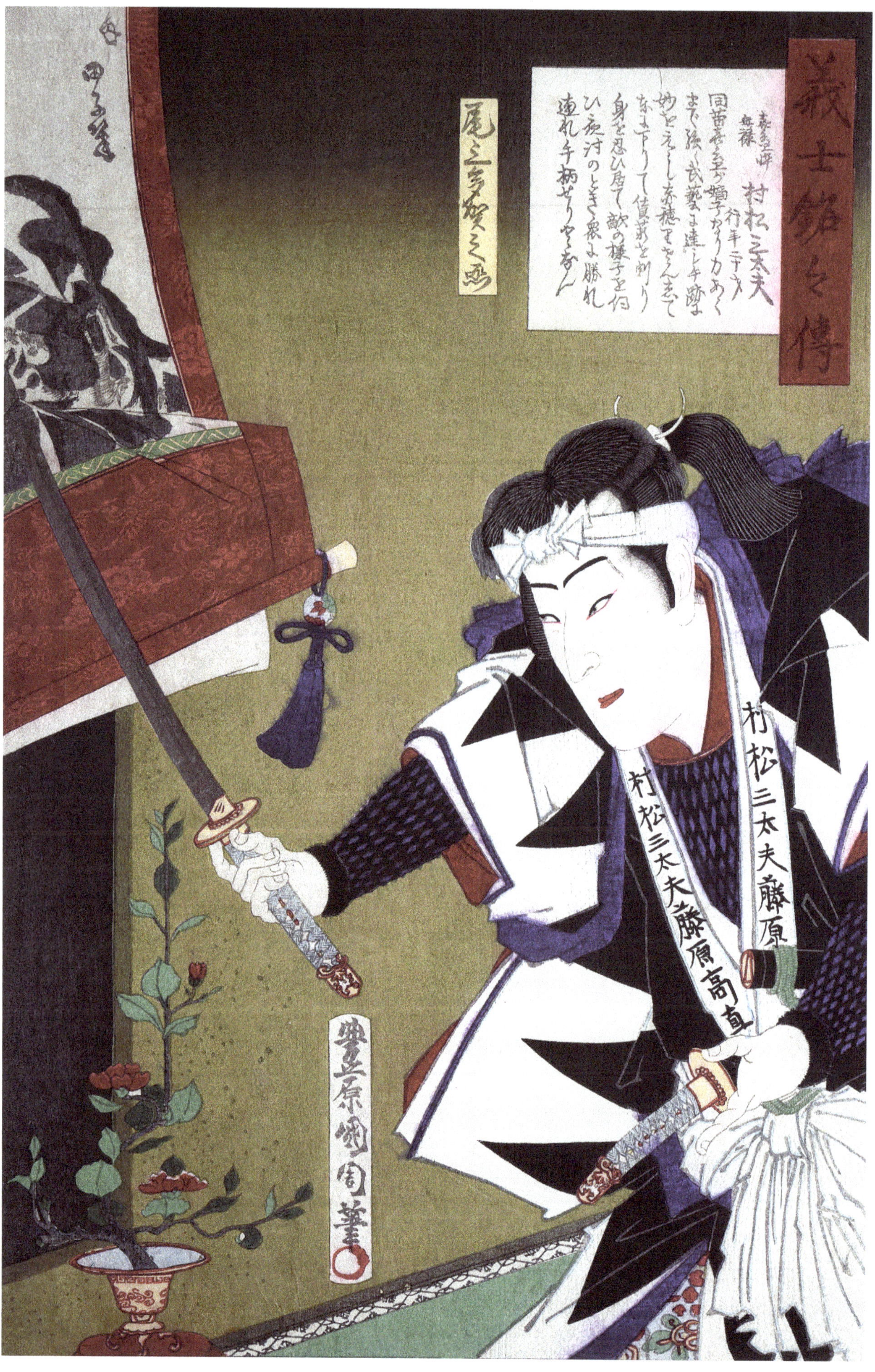
義士銘々傳

尾上多賀之丞

村松三太夫
秀色丈野
無様

豐原國周筆

村松三太夫藤原高直

村松三太夫藤原高直

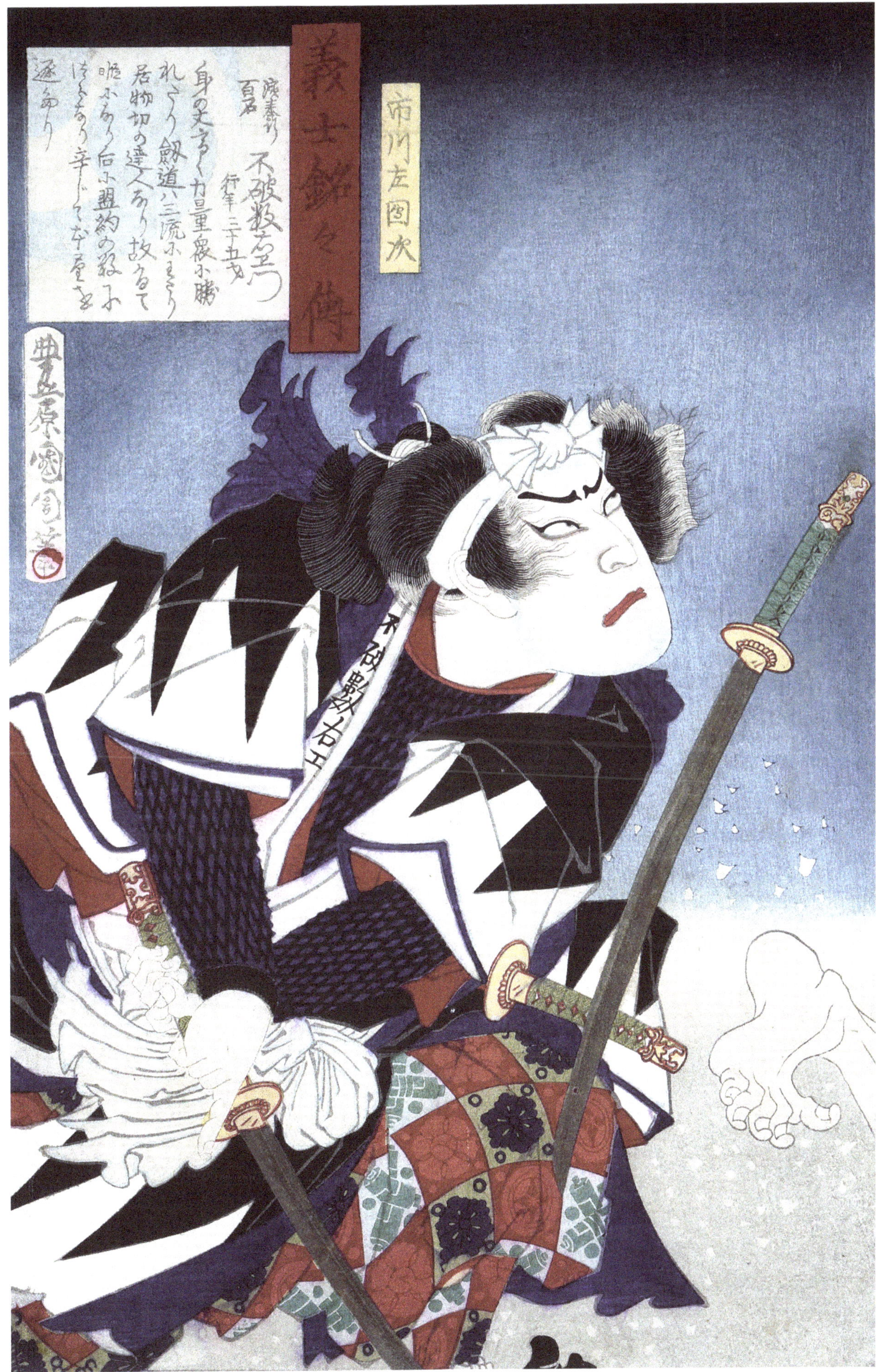

義士銘々傳

市川左団次

不破数右エ門
行年三十五才

演義抄
百石

身の丈高く力量衆に勝
れさり劔道八三流に至り
居物切の達人なり故に
眠ふるくて右ふ盟約の後不
ほとんどり辛ドして本意を
遂るなり

豊原國周画

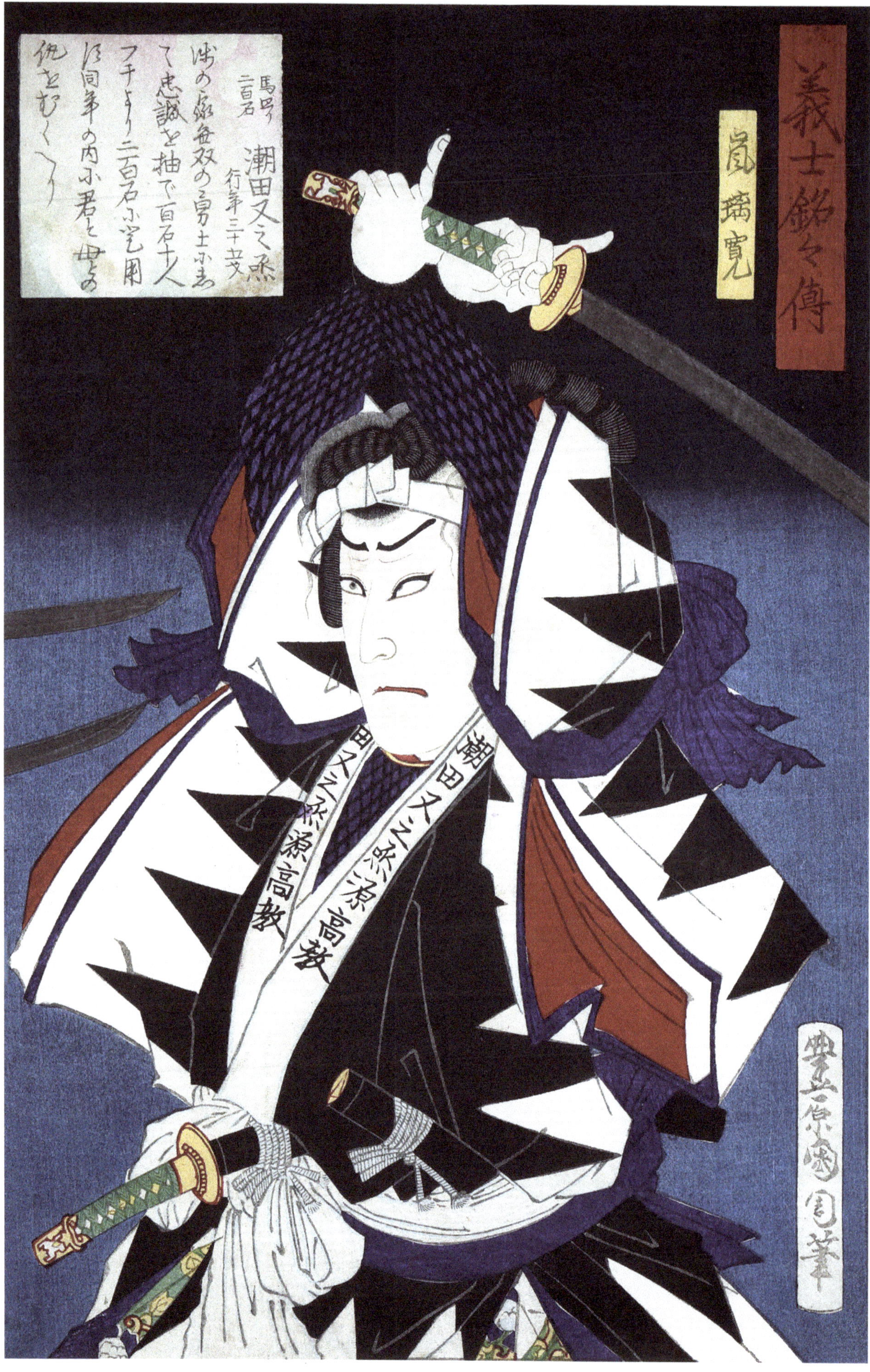

義士銘々傳
嵐璃寛
馬号
二百石
潮田又之丞
行年三十五
沖の石義勇双の勇士小高
て忠誠を抽で百石十人
フチより二百石小宅用
に同年の内小君を母との
仇をむくつ
豊原國周筆

112

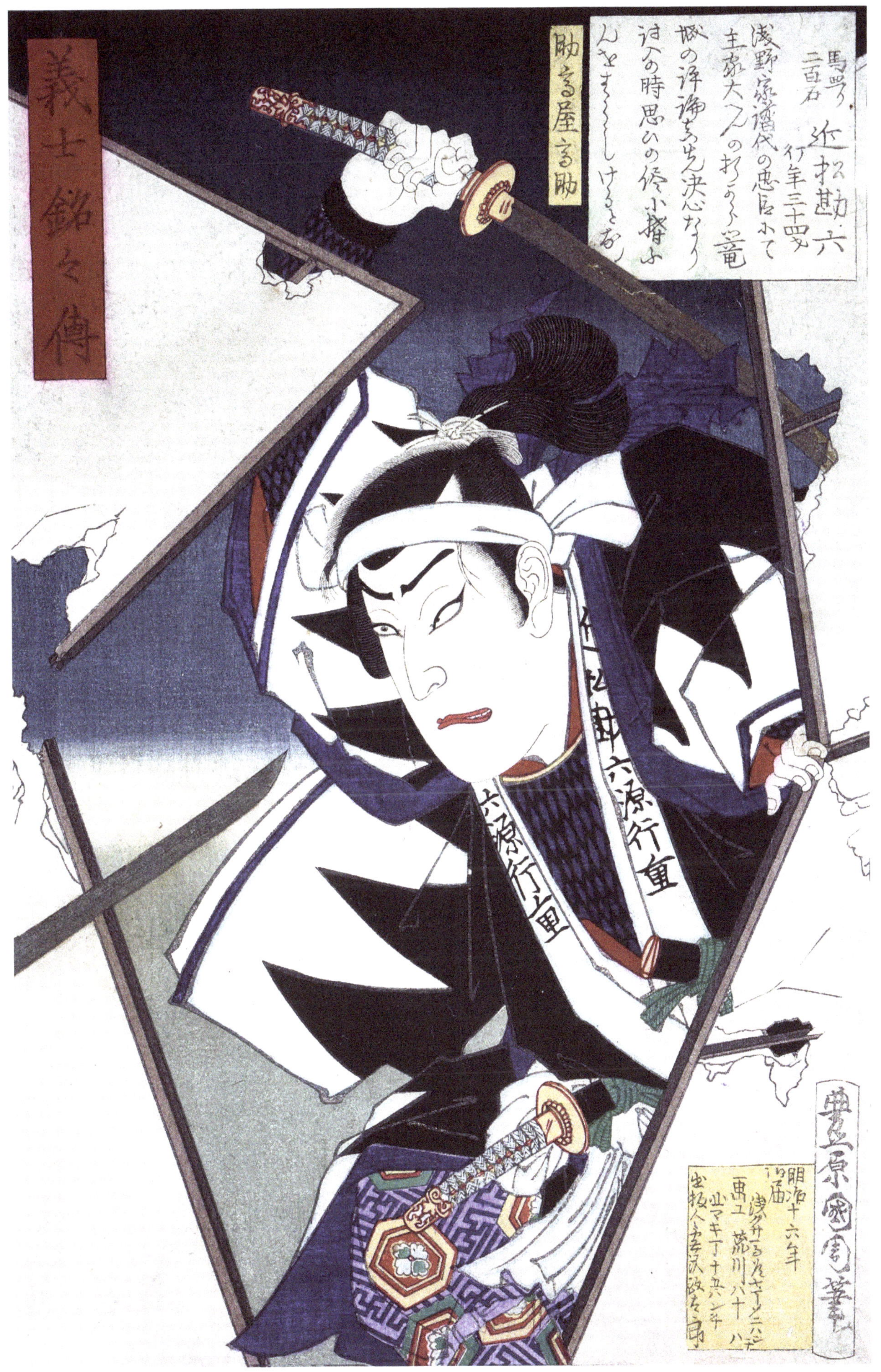

義士銘々傳
馬弓　二番石　近松勘六
行年三十四歳
助る屋言助
淺野家譜代の忠臣ふて
主恭大刀の打つゝ竜
城の評論ちち決心なり
討入の時思ひの修小楮ふ
んをすゝゝゝしけるとも
明治十六年
浅升ゐるさゝ二六八十
再ユ　荒川八十八
山マキ丁十五ハンチ
出扨人亭沢政を郎
豊原國周筆

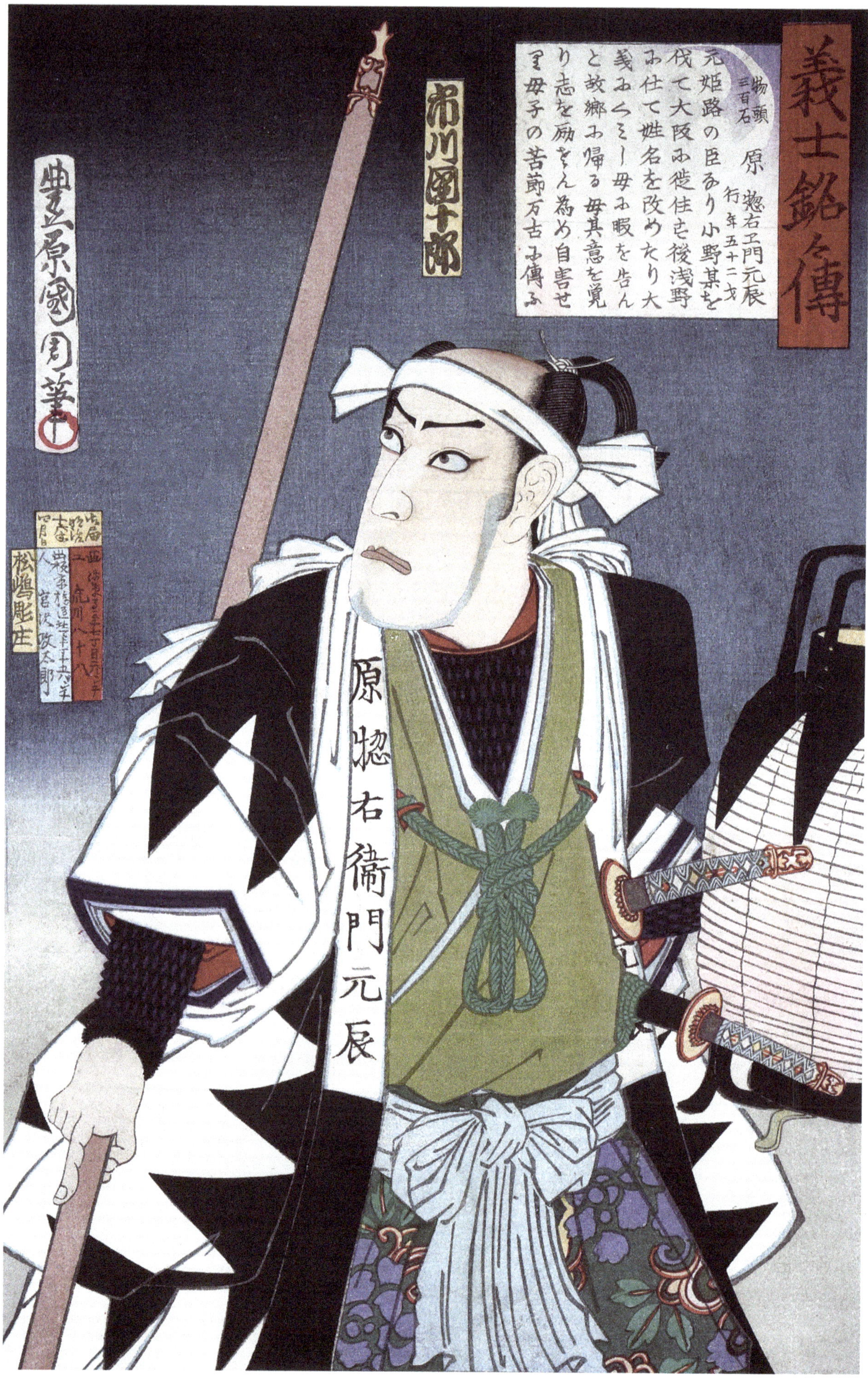
義士銘々傳
物頭
三百石
原　惣右エ門元辰
行年五十二戈
元姫路の臣なり小野某を
伐て大阪へ徙住さ後浅野
に仕て姓名を改めたり大
義ふくミ一母ふ暇を告ん
と故郷ふ帰る母其意を覚
り志を励さん為め自害せ
ゝ母子の苦節万古ふ傳ふ
市川團十郎
豊原國周筆
原惣右備門元辰
松嶋彫庄

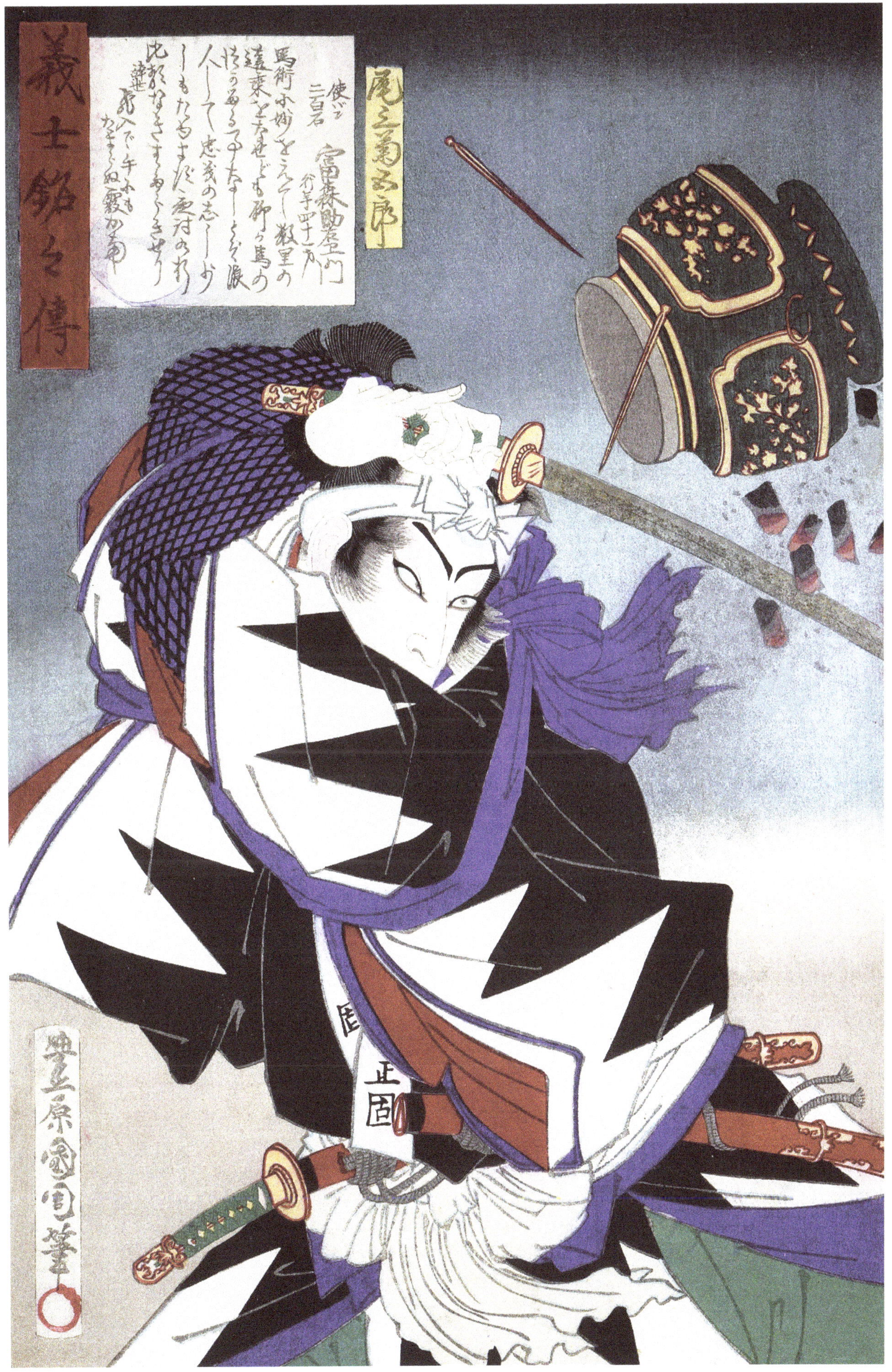
義士銘々傳

尾三菊五郎

富森助右衛門
使に二百石

馬術小性をえらび
遠来ともなせども御々馬の
人一て忠義の志一�び
此都なるますに変著のれ
尾八ぢー手かける

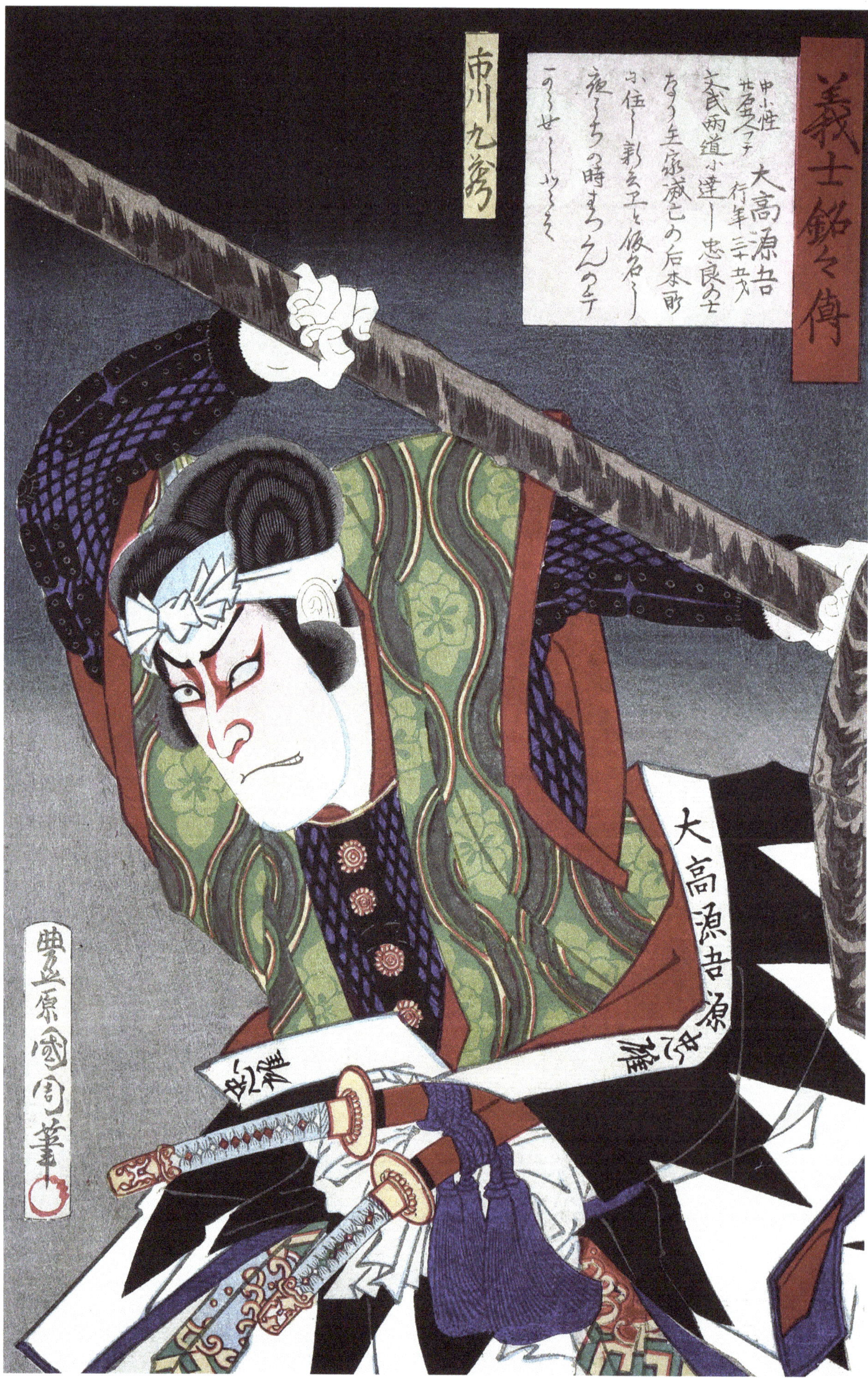

義士銘々傳
市川九蔵
大高源吾
大高源吾源忠雄
豊原國周筆

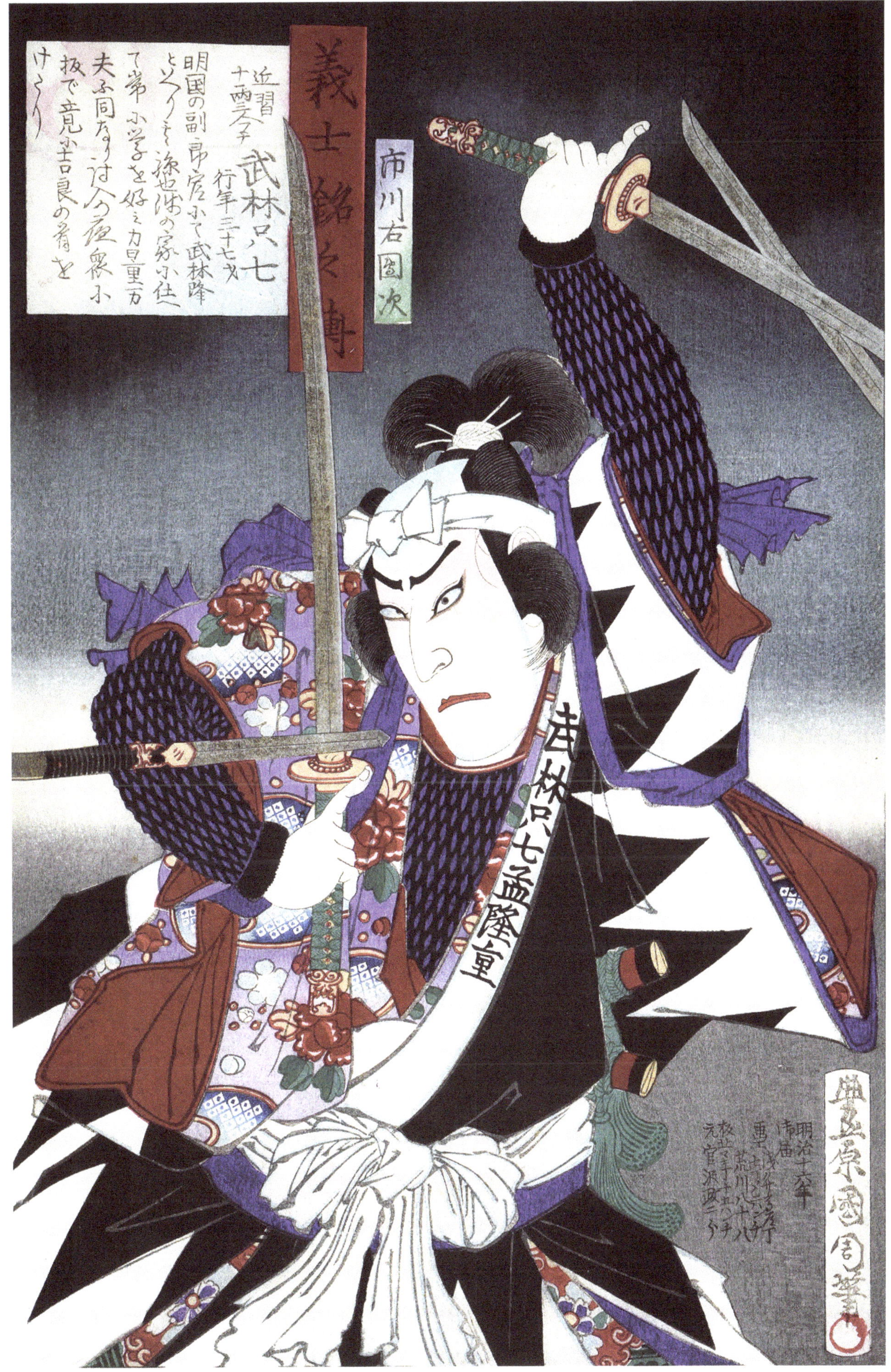

義士銘々傳
市川右團次
近習
十两三人子　武林只七　行年三十七才
明国の副昂宕ふて武林隆
とゝ）を淥地沖の家小仕
て常小學を好ミ力旦里二方
夫ふ同なり过今座衆小
抜で竟此吉良の肴を
けくり
武林只七盈隆宣
豊原國周筆

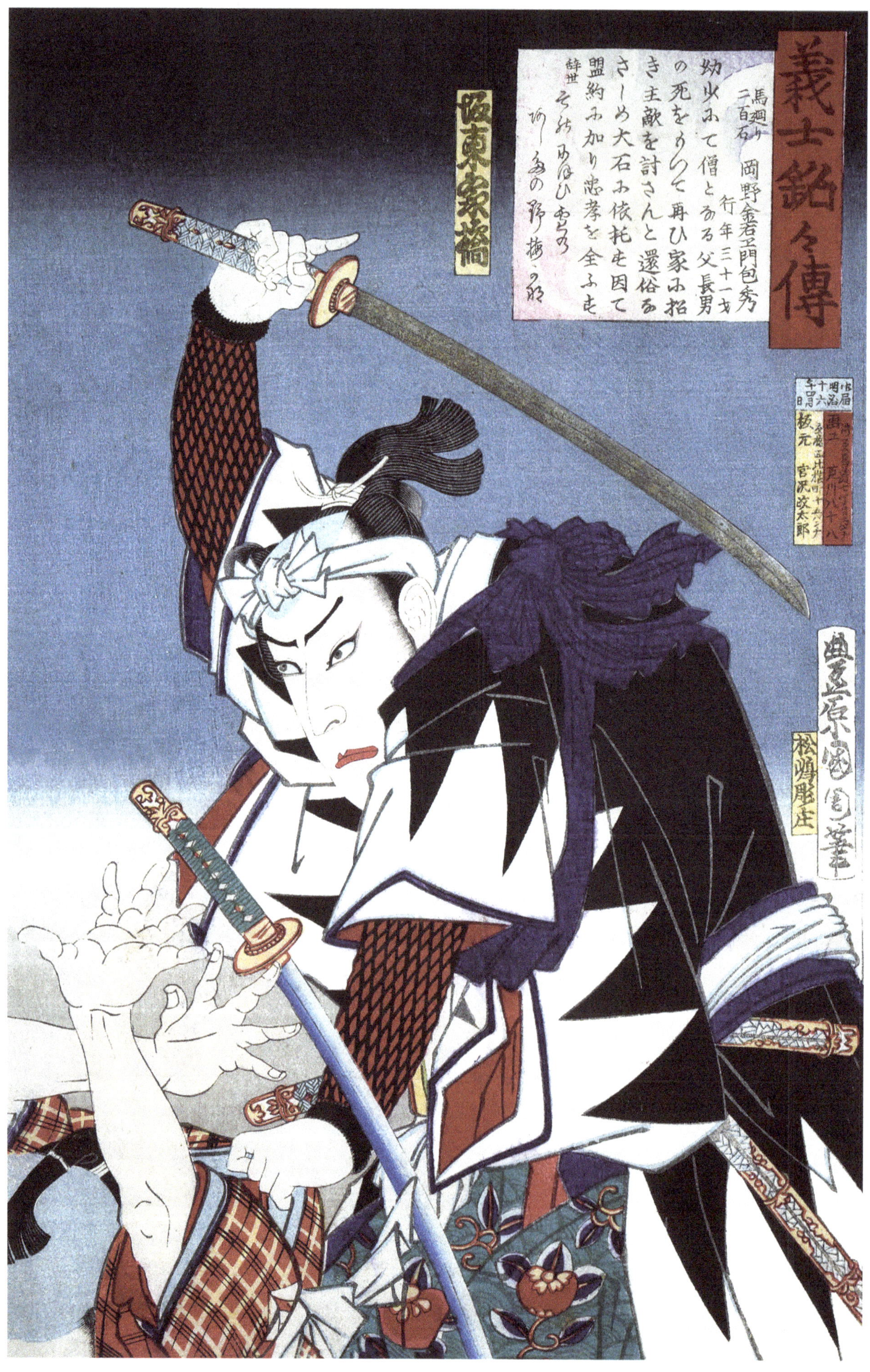

義士銘々傳
坂東家橘
馬廻り　二百石　岡野金右衛門包秀　行年三十一戈
幼少ふて僧とあるゝ父長男
の死をゝりて再ひ家ふ招
き主敵を討さんと還俗ゐ
さしめ大石ふ依托を因て
盟約ふ加り忠孝を全ふゑ
辞世
そゝみゆひもらゝ
ゝ多の野梅の名
陽斎豊原國周筆
松嶋彫庄

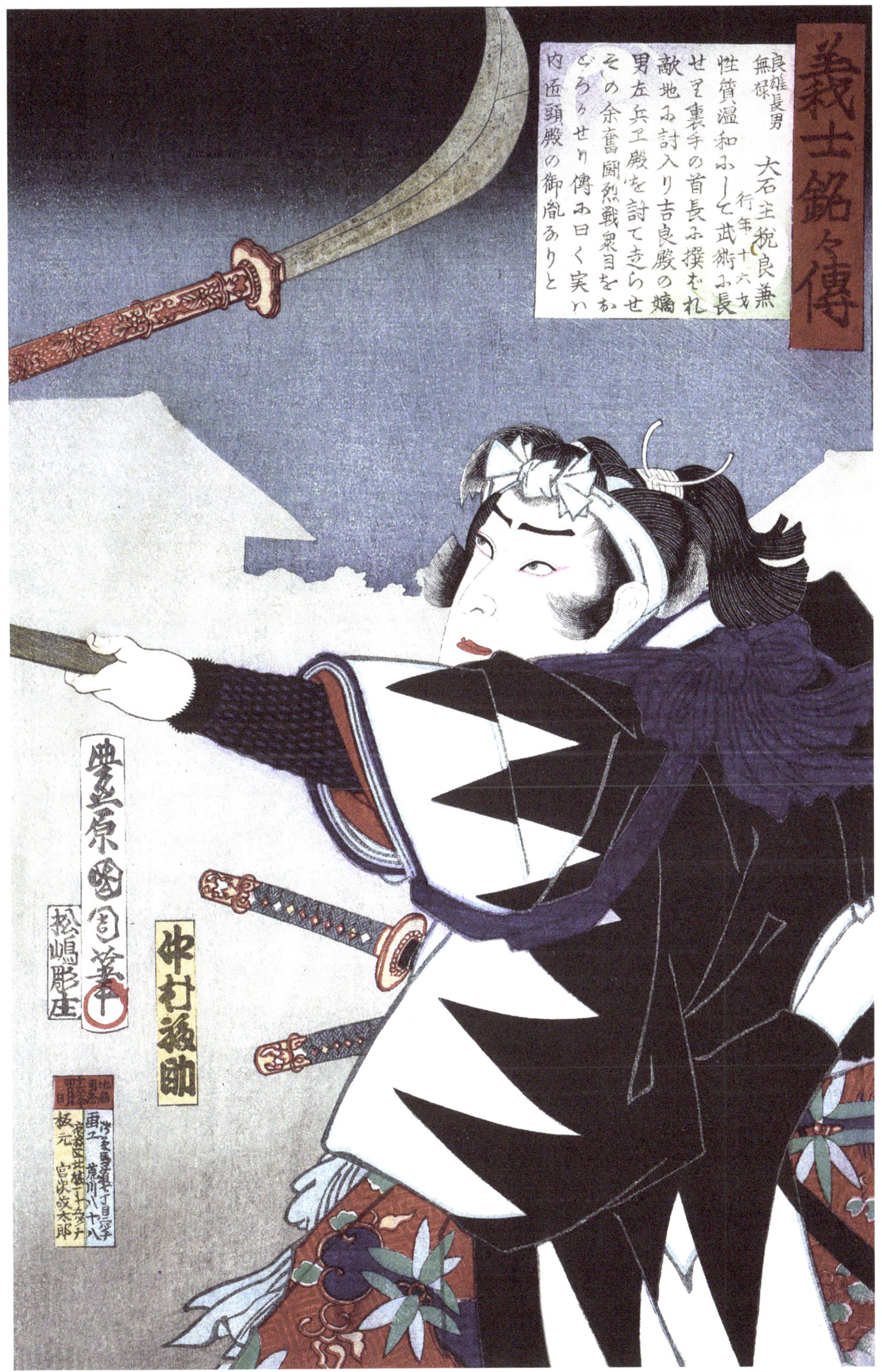
義士銘々傳
良雄長男
無禄　大石主税良兼　行年十六才
性質温和ふして武術ふ長
せず裏手の首長ふ撰ぶれ
敵地ふ討入り吉良殿の嫡
男左兵エ殿を討て走らせ
その余奮闘烈戦衆目をお
どろゞせり傅ふ曰く実ひ
内匠頭殿の御胤ありと
豊原國周筆
松嶋彫庄
中村福助

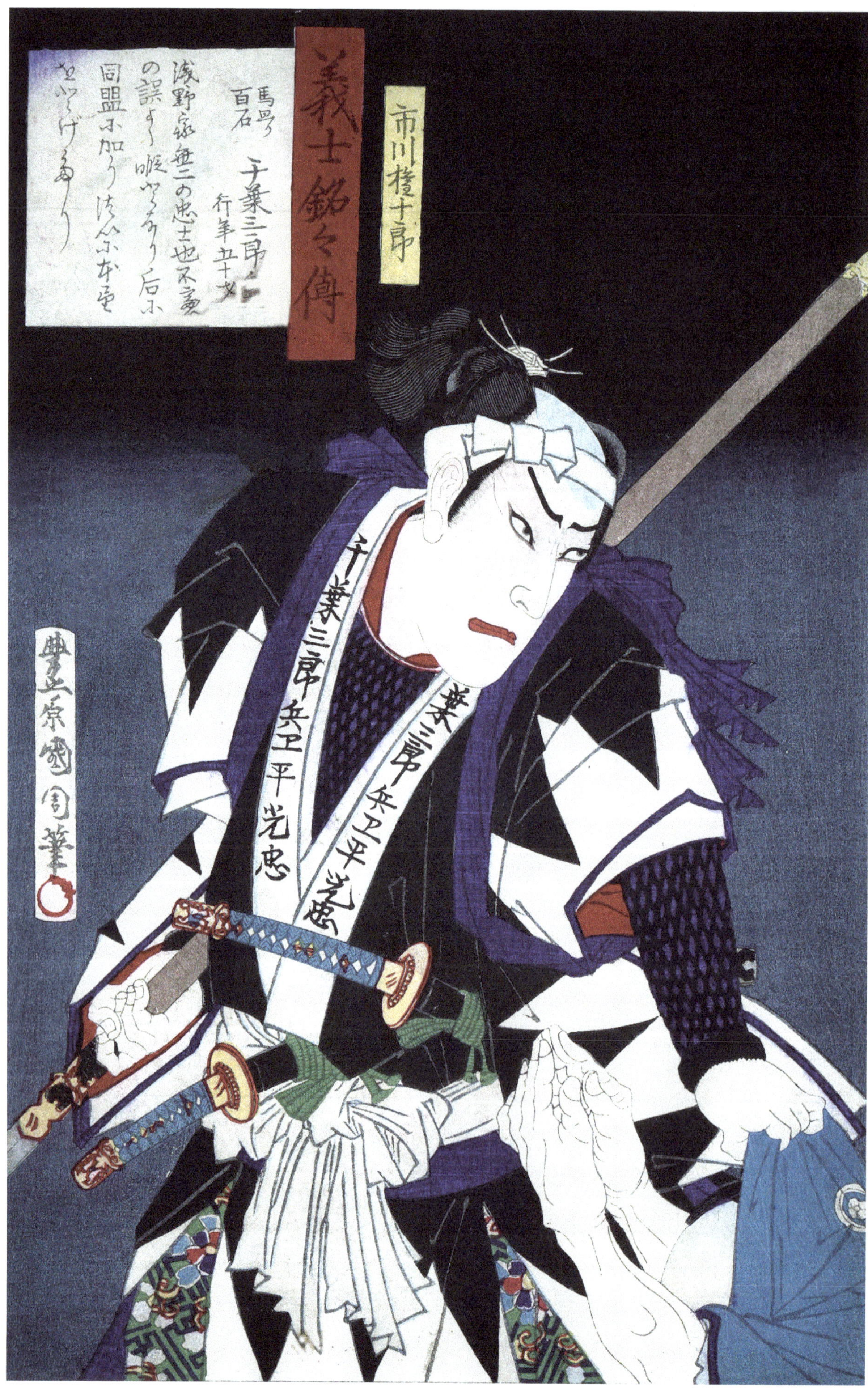

義士銘々傳
市川權十郎
千葉三郎兵工平光忠
千葉三郎兵工平光忠
馬乗
百石
千葉三郎
行年五十文
浅野家無二の忠士也不幸
の誤より喧嘩あり后不
同盟に加らはんぶ本意
とぶつげてあり
豊原國
周筆

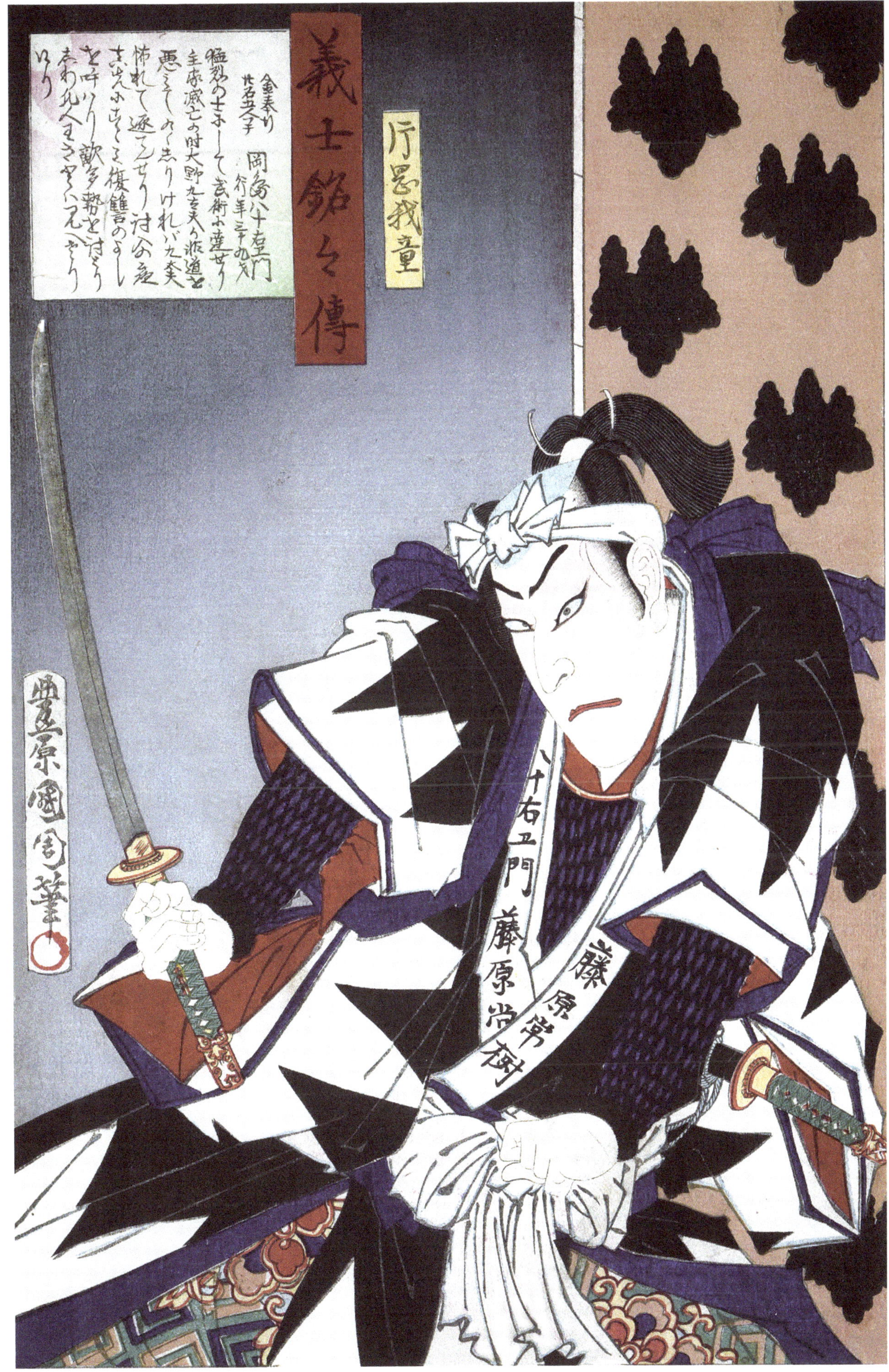

義士銘々傳
行晋我童
八十右ヱ門藤原常樹
藤原常樹
豊原國周筆

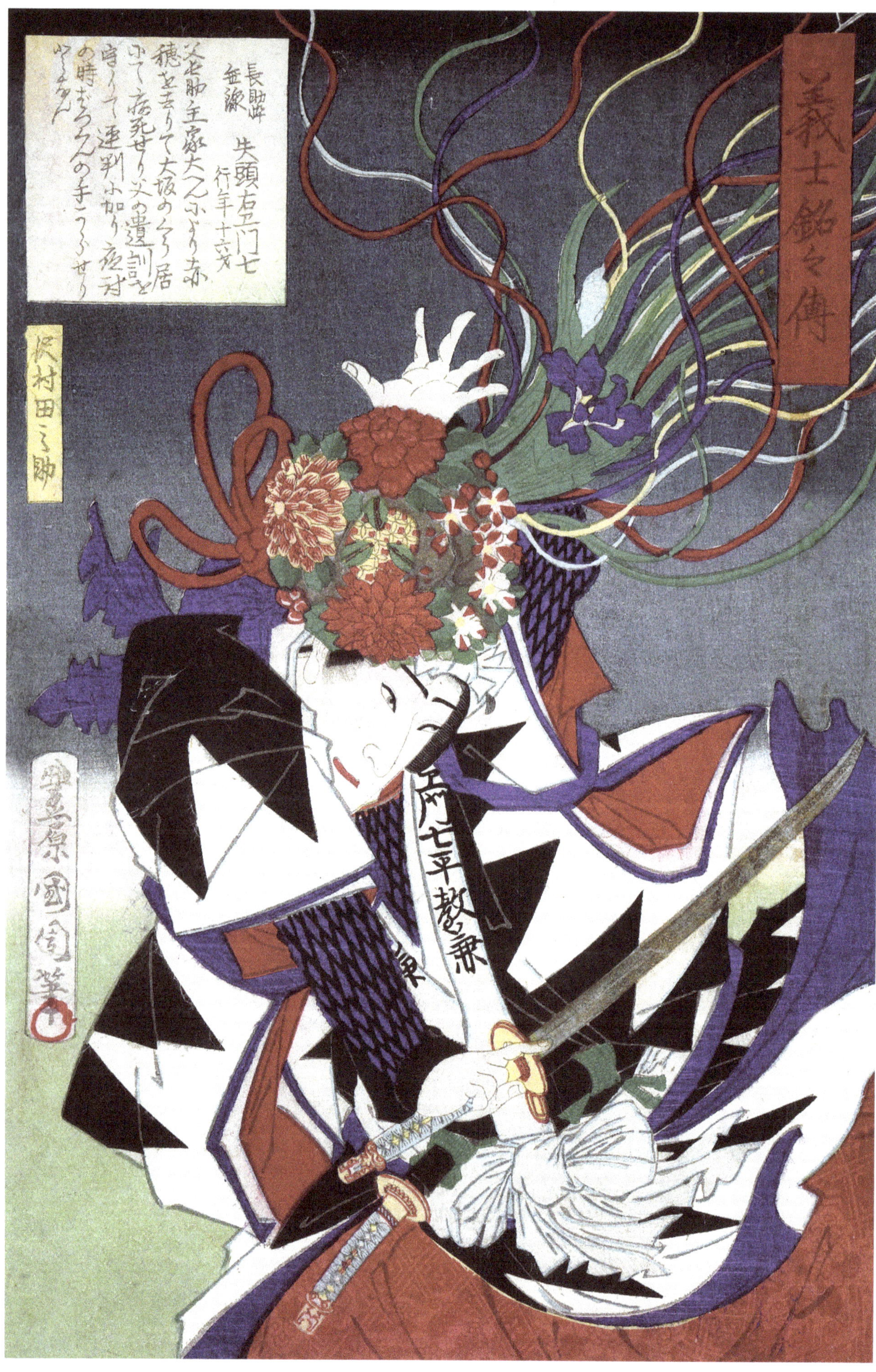

義士銘々傳
長則眸 矢頭右衛門七
並線 失頭右衛門七 行年十六歳
父七胸主家大乙ふより赤
穂を去りて大坂のくら居
ふて病死せり父の遺訓を
守りて運判ふ加り夜対
の時ぎろ九の手こつふせり
かるゝ
坂村田三助
豊原國周筆

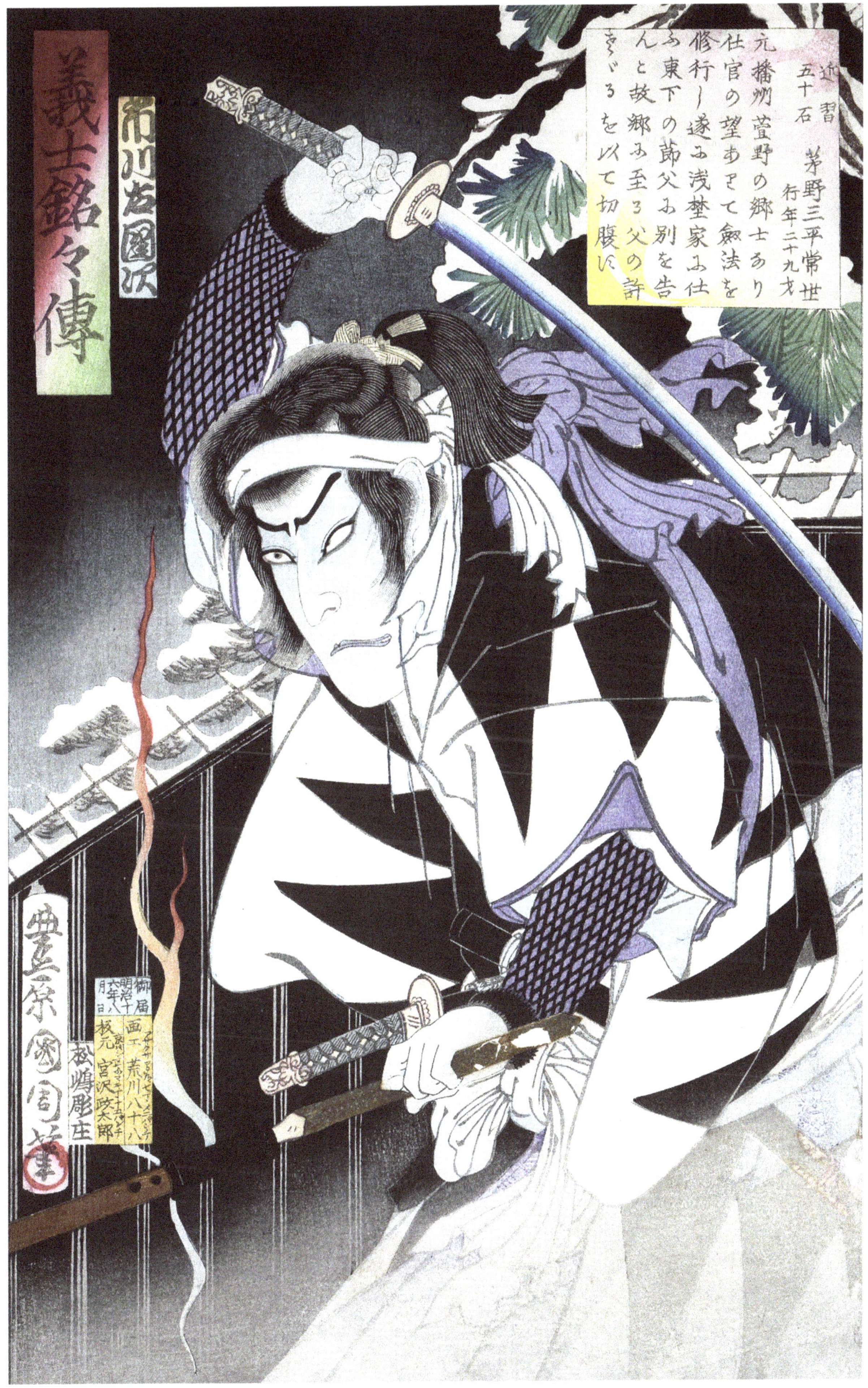

義士銘々傳
市川左團次
近習
五十石　茅野三平常世　行年二十九才
元播州萱野の郷士あり仕官の望あて剱法を修行し遂ふ浅墊家ふ仕ふ東下の節父ふ別を告んと故郷ふ至る父の許きぐるを以て切腹い
豊原國周筆

PICTURE DETAILS

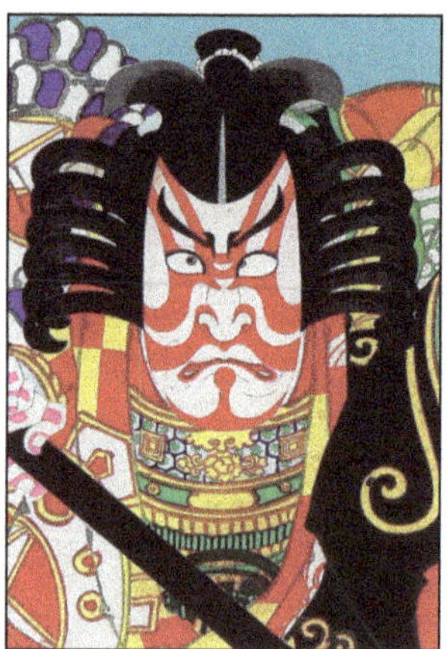

THE ACTOR ICHIKAWA DANJURO IX
AS YANONE, FROM THE SERIES
**ICHIKAWA DANJURO ENGEI
HYAKUBAN** (1893).

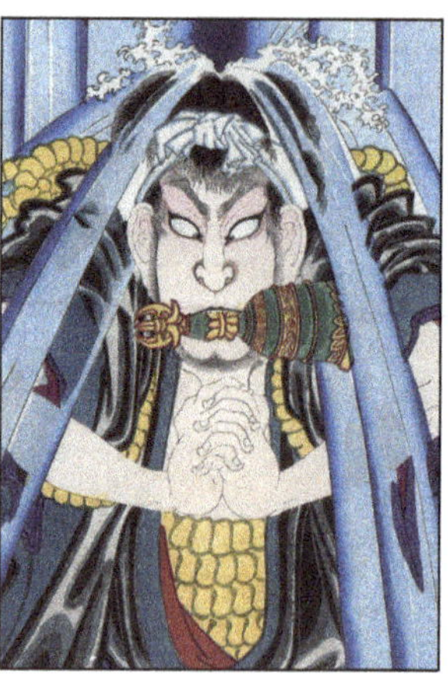

THE ACTOR NAKAMURA SHIKAN IV
AS MONGAKU SHONIN, FROM AN
UNTITLED SERIES (1875).

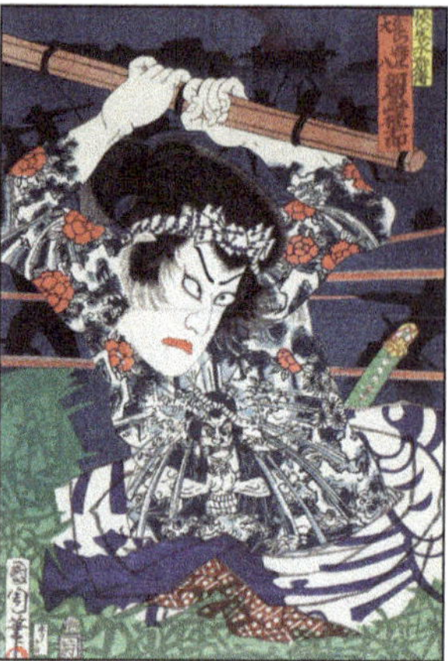

THE ACTOR KAWARAZAKI GONJURO
I AS KAKURA SHISHI, FROM THE
SERIES **SHI-KYAKU SUIKODEN**
(1868).

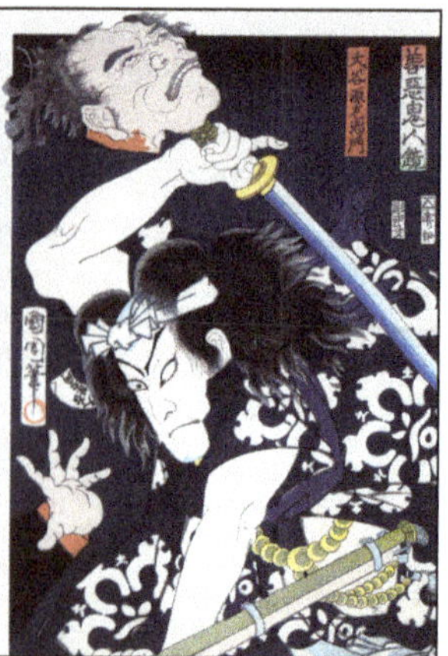

THE ACTOR NAKAMURA SHIKAN IV
AS OTANI GENZAEMON, FROM THE
SERIES **ZEN-AKU KIJIN KAGAMI**
(1868).

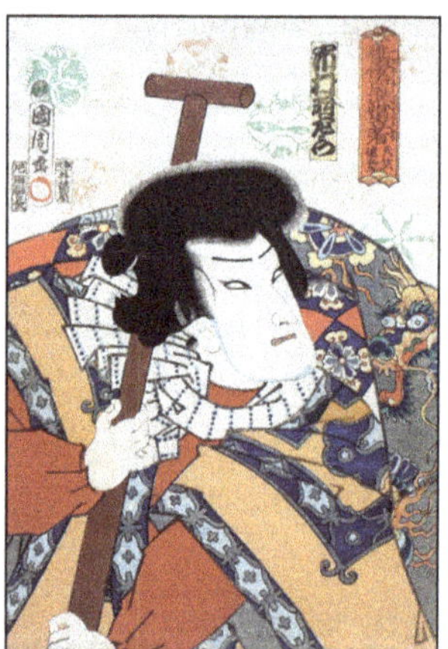

THE ACTOR ICHIMURA UZAEMON AS
TENJIKU TOKUBEI, FROM THE SERIES
**HAIYU SHIRANAMI ATARI
GOKETSU** (1864).

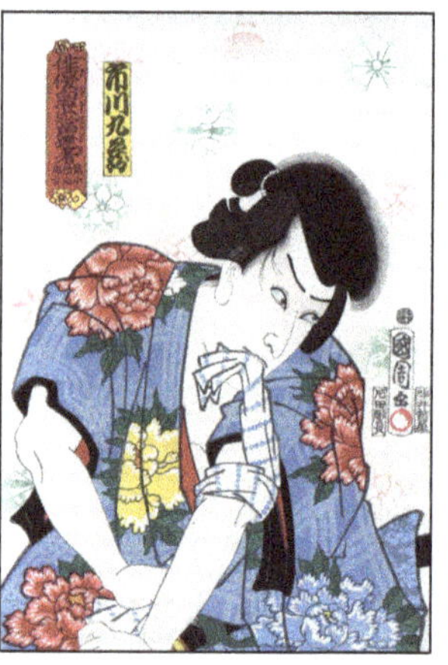

THE ACTOR ICHIKAWA KUZO AS
NEZUMI KOZO JIROKICHI, FROM THE
SERIES **HAIYU SHIRANAMI ATARI
GOKETSU** (1864).

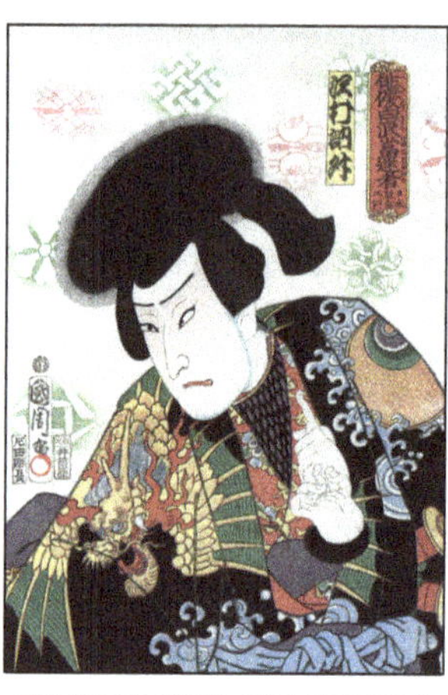

THE ACTOR SAWAMURA TOSSHO II
AS NIHONDAEMON, FROM THE
SERIES **HAIYU SHIRANAMI ATARI
GOKETSU** (1864).

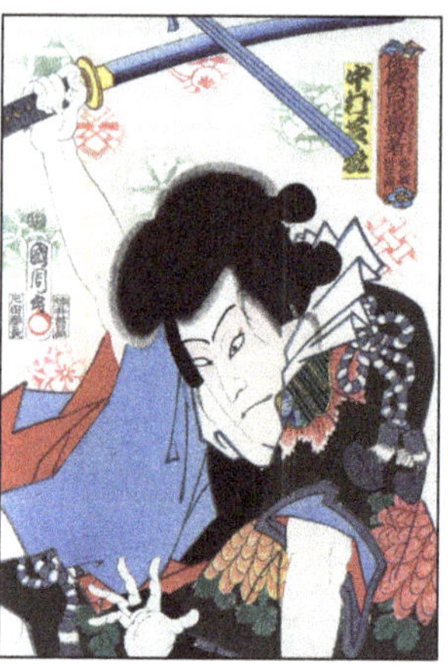

THE ACTOR NAKAMURA SHIKAN IV
AS SHIKEN TANZAEMON, FROM THE
SERIES **HAIYU SHIRANAMI ATARI
GOKETSU** (1864).

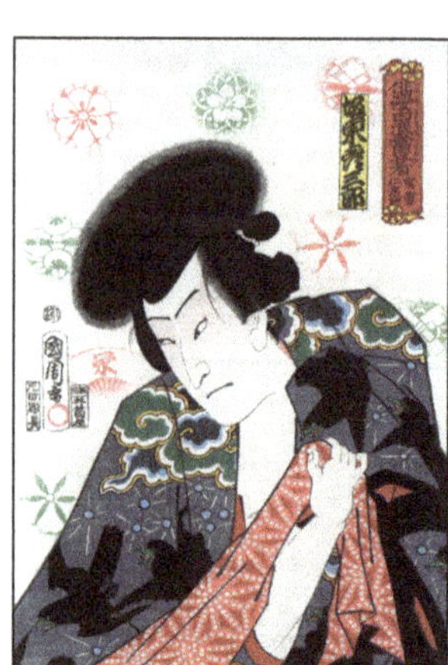

THE ACTOR BANDO HIKOSABURO V
AS KUMOKIRI NIZAEMON, FROM
THE SERIES **HAIYU SHIRANAMI
ATARI GOKETSU** (1864).

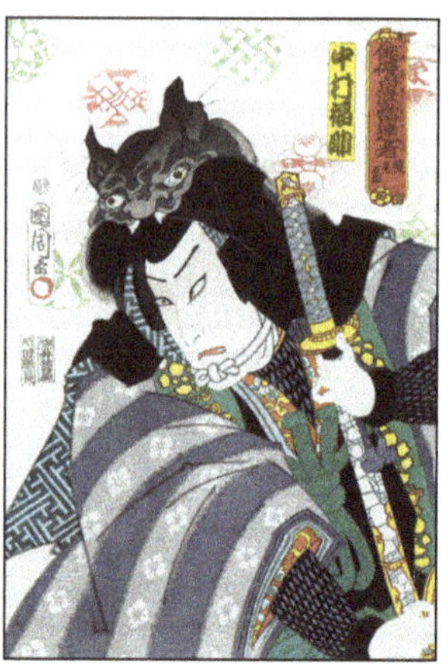

THE ACTOR NAKAMURA FUKUSUKE
II AS AKATSUKI HOSHIGORO, FROM
THE SERIES **HAIYU SHIRANAMI
ATARI GOKETSU** (1864).

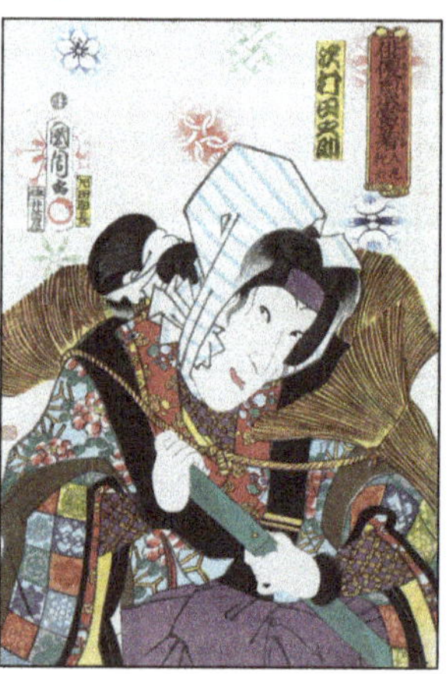

THE ACTOR SAWAMURA TANOSUKE
III AS HITOMARU OROKU, FROM THE
SERIES **HAIYU SHIRANAMI ATARI
GOKETSU** (1864).

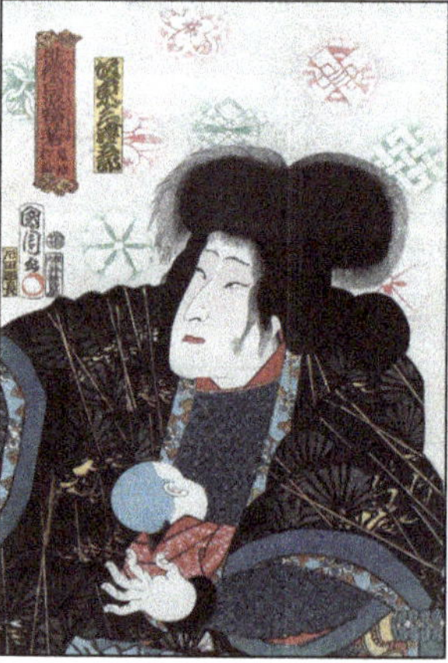

THE ACTOR BANDO MITSUGORO VI
AS KIJIN OMATSU, FROM THE SERIES
**HAIYU SHIRANAMI ATARI
GOKETSU** (1864).

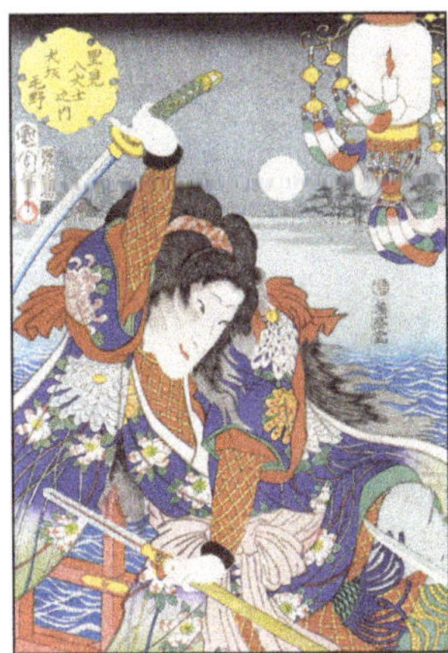

THE ACTOR SAWAMURA TANOSUKE III AS INUZAKA KENO, FROM THE SERIES **SATOMI HAKKENSHI NO UCHI** (1865-66).

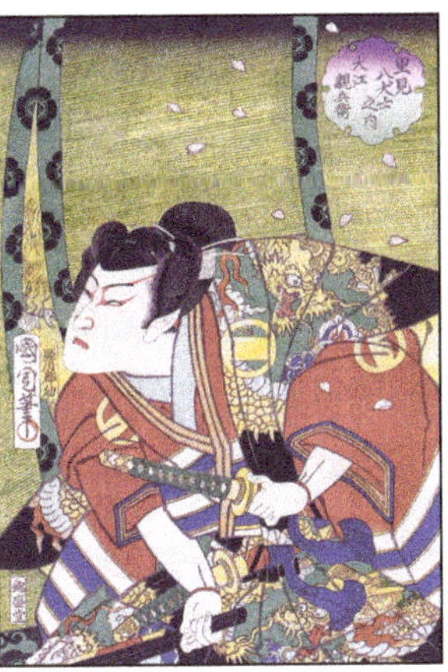

THE ACTOR NAKAMURA FUKUSUKE II AS INUE SHINBEI, FROM THE SERIES **SATOMI HAKKENSHI NO UCHI** (1865-66).

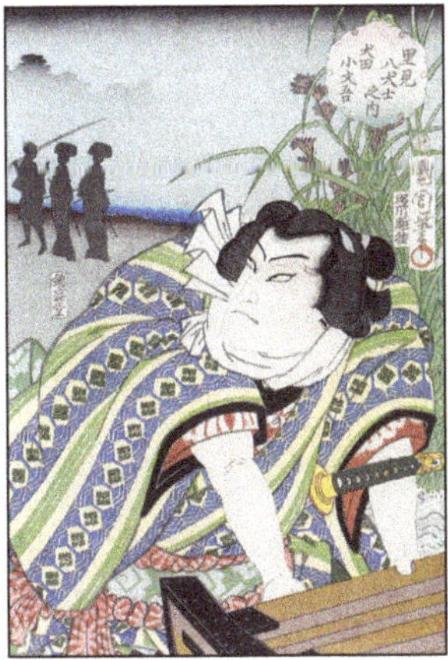

THE ACTOR NAKAMURA SHIKAN IV AS INUDA KOBUNGO, FROM THE SERIES **SATOMI HAKKENSHI NO UCHI** (1865-66).

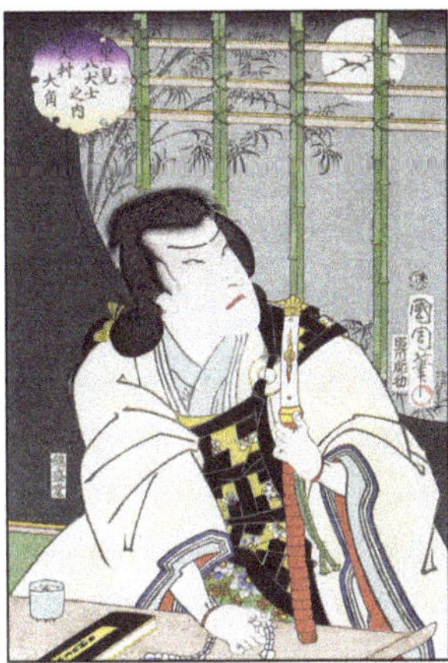

THE ACTOR SAWAMURA TOSSHO II AS INUMURA DAIKAKU, FROM THE SERIES **SATOMI HAKKENSHI NO UCHI** (1865-66).

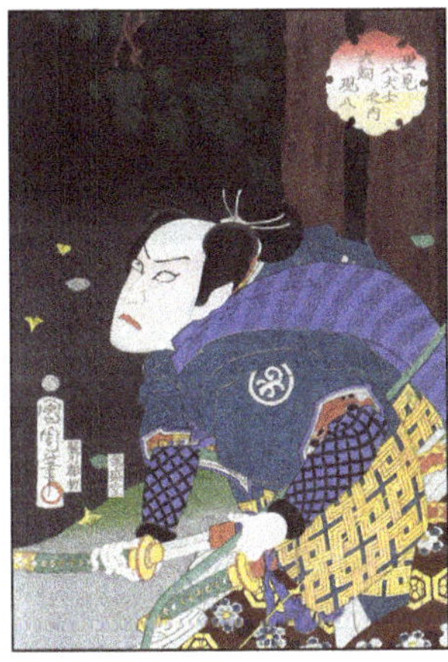

THE ACTOR KAWARAZAKI GONJURO I AS INUKAI GENPACHI, FROM THE SERIES **SATOMI HAKKENSHI NO UCHI** (1865-66).

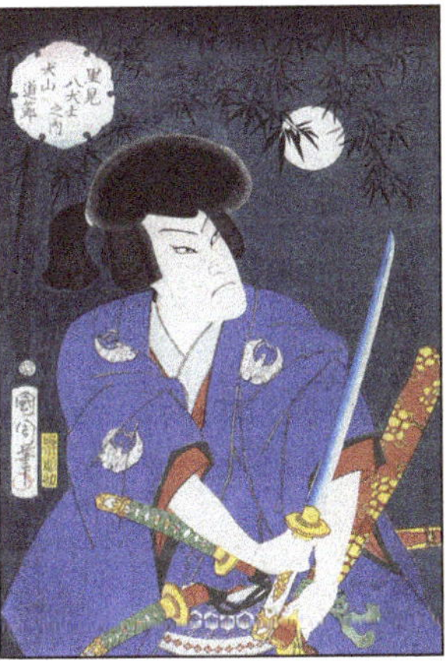

THE ACTOR BANDO HIKOSABURO V AS INUYAMA DOSETSU, FROM THE SERIES **SATOMI HAKKENSHI NO UCHI** (1865-66).

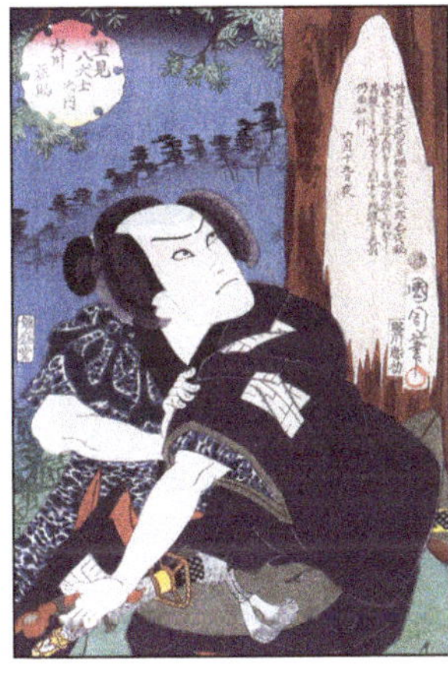

THE ACTOR ICHIKAWA KUZO III AS INUKAWA SOSUKE, FROM THE SERIES **SATOMI HAKKENSHI NO UCHI** (1865-66).

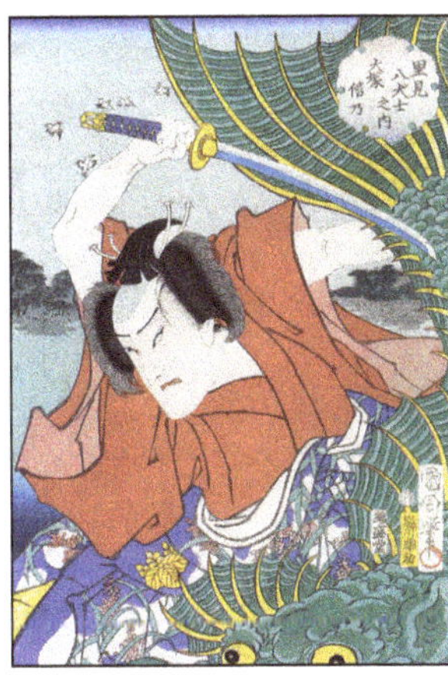

THE ACTOR ICHIMURA KAKITSU IV AS INUZUKA SHINO, FROM THE SERIES **SATOMI HAKKENSHI NO UCHI** (1865-66).

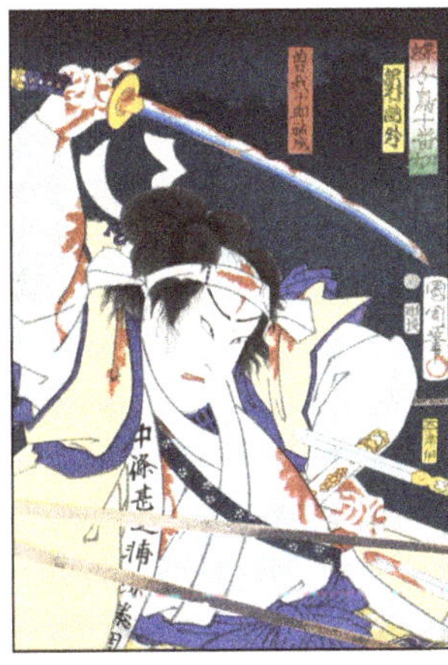

THE ACTOR SAWAMURA TOSSHO II AS SOGA JURO SUKENARI, FROM THE SERIES **CHOCHIDORI JUBAN KIRI** (1868).

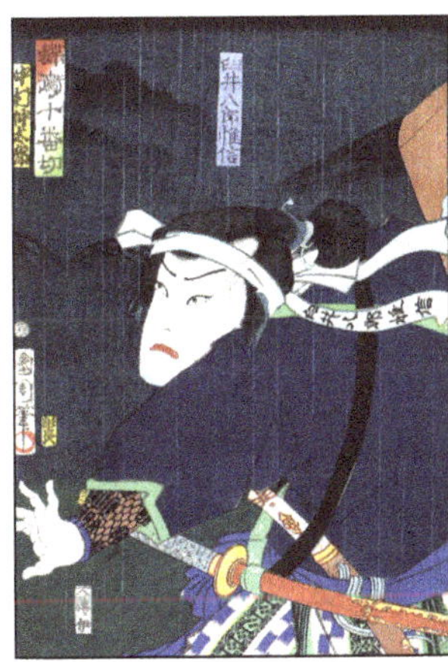

THE ACTOR NAKAMURA NAKATARO AS USUI HACHIRO TADANOBU, FROM THE SERIES **CHOCHIDORI JUBAN KIRI** (1868).

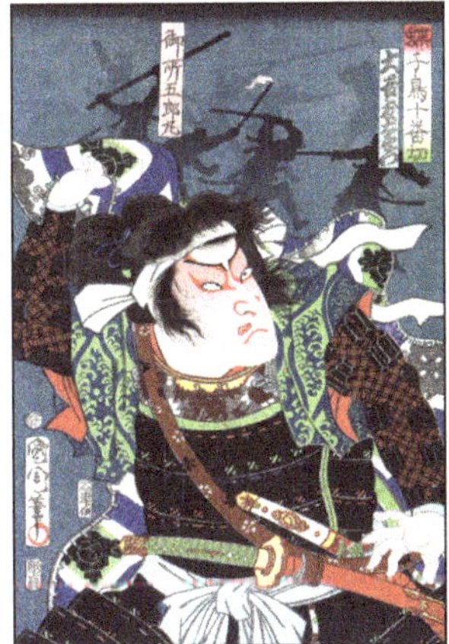

THE ACTOR OTANI TOMOEMON V AS GOSHO GOROMARU, FROM THE SERIES **CHOCHIDORI JUBAN KIRI** (1868).

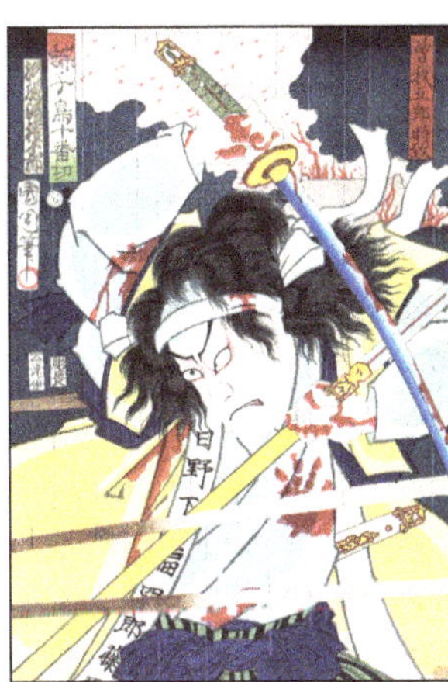

THE ACTOR KAWARAZAKI GONJURO I AS SOGA GORO TOKIMUNE, FROM THE SERIES **CHOCHIDORI JUBAN KIRI** (1868).

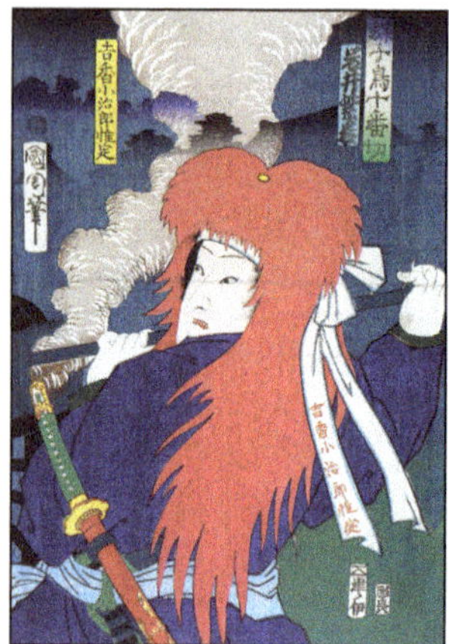

THE ACTOR IWAI SHIJAKU II AS YOSHIKO KOJIRO TADASHIGE, FROM THE SERIES **CHOCHIDORI JUBAN KIRI** (1868).

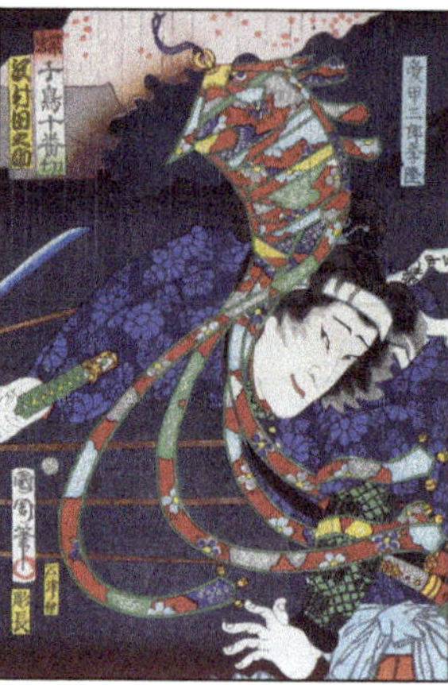

THE ACTOR SAWAMURA TANOSUKE III AS AIKOSABURO SUETAKA, FROM THE SERIES **CHOCHIDORI JUBAN KIRI** (1868).

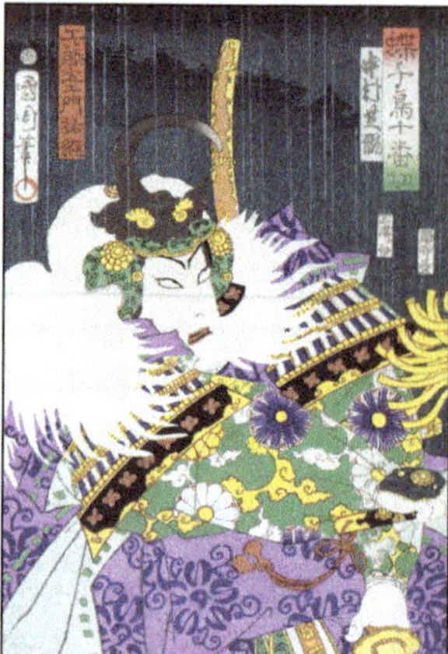

THE ACTOR NAKAMURA SHIKAN IV AS KUDOZAEMON SUKETSUNE, FROM THE SERIES **CHOCHIDORI JUBAN KIRI** (1868).

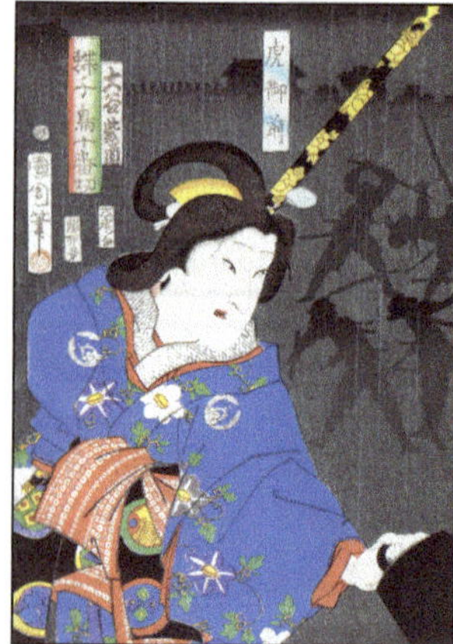

THE ACTOR OTANI MURASAKI AS TORA GOZEN, FROM THE SERIES **CHOCHIDORI JUBAN KIRI** (1868).

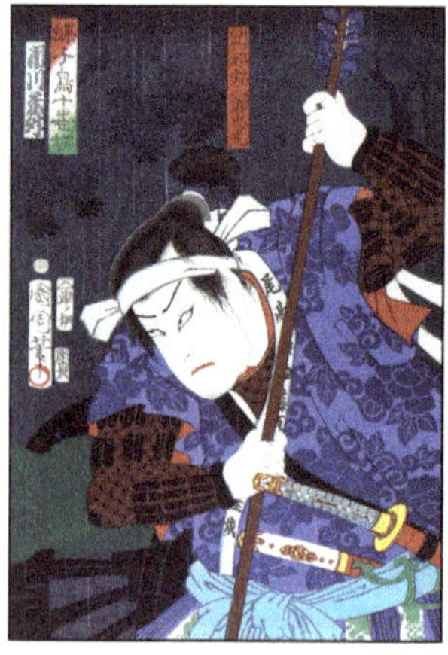

THE ACTOR ICHIKAWA YONEMASU AS OKABE YASABURO TADAMITSU, FROM THE SERIES **CHOCHIDORI JUBAN KIRI** (1868).

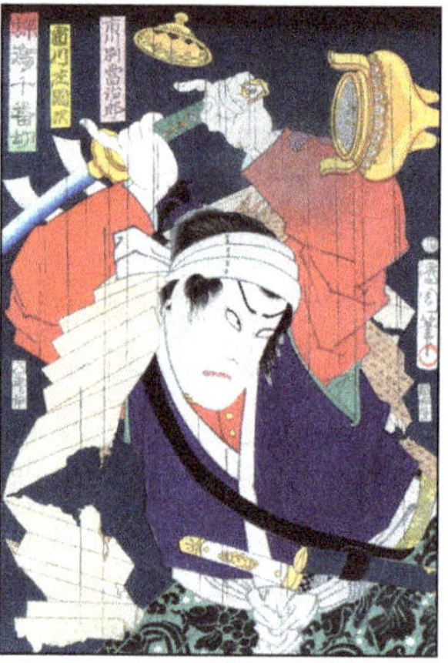

THE ACTOR ICHIKAWA SADANJI I AS ICHIKAWA BETTO JIRO, FROM THE SERIES **CHOCHIDORI JUBAN KIRI** (1868).

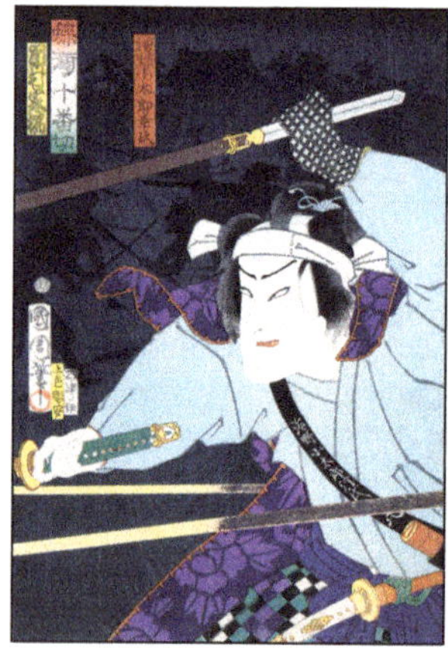

THE ACTOR ICHIMURA KAKITSU IV AS UMINO KOTARO TSUKIUJI, FROM THE SERIES **CHOCHIDORI JUBAN KIRI** (1868).

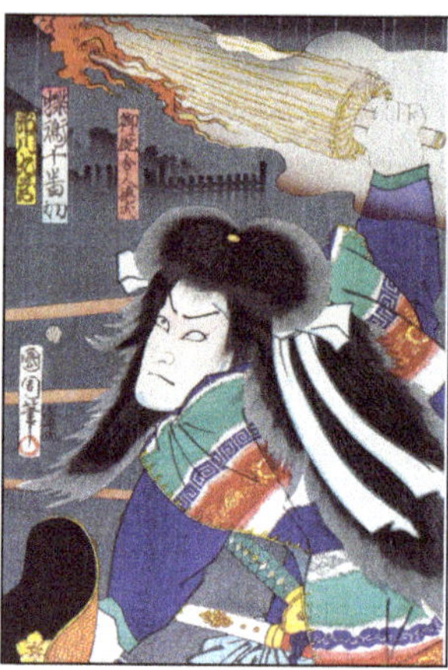

THE ACTOR ICHIKAWA KUZO III AS TOKUTAKE, FROM THE SERIES **CHOCHIDORI JUBAN KIRI** (1868).

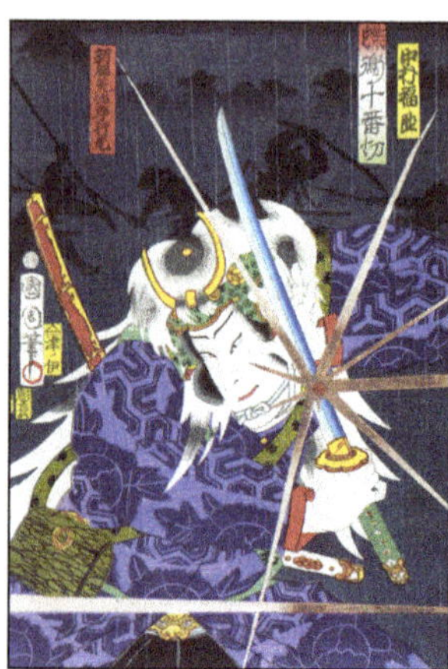

THE ACTOR NAKAMURA FUKUSUKE III AS SHINKAI KOJIRO YUKIMITSU, FROM THE SERIES **CHOCHIDORI JUBAN KIRI** (1868).

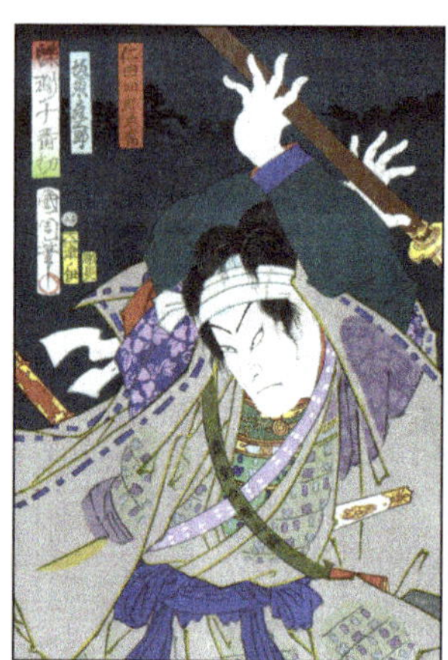

THE ACTOR BANDO HIKOSABURO V AS NITTO SHIRA TADATSUNE, FROM THE SERIES **CHOCHIDORI JUBAN KIRI** (1868).

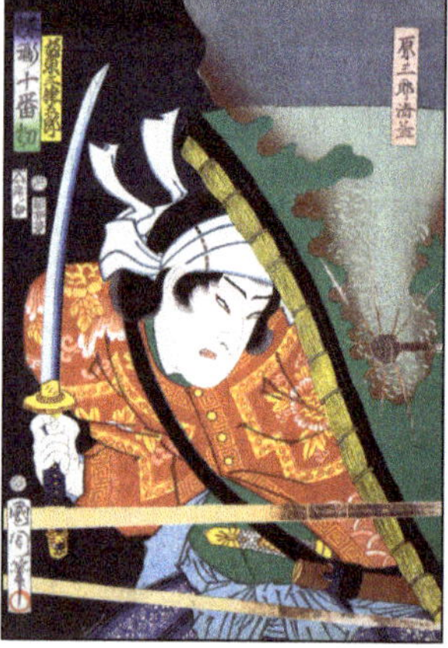

THE ACTOR BANDO MITSUGORO VI AS KIYOMASU HARASABURO, FROM THE SERIES **CHOCHIDORI JUBAN KIRI** (1868).

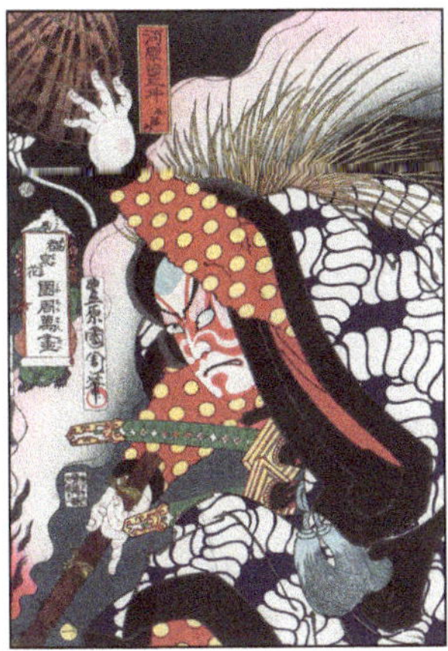

THE ACTOR KAWARAZAKI GONJURO I AS WATONAI, FROM THE SERIES **TOKYO HANA KUNICHIKA MANGA** (1872).

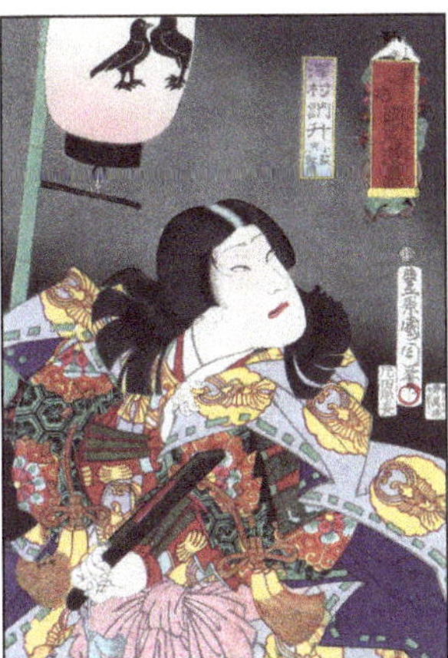

THE ACTOR SAWAMURA TOSSHO II AS KOHAGI (ACTUALLY ATSUMORI), FROM THE SERIES **TOKYO HANA KUNICHIKA MANGA** (1872).

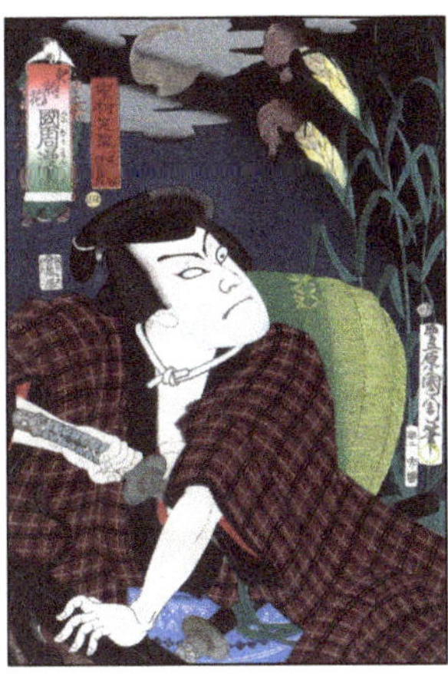

THE ACTOR AKAMURA SHIKAN IV AS TAMIYA IEMON, FROM THE SERIES **TOKYO HANA KUNICHIKA MANGA** (1872).

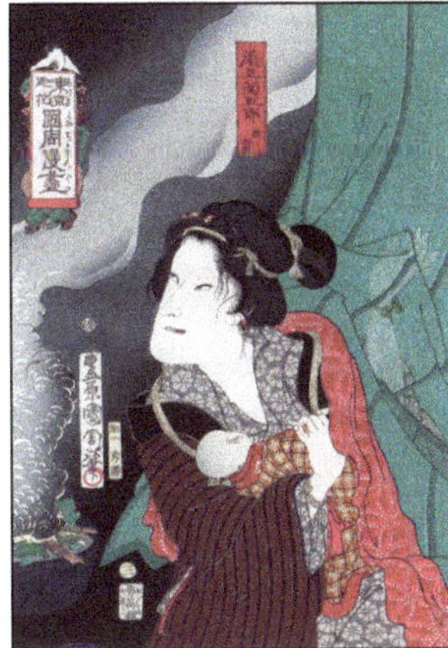

THE ACTOR ONOE KIKUGORO V AS OIWA, FROM THE SERIES **TOKYO HANA KUNICHIKA MANGA** (1872).

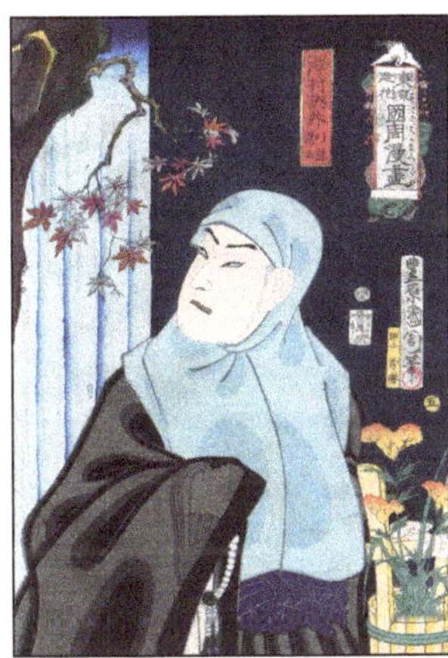

THE ACTOR SAWAMURA TOSSHO II AS KARUKAYA DOSHIN, FROM THE SERIES **TOKYO HANA KUNICHIKA MANGA** (1872).

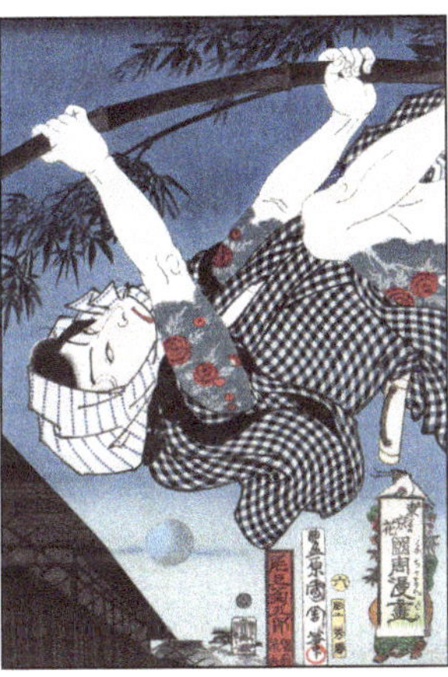

THE ACTOR ONOE KIKUGORO V AS ONIAZAMI SEKICHI, FROM THE SERIES **TOKYO HANA KUNICHIKA MANGA** (1872).

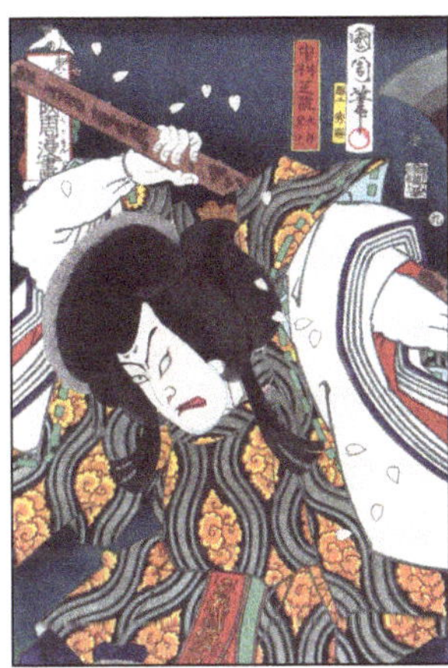

THE ACTOR NAKAMURA SHIKAN IV AS OTOMO KURONUSHI, FROM THE SERIES **TOKYO HANA KUNICHIKA MANGA** (1872).

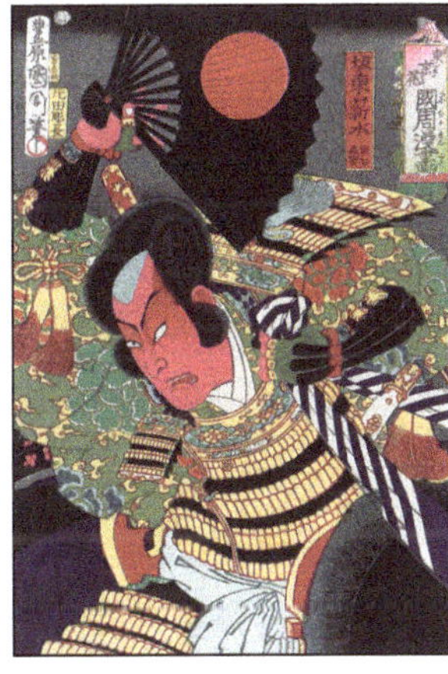

THE ACTOR BANDO HIKOSABURO V AS KUMAGAI NAOZANE, FROM THE SERIES **TOKYO HANA KUNICHIKA MANGA** (1872).

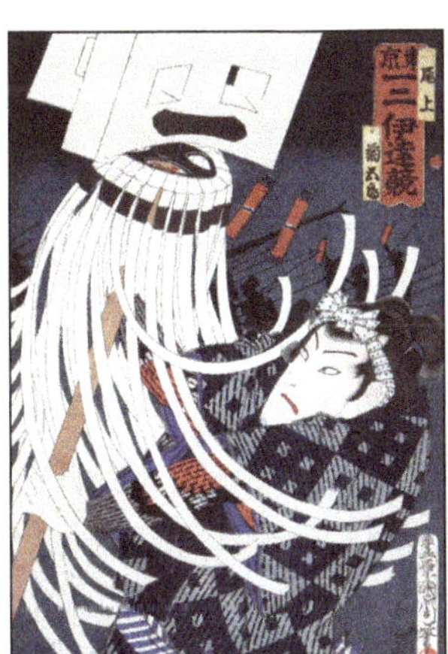

THE ACTOR ONOE KIKUGORO V AS A TOKYO FIREFIGHTER, FROM THE SERIES **TOKYO ICHINI DATE KURABE** (1874).

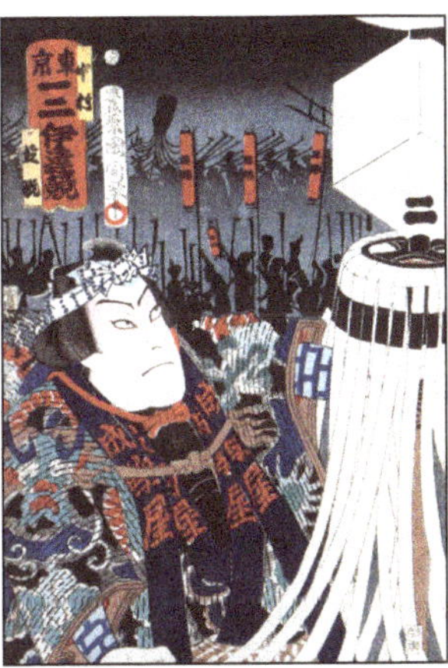

THE ACTOR NAKAMURA SHIKAN IV AS A TOKYO FIREFIGHTER, FROM THE SERIES **TOKYO ICHINI DATE KURABE** (1874).

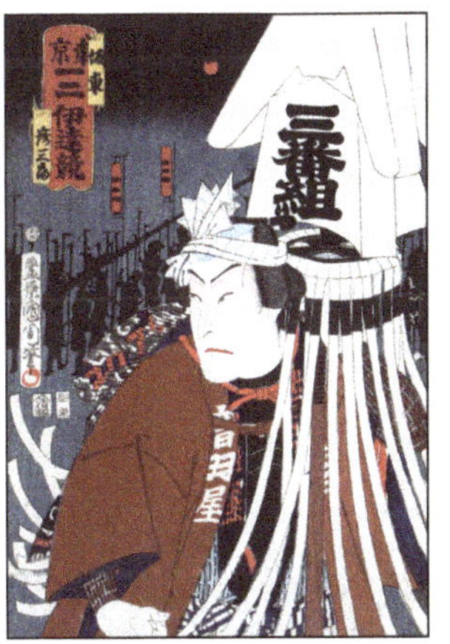

THE ACTOR BANDO HIKASABURO V AS A TOKYO FIREFIGHTER, FROM THE SERIES **TOKYO ICHINI DATE KURABE** (1874).

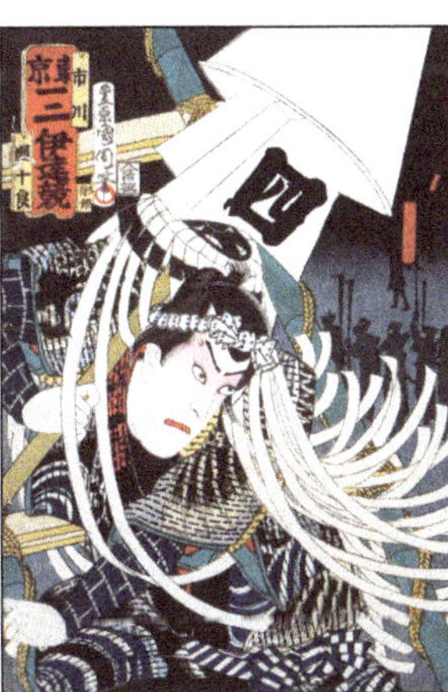

THE ACTOR ICHIKAWA DANJURO IX AS A TOKYO FIREFIGHTER, FROM THE SERIES **TOKYO ICHINI DATE KURABE** (1874).

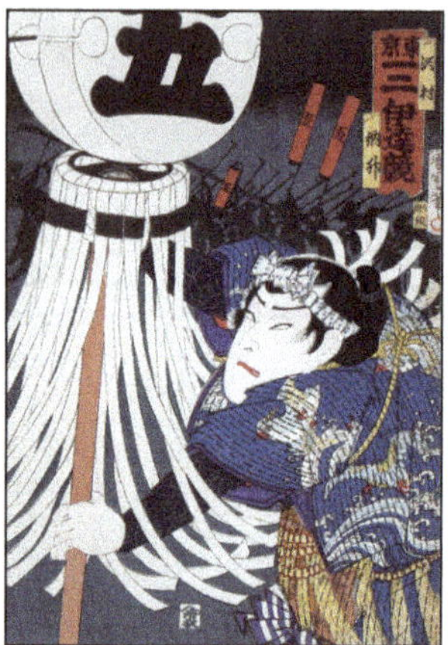

THE ACTOR SAWAMURA TOSSHO II AS A TOKYO FIREFIGHTER, FROM THE SERIES **TOKYO ICHINI DATE KURABE** (1874).

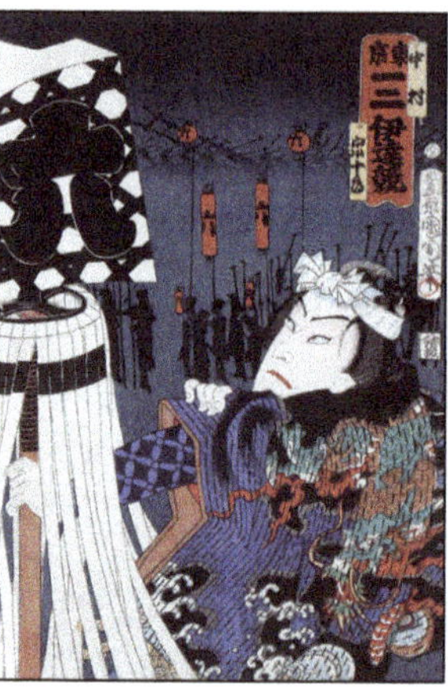

THE ACTOR NAKAMURA SOJURO AS A TOKYO FIREFIGHTER, FROM THE SERIES **TOKYO ICHINI DATE KURABE** (1874).

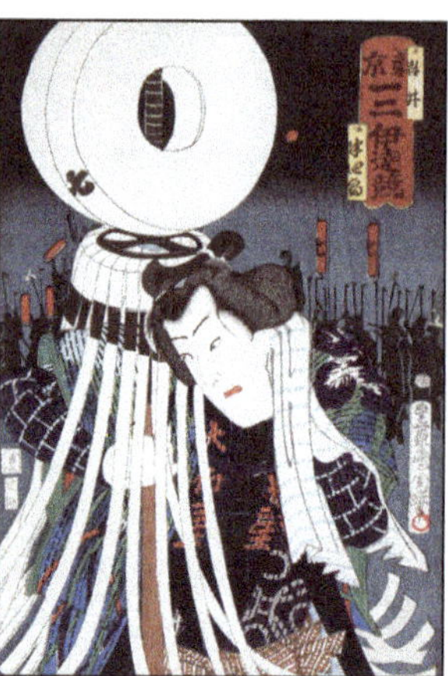

THE ACTOR IWAI HANSHIRO AS A TOKYO FIREFIGHTER, FROM THE SERIES **TOKYO ICHINI DATE KURABE** (1874).

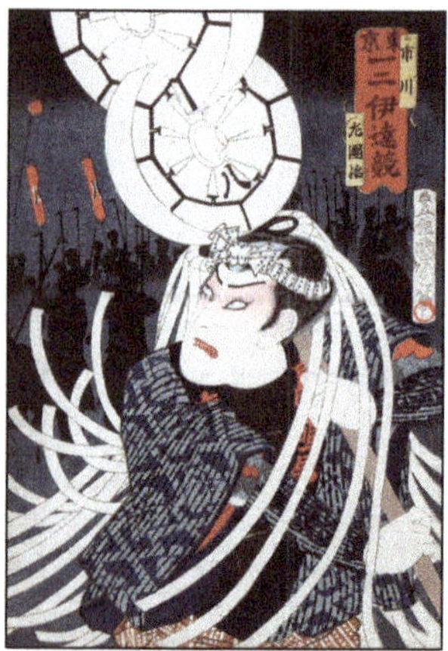

THE ACTOR ICHIKAWA SADANJI I AS A TOKYO FIREFIGHTER, FROM THE SERIES **TOKYO ICHINI DATE KURABE** (1874).

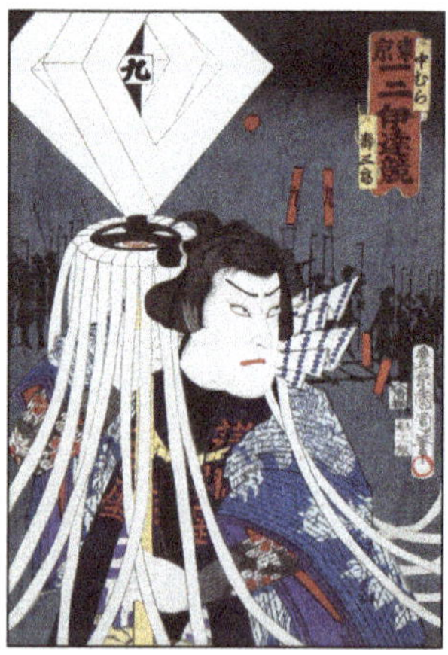

THE ACTOR NAKAMURA JUSABURO AS A TOKYO FIREFIGHTER, FROM THE SERIES **TOKYO ICHINI DATE KURABE** (1874).

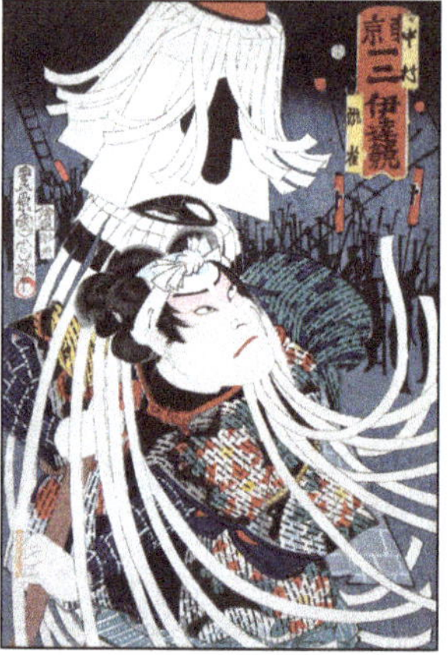

THE ACTOR NAKAMURA SHIJAKU AS A TOKYO FIREFIGHTER, FROM THE SERIES **TOKYO ICHINI DATE KURABE** (1874).

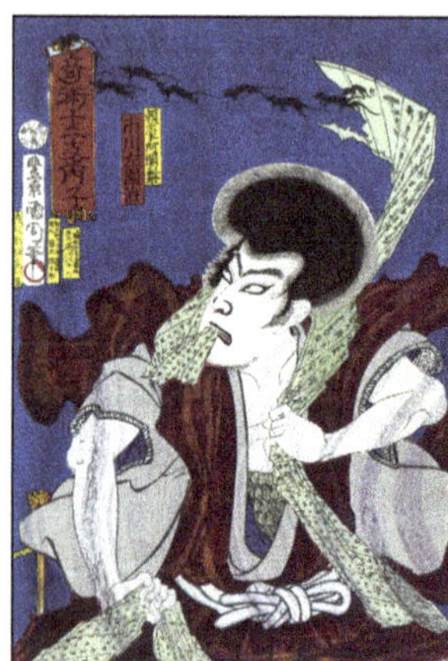

RAT – THE ACTOR ICHIKAWA SADANI I AS RAIGO AJARI, FROM THE SERIES **KIJUTSU JUNISHI NO UCHI** (1877).

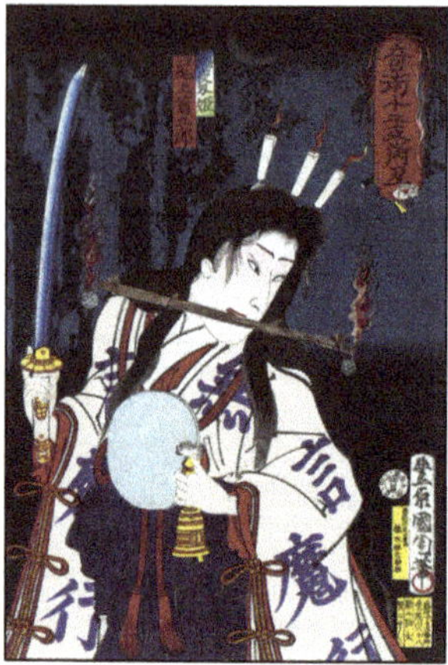

OX – THE ACTOR ONOE KIKUGORO V AS TAKIYASHA-HIME, FROM THE SERIES **KIJUTSU JUNISHI NO UCHI** (1877).

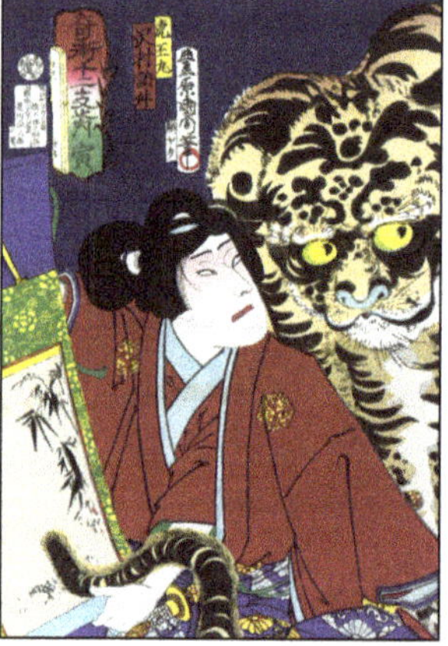

TIGER – THE ACTOR SAWAMURA TOSSHO II AS TORAOMARU, FROM THE SERIES **KIJUTSU JUNISHI NO UCHI** (1877).

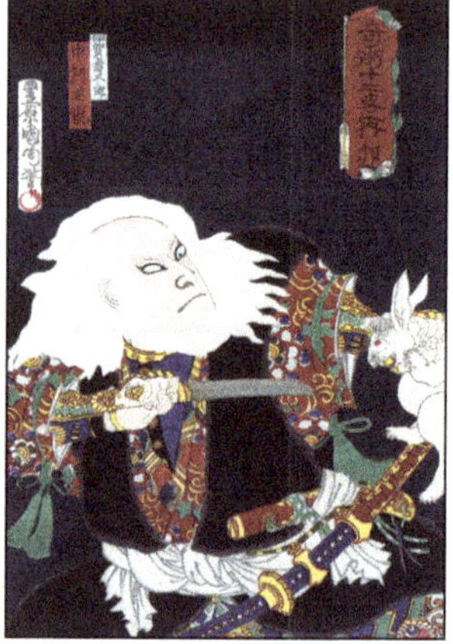

HARE – THE ACTOR NAKAMURA SHIKAN IV AS JUTARO IGA, FROM THE SERIES **KIJUTSU JUNISHI NO UCHI** (1877).

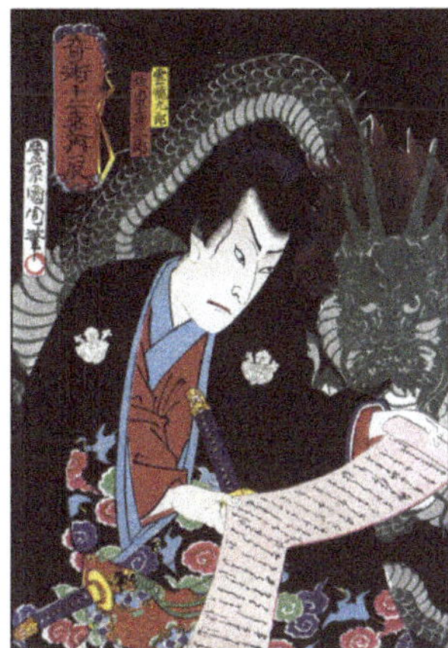

DRAGON – THE ACTOR BANDO HIKOSABURO V AS KURO UNRYU, FROM THE SERIES **KIJUTSU JUNISHI NO UCHI** (1877).

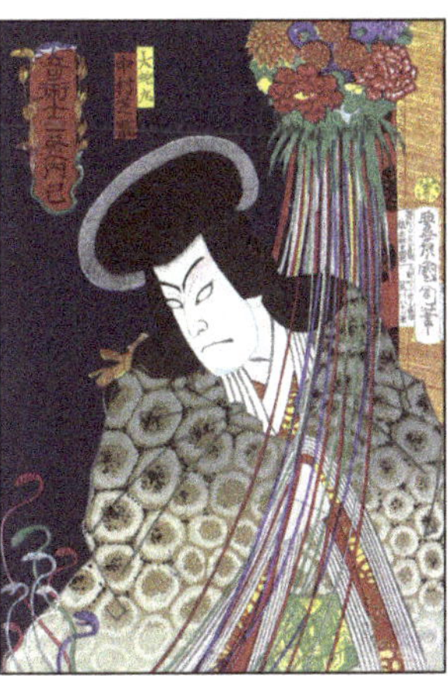

SNAKE – THE ACTOR NAKAMURA SHIKAN IV AS OCHIMARU, FROM THE SERIES **KIJUTSU JUNISHI NO UCHI** (1877).

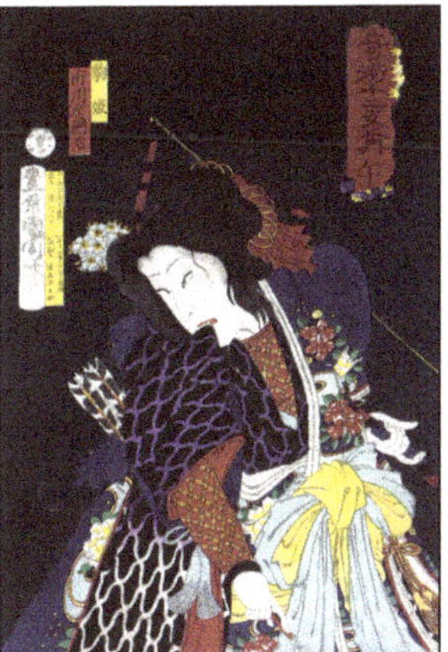

HORSE – THE ACTOR ICHIKAWA SADANJI I AS KOMA-HIME, FROM THE SERIES **KIJUTSU JUNISHI NO UCHI** (1877).

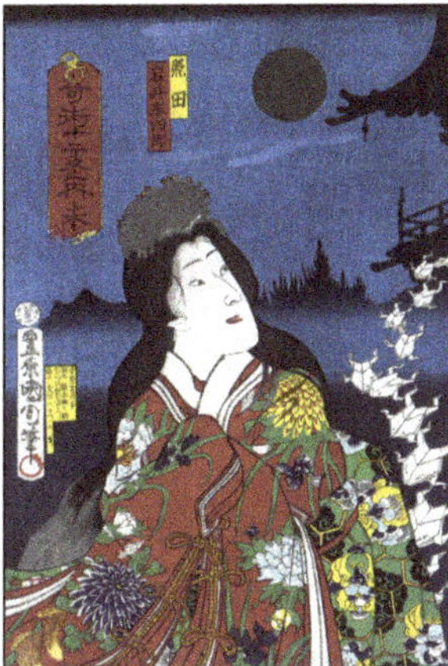

RAM – THE ACTOR IWAI HANSHIRO AS TERUDA, FROM THE SERIES **KIJUTSU JUNISHI NO UCHI** (1877).

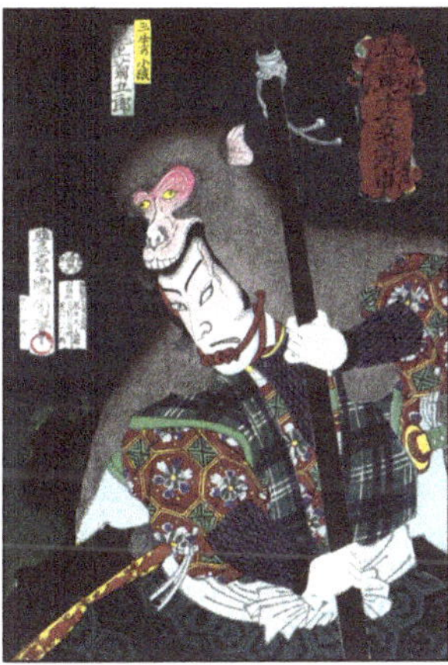

MONKEY – THE ACTOR ONOE KIKUGORO V AS SANSHO NO KOSARU, FROM THE SERIES **KIJUTSU JUNISHI NO UCHI** (1877).

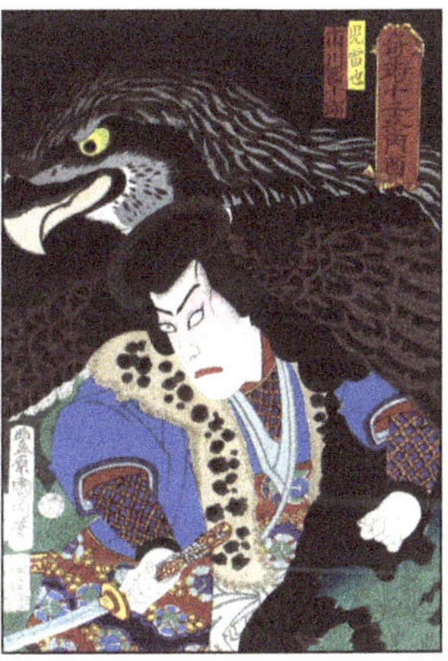

BIRD – THE ACTOR ICHIKAWA DANJURO IX AS JIRAIYA, FROM THE SERIES **KIJUTSU JUNISHI NO UCHI** (1877).

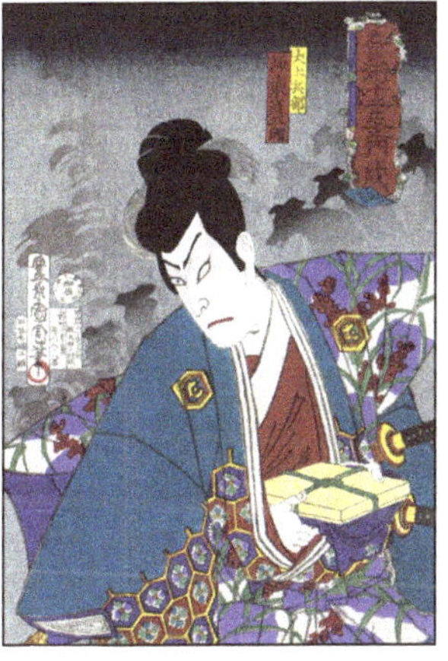

DOG – THE ACTOR BANDO HIKOSABURO V AS INUKAMI HYOBU, FROM THE SERIES **KIJUTSU JUNISHI NO UCHI** (1877).

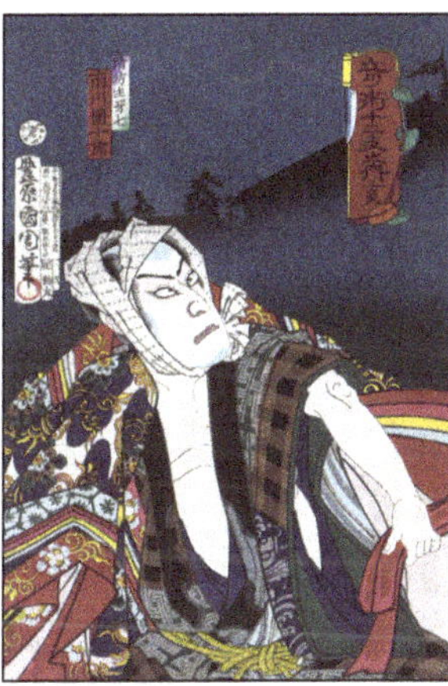

BOAR – THE ACTOR ICHIKAWA DANJURO IX AS IBOZO KIBAHACHI, FROM THE SERIES **KIJUTSU JUNISHI NO UCHI** (1877).

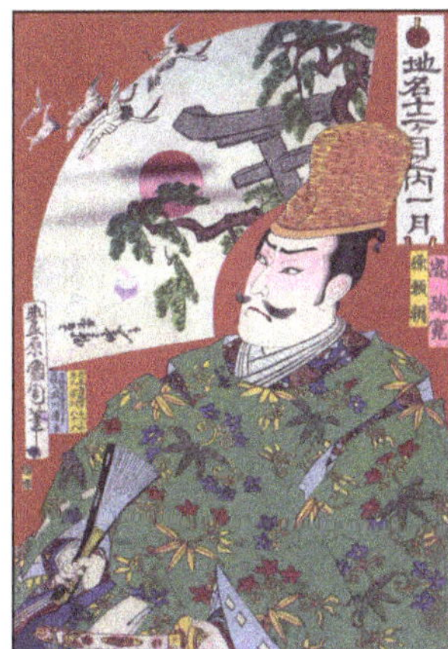

THE ACTOR ARASHI RIKAN IV AS MINAMOTO YORITOMO, FROM THE SERIES **CHIMEI JUNIKAGETSU NO UCHI** (1882).

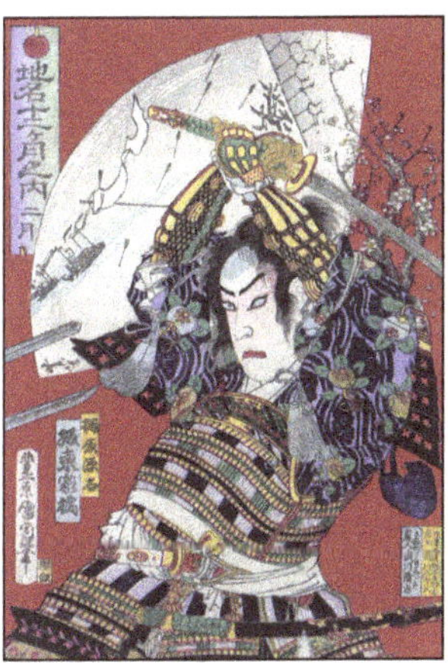

THE ACTOR BANDO KAKITSU AS KAJIWARA GENTA, FROM THE SERIES **CHIMEI JUNIKAGETSU NO UCHI** (1882).

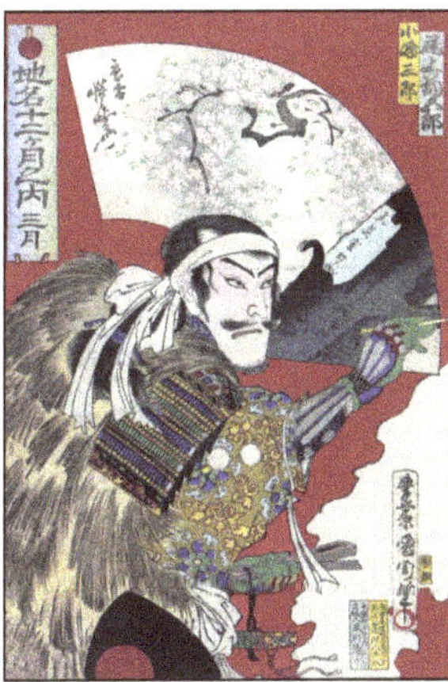

THE ACTOR ONOE KIKUGORO V AS KOJIMA SABURO, FROM THE SERIES **CHIMEI JUNIKAGETSU NO UCHI** (1882).

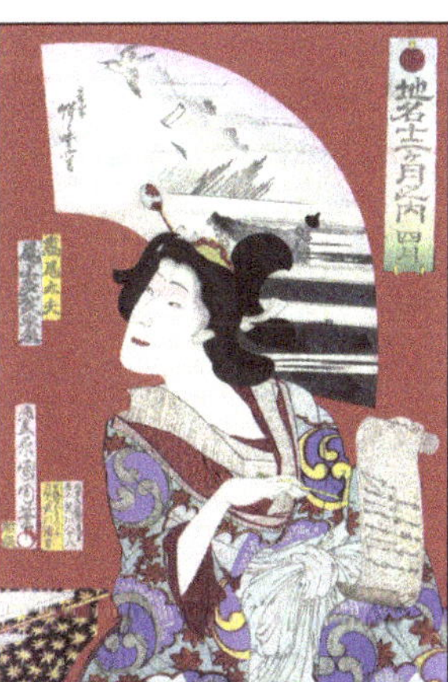

THE ACTOR ONOE TAGANOJO AS TAKAO-DAIYU, FROM THE SERIES **CHIMEI JUNIKAGETSU NO UCHI** (1882).

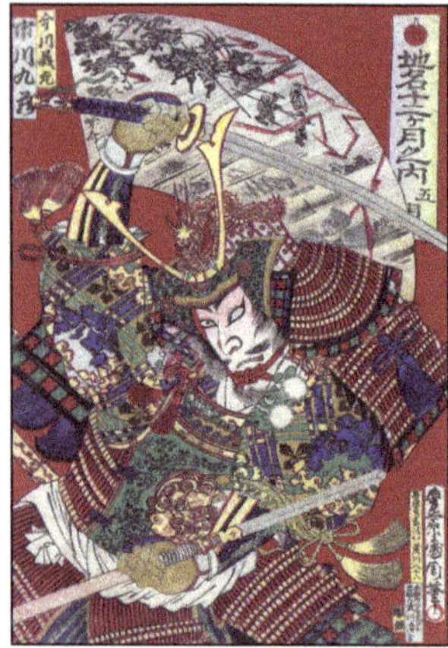

THE ACTOR ICHIKWA KUZO III AS IMAGAWA YOSHIMOTO, FROM THE SERIES **CHIMEI JUNIKAGETSU NO UCHI** (1882).

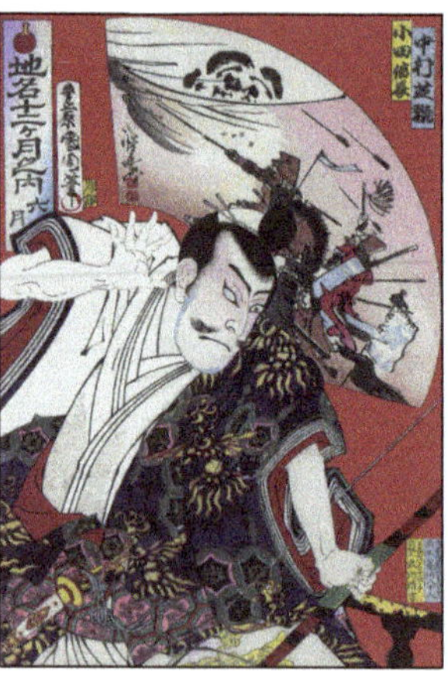

THE ACTOR NAKAMURA SHIKAN IV AS ODA NOBUNAGA, FROM THE SERIES **CHIMEI JUNIKAGETSU NO UCHI** (1882).

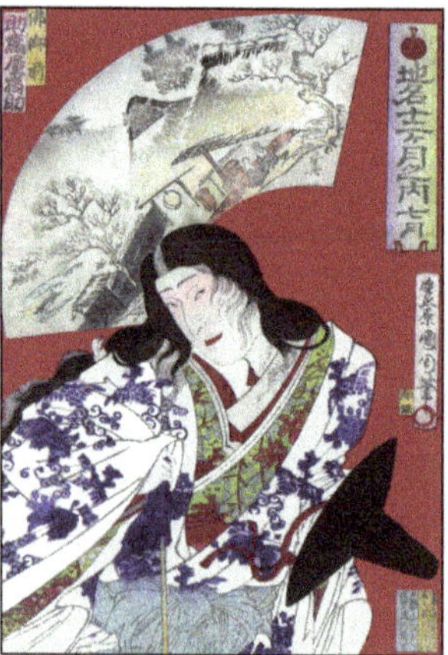

THE ACTOR SAWAMURA TOSSHI II AS HOTOKE GOZEN, FROM THE SERIES **CHIMEI JUNIKAGETSU NO UCHI** (1882).

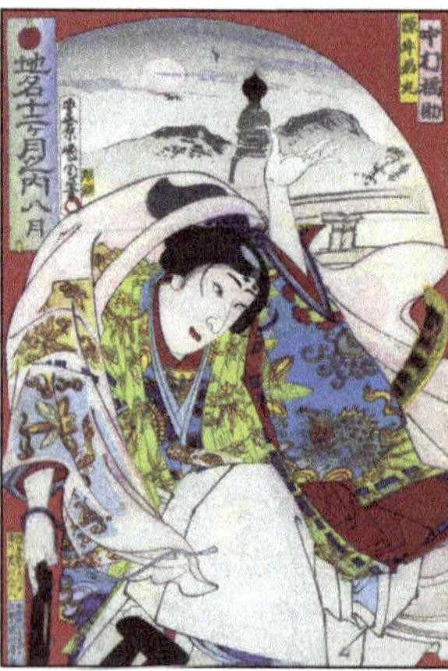

THE ACTOR NAKAMURA FUKUSUKE I AS USHIWAKAMARU, FROM THE SERIES **CHIMEI JUNIKAGETSU NO UCHI** (1882).

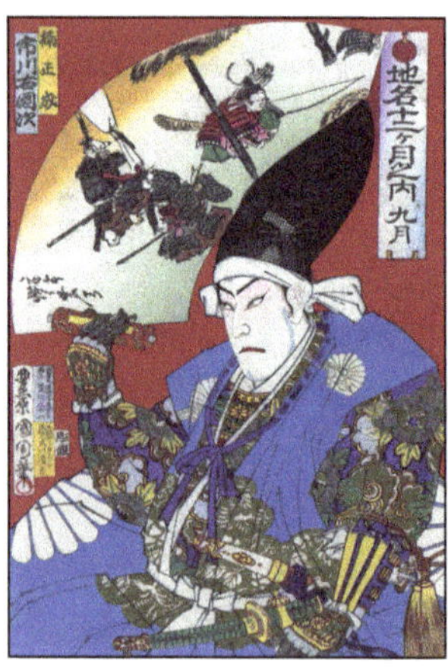

THE ACTOR ICHIKAWA UDANJI AS KUSUNOKI MASAHIGE, FROM THE SERIES **CHIMEI JUNIKAGETSU NO UCHI** (1882).

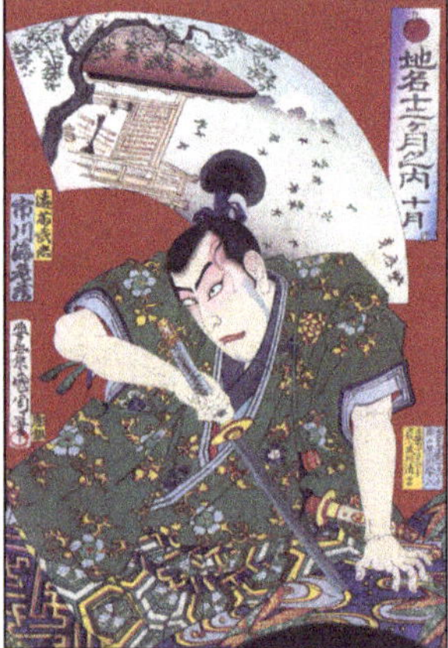

THE ACTOR ICHIKAWA EBIZO AS ENDO MORITO, FROM THE SERIES **CHIMEI JUNIKAGETSU NO UCHI** (1882).

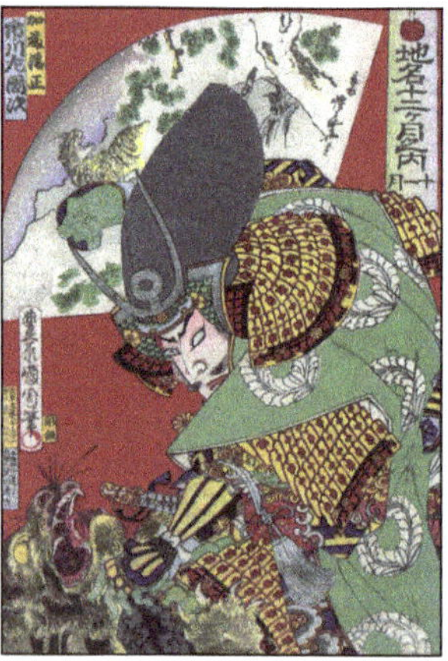

THE ACTOR ICHIKAWA SADANJI I AS KATO KIYOMASA, FROM THE SERIES **CHIMEI JUNIKAGETSU NO UCHI** (1882).

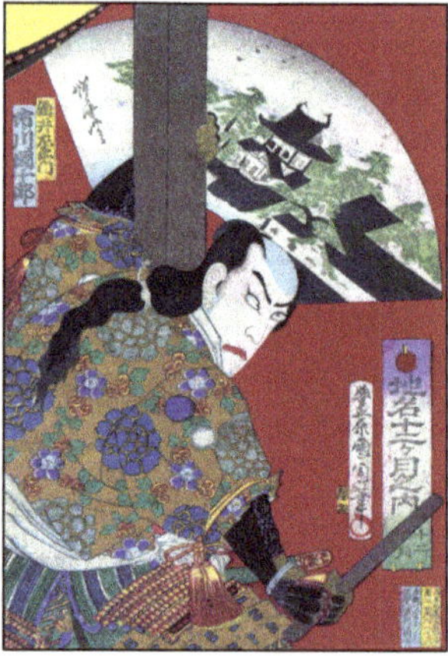

THE ACTOR ICHIKAWA DANJURO IX AS SAKAI SAEMON, FROM THE SERIES **CHIMEI JUNIKAGETSU NO UCHI** (1882).

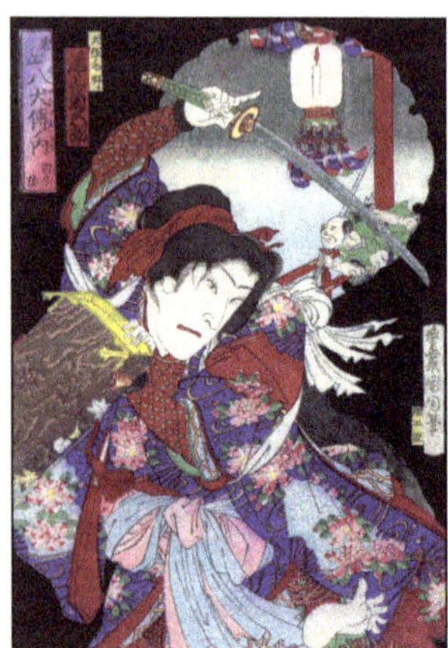

THE ACTOR ONOE KIKUGORO V AS INUZAKA KENO, FROM THE SERIES **MITATE HAKKENDEN NO UCHI** (1883).

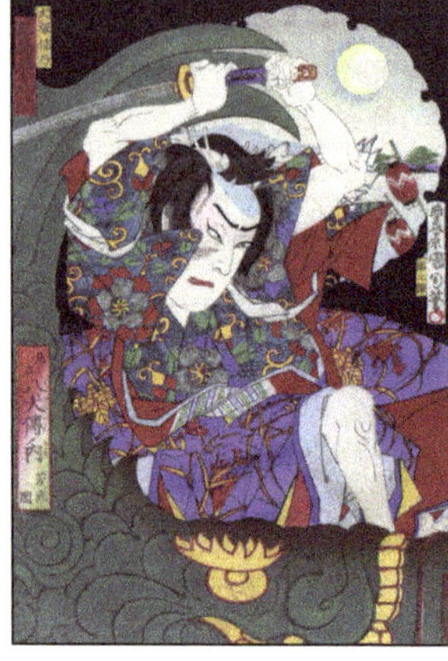

THE ACTOR SUKEYAKAYA TAKESUKE AS INUZUKA SHINO, FROM THE SERIES **MITATE HAKKENDEN NO UCHI** (1883).

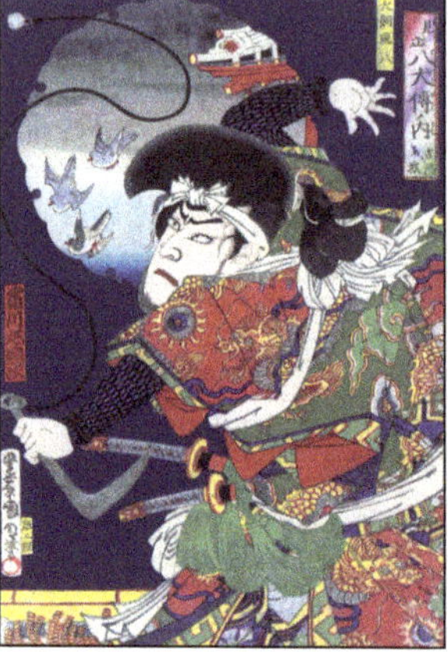

THE ACTOR ICHIKAWA SADANJI I AS INUKAI GENPACHI, FROM THE SERIES **MITATE HAKKENDEN NO UCHI** (1883).

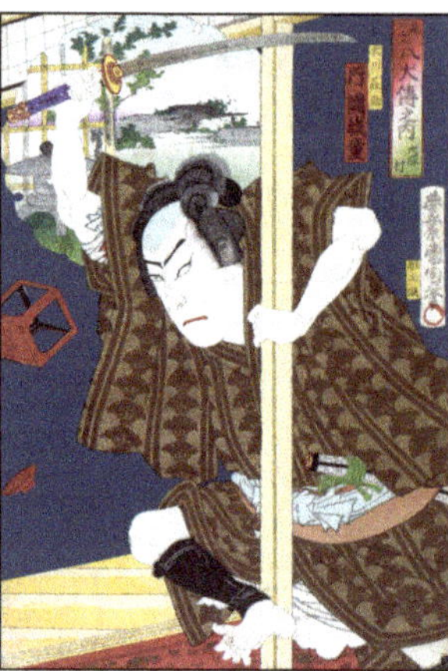

THE ACTOR KATAOKA GADO III AS INUKAWA SOSUKE, FROM THE SERIES **MITATE HAKKENDEN NO UCHI** (1883).

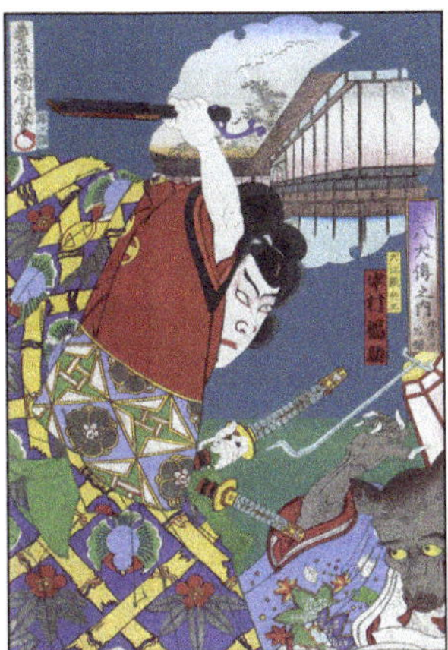

THE ACTOR NAKAMURA FUKUSUKE IV AS INUE SHINBEI, FROM THE SERIES **MITATE HAKKENDEN NO UCHI** (1883).

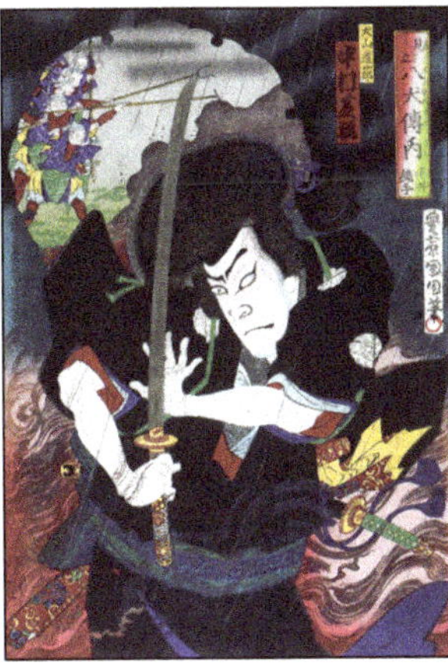

THE ACTOR NAKAMURA SHIKAN IV AS INUYAMA DOSETSU, FROM THE SERIES **MITATE HAKKENDEN NO UCHI** (1883).

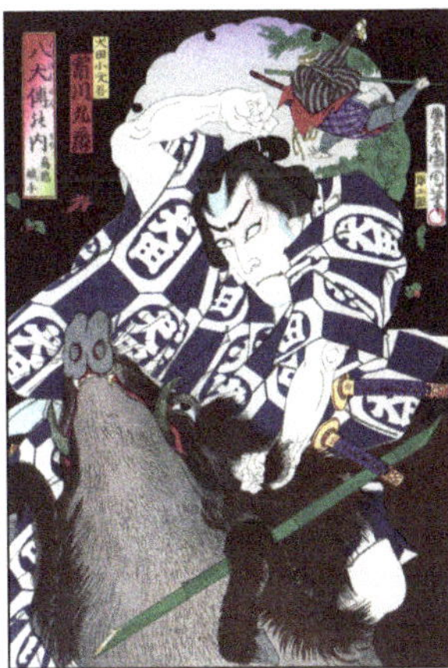

THE ACTOR ICHIKAWA KUZO III AS INUTA KOBUNGO, FROM THE SERIES **MITATE HAKKENDEN NO UCHI** (1883).

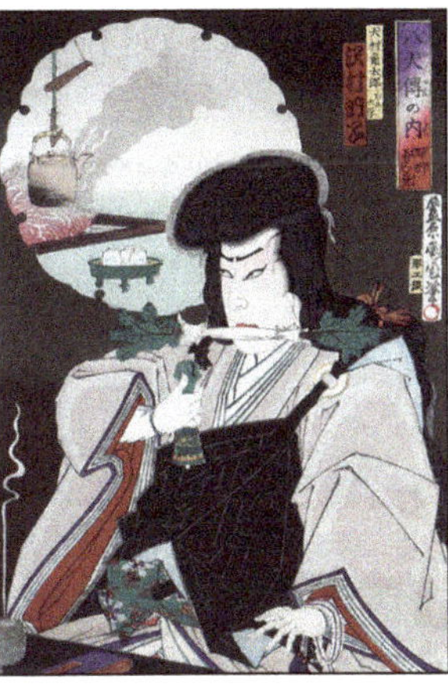

THE ACTOR SAWAMURA TOSSHO II AS INUMURA DAIKAKU, FROM THE SERIES **MITATE HAKKENDEN NO UCHI** (1883).

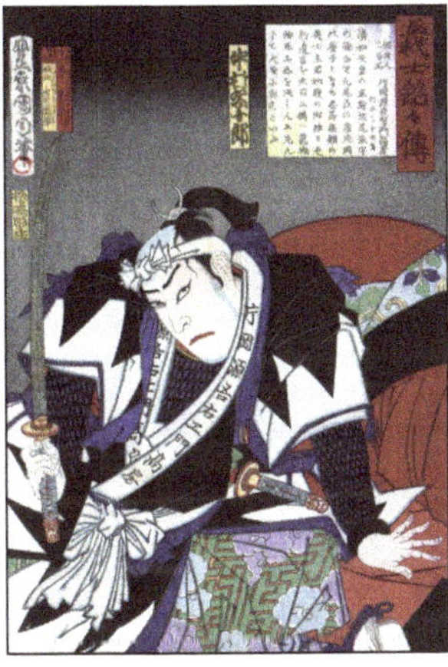

THE ACTOR NAKAMURA SOJURO I AS KATAOKA GENGOEMON TAKAFUSA, FROM THE SERIES **GISHI MEIMEI-DEN** (1883).

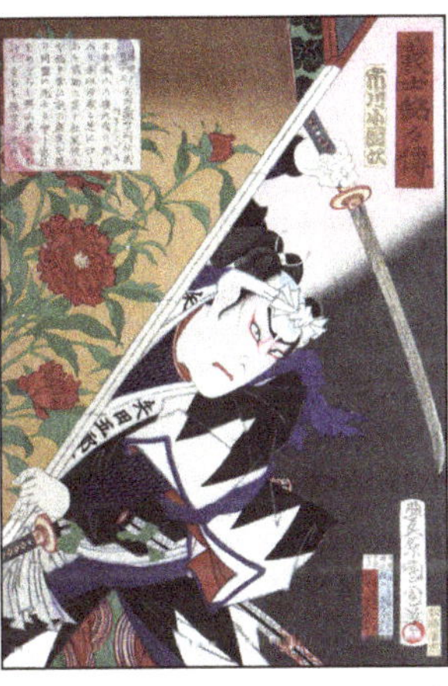

THE ACTOR ICHIKAWA KODANJI V AS YADA GOROZAEMON SUKETAKE, FROM THE SERIES **GISHI MEIMEI-DEN** (1883).

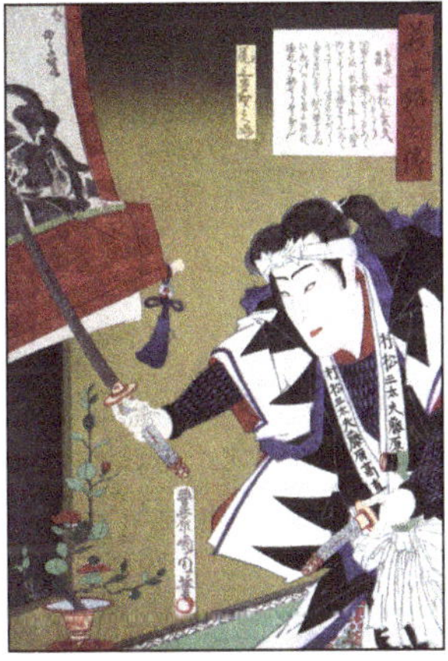

THE ACTOR ONOE TAGANOJO II AS MURAMATSU SANDAYU TAKANAO, FROM THE SERIES **GISHI MEIMEI-DEN** (1883).

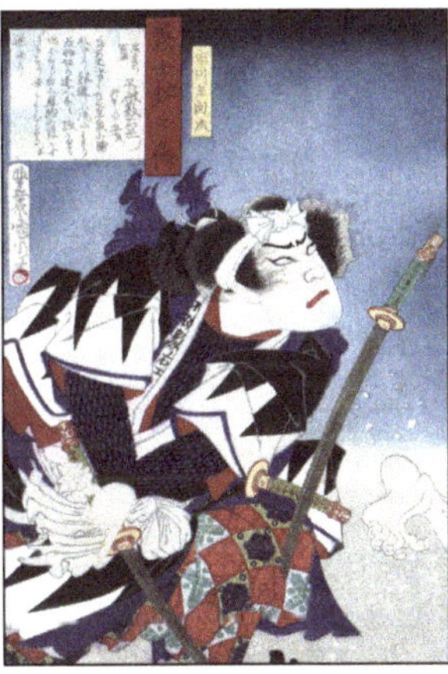

THE ACTOR ICHIKAWA SADANJI I AS FUWA KAZUEMON MASATANE, FROM THE SERIES **GISHI MEIMEI-DEN** (1883).

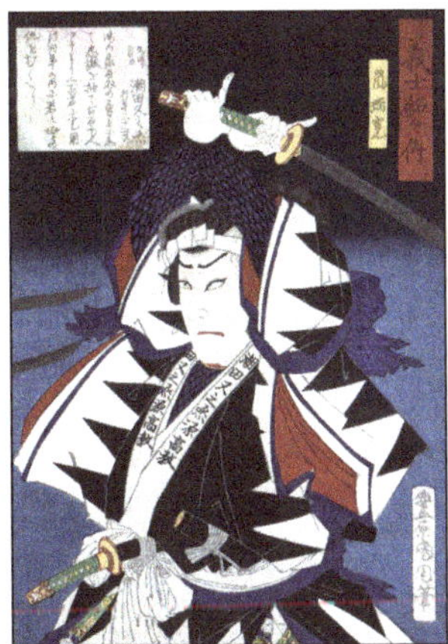

THE ACTOR ARASHI RIKAN IV AS USHIODA MATANOJO TAKANORI, FROM THE SERIES **GISHI MEIMEI-DEN** (1883).

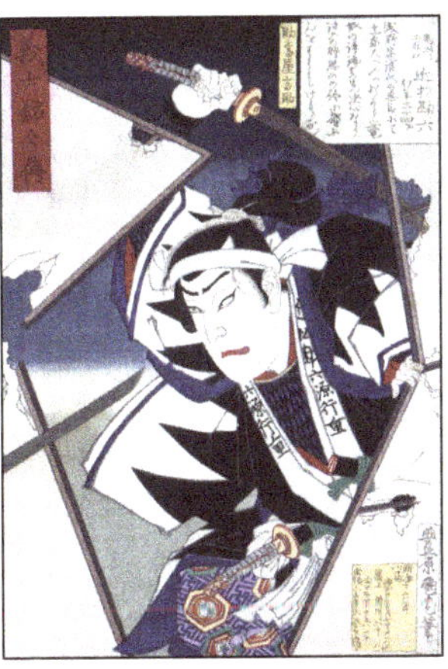

THE ACTOR SUKETAKAYA TAKASUKE IV AS CHIKAMATSU KANROKU YUKISHIGE, FROM THE SERIES **GISHI MEIMEI-DEN** (1883).

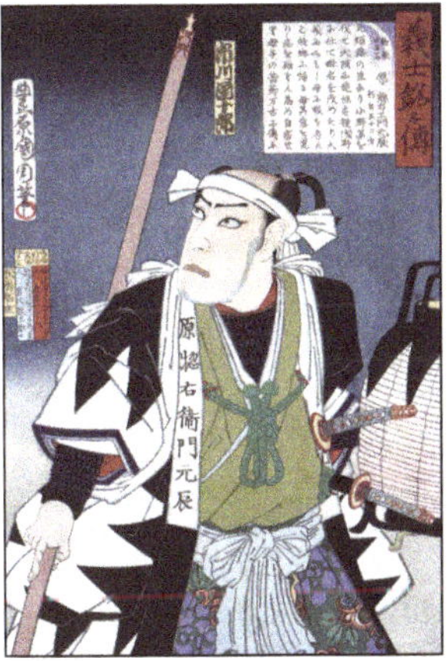

THE ACTOR ICHIKAWA DANJURO IX AS HARA SUEMON MOTOTOKI, FROM THE SERIES **GISHI MEIMEI-DEN** (1883).

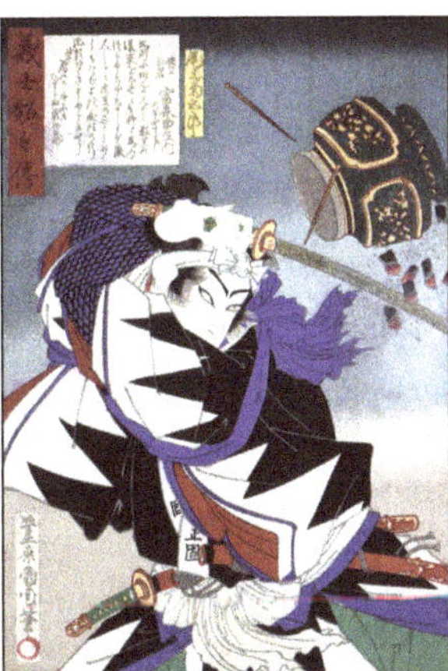

THE ACTOR ONOE KIKUGORO V AS TOMIMORI SUKEEMON MASAYORI, FROM THE SERIES **GISHI MEIMEI-DEN** (1883).

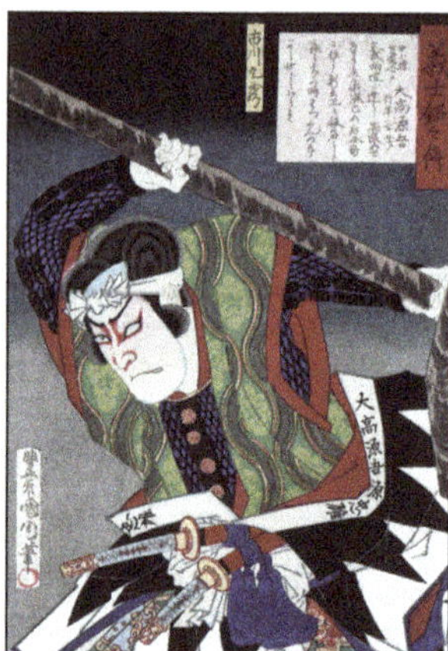

THE ACTOR ICHIKAWA KUZO III AS OTAKA GENGO TADAO, FROM THE SERIES **GISHI MEIMEI-DEN** (1883).

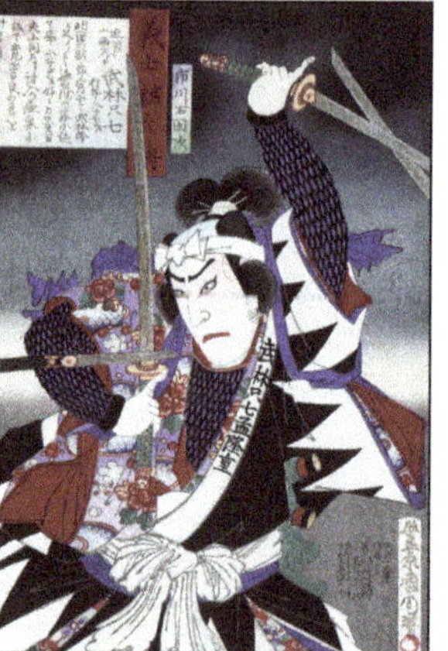

THE ACTOR ICHIKAWA UDANJI I AS TAKEBAYASHI TADASHICHI TAKASHIGE, FROM THE SERIES **GISHI MEIMEI-DEN** (1883).

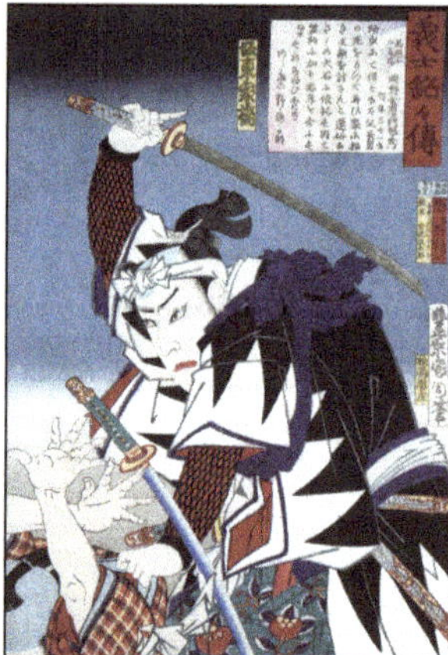

THE ACTOR BANDO KAKITSU I AS OKANO KINEMON KANEHIDE, FROM THE SERIES **GISHI MEIMEI-DEN** (1883).

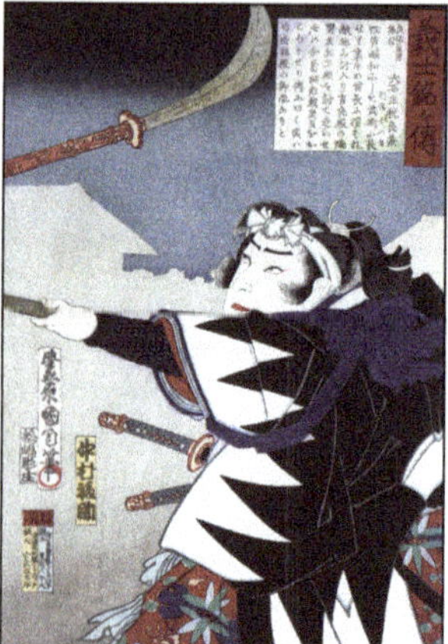

THE ACTOR NAKAMURA FUKUSUKE IV AS OISHI CHIKARA YOSHIKANE, FROM THE SERIES **GISHI MEIMEI-DEN** (1883).

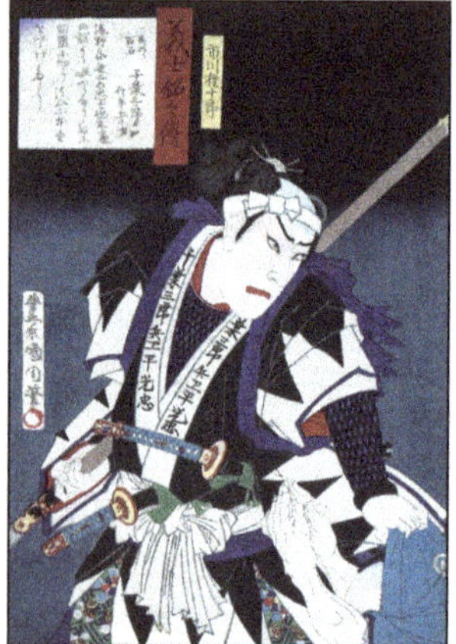

THE ACTOR ICHIKAWA GONJURO I AS CHIBA SABUROBEI MITSUTADA, FROM THE SERIES **GISHI MEIMEI-DEN** (1883).

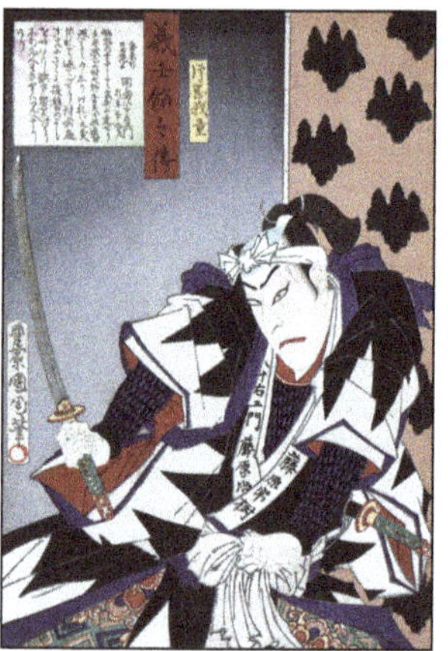

THE ACTOR KATAOKA GADO III AS OKAJIMA YASOEMON TSUNESHIGE, FROM THE SERIES **GISHI MEIMEI-DEN** (1883).

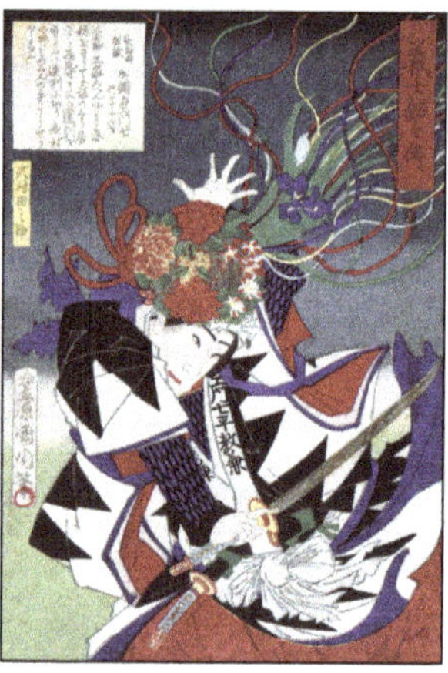

THE ACTOR SAWAMURA TANOSUKE IV AS YATO EMOSHICHI NORIKANE, FROM THE SERIES **GISHI MEIMEI-DEN** (1883).

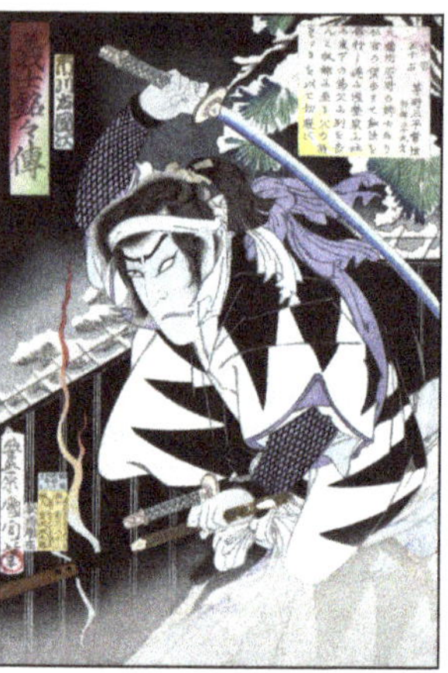

THE ACTOR ICHIKAWA SADANJI I AS THE GHOST OF KAYANO SANPEI SHIGEZANE, FROM THE SERIES **GISHI MEIMEI-DEN** (1883).

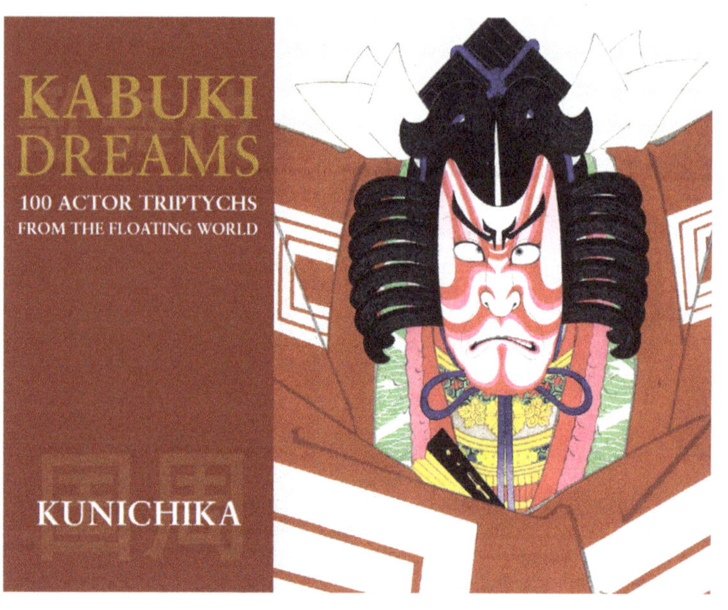

KABUKI DREAMS

100 Actor Triptychs By Kunichika

Toyohara Kunichika (1835-1900) is renowned as one of the greatest *ukiyo-e* artists of the 19th century. Almost his entire artistic life was dedicated to creating image records of *kabuki* theatre productions and the actors who starred in them, including such notables as Ichikawa Danjuro IX, Nakamura Shikan IV, and Onoe Kikugoro V. Kunichika constantly developed his own unique aesthetic style, always pushing the boundaries of *ukiyo-e* in bold and provocative new directions. KABUKI DREAMS collects 100 of Kunichika's innovative, vivid and dynamic *kabuki* designs in the triptych format, in which he found the freedom to express his visions as narratives in a proto-cinematic image frame. These classic works, produced between 1863 and 1896, are reproduced in full-color throughout.

ISBN 978-1-917285-28-5

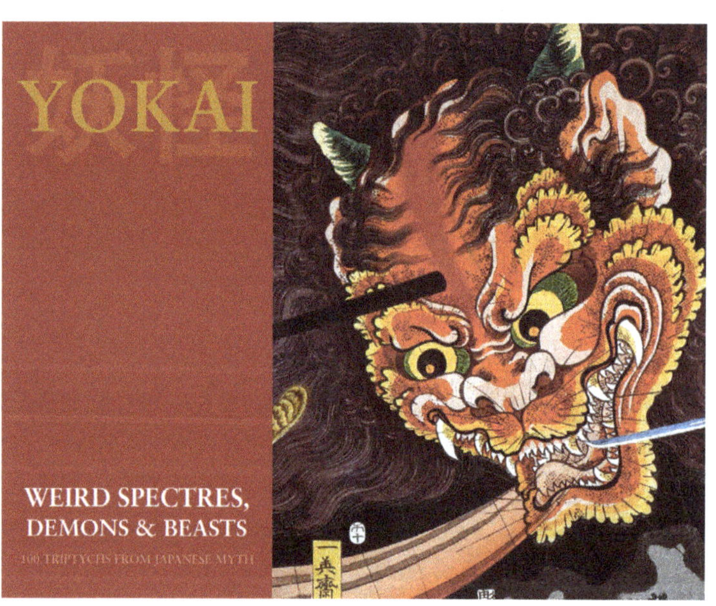

YOKAI

(WEIRD SPECTRES, DEMONS & BEASTS)

100 Triptychs From Japanese Myth

YOKAI collects more than 100 19th century Japanese woodblock prints whose subject matter covers the entire spectrum of the supernatural, all in the triptych format which gave *ukiyo-e* artists the freedom to express their phantasies as narratives in a kinetic, detailed image frame. The work of over twenty different artists is featured, spread over five different categories – *kaiju* ("strange beasts"), *yurei* ("ghosts"), *oni* ("demons"), *juryoku* ("mystic forces"), and *yojutsu* ("black magic"). The book also has a special section for *yakusha-e*, prints directly depicting supernatural scenes from the *kabuki* theatre. The artists featured include Kyosai, Yoshitoshi, Kunichika, Kuniyoshi, Yoshikazu, Kunisada, Yoshitsuya, and many others. Full color throughout.

ISBN 978-1-917285-27-8

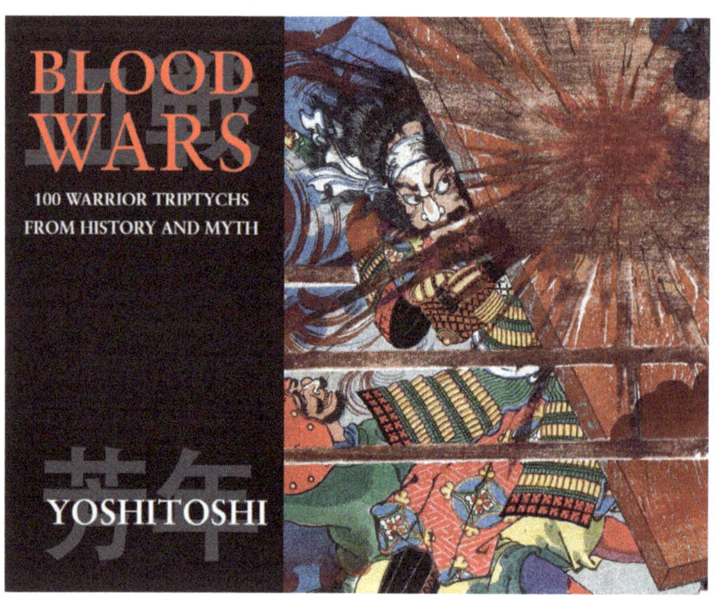

BLOOD WARS

100 Warrior Triptychs By Yoshitoshi

Yoshitoshi Tsukioka, perhaps the best-known of all 19th century *ukiyo-e* artists, created illustrations of mythic warriors and legendary battles throughout his career, including years spent documenting contemporaneous civil conflicts. BLOOD WARS collects 100 such prints by Yoshitoshi, all in triptych format, often violent and bloody in nature Subjects range from the internecine decapitation wars of the 12th to 16th centuries to the uprising of the Satsuma Rebellion in 1877, the last stand of Japan's *samurai* class against the new imperial government. Within the aesthetic discipline of the triptych, Yoshitoshi was able to express the blood-drenched chaos of war in an unmatched body of vivid, high-impact depictions. Full color throughout.

ISBN 978-1-84068-336-3